PRACTICAL INTRANET SECURITY

PRACTICAL INTRANET SECURITY

Overview of the State of the Art
and Available Technologies

by

PAUL ASHLEY
Queensland University of Technology,
Brisbane, Australia

and

MARK VANDENWAUVER
K.U. Leuven,
Belgium

KLUWER ACADEMIC PUBLISHERS
BOSTON / DORDRECHT / LONDON

Library of Congress Cataloging-in-Publication Data

ISBN 0-7923-8354-0

Published by Kluwer Academic Publishers,
P.O. Box 17, 3300 AA Dordrecht, The Netherlands.

Sold and distributed in North, Central and South America
by Kluwer Academic Publishers,
101 Philip Drive, Norwell, MA 02061, U.S.A.

In all other countries, sold and distributed
by Kluwer Academic Publishers,
P.O. Box 322, 3300 AH Dordrecht, The Netherlands.

Printed on acid-free paper

Printed in the Netherlands

Contents

Foreword

As we approach the millennium it is clear that the vast increase in the use of information technology will continue well into the next century. Corporations are being reengineered with increasing use of information technology in all aspects of their processes. On the positive side, this helps corporations to become more competitive, the negative side is that new risks to businesses are emerging.

In the closed communication scenarios of the past, information security was obtained through physical security: sealed envelopes, safes storing documents, and other means. In these cases the risk to the information was generally very low, and people understood what precautions needed to be taken.

In the era of information technology the risks and solutions are very different and unfortunately not always so well understood. A popular answer to the problem of introducing security in information technologies is to use cryptography. However even the strongest cryptographic algorithm does not give security if it is used in a wrong way. What is needed is a broad understanding of a range of information security areas including cryptography, but also the protocols used, the different attack scenarios, and other security architectures.

This book concentrates on the Intranet, the computer network owned by corporations, and used for their essential processes. Intranets are a big risk for companies. Data transmitted over these networks can be destroyed, intercepted and even modified in some cases. Such attacks are even more dangerous when executed by employees, people inside the organization and only a careful design can prevent these.

The aim of this book is to provide knowledge to businesses on how to protect their information against all attacks. It gives an excellent description of a range of Intranet security solutions and what services they provide to the organization. In the first part of the book the authors give a concise summary of contemporary cryptography and network security. The second part of the book explains in details two architectures, the well-known Kerberos and the more advanced SESAME. In the third and last part of the book the authors describe all other important security architectures, including PEM, PGP, S/MIME and SSL.

This book is a valuable contribution to the Intranet security field. It provides a comprehensive and highly readable explanation of the issues and the solutions for securing an organization's intranet. The included CD-ROM with the SESAME security architecture sources and secured applications developed by the authors will undoubtedly be useful for many businesses. The authors should be congratulated for their work.

Prof. Dr. Lars R. Knudsen
Department of Informatics
University of Bergen
N-5020 Bergen, Norway

To Kellie and Zakia

Acknowledgments

It is a real pleasure for us to be able to thank everyone who has helped us during the preparation of this book.

We first want to thank Lars Knudsen for reviewing the book and writing the excellent foreword. His input was much appreciated.

We also want to express our sincerest thanks to the people who have edited the drafts of this book and have made invaluable corrections and suggestions:

Colin Boyd	Bradley Broom	Andrew Clark	Alex Duncan
Ravi Ganesan	Gary Gaskell	Per Kaijser	Mark Looi
Bradley MacKenzie	Doug Maughan	Scott Mewett	Vincent Rijmen

In addition we acknowledge the efforts of all the people involved in porting SESAME to other platforms and co-authoring the applications that are described in this book: Sebastien Boving, Shaw Innes, Wayne Meissner, Mark Rutherford and Isabel Snoeckx. Also thanks to Joris Claessens for working on the SESAME CD-ROM that accompanies this book and also on the SESAME web pages.

Mark says: for the great working atmosphere in COSIC, I thank my former and current colleagues: Erik De Win, Bart Van Rompay, Joris Claessens, Antoon Bosselaers, Vincent Rijmen, Keith Martin, Johan Borst, Cristian Radu, Stefan Hoeben, Danny De Cock, Filip Mertens, Joan Daemen, Jan Verschuren and Luc Van Linden. Special thanks have to go out to Prof. Joos Vandewalle, Prof. René Govaerts and Prof. Bart Preneel for guiding me throughout my research.

Zakia, I realize there is no way that I can tell you how grateful I am for the way you have changed my life. Thanks a million for all you mean to me.

Finally a sincere thank you to my parents, sister, and family, and all my friends for providing me with ample opportunities to divert my mind and for reminding me that there is always life beyond work.

Paul says: Thank you to Prof. William Caelli, Prof. Edward Dawson and Prof. Dennis Longley for their efforts in making the ISRC such an inspiring place to work. A sincere thanks must go out to Bradley Broom for guiding me throughout my research. I would also like to thank my other colleagues in the

ISRC for their friendship and motivation: Colin Boyd, Andrew Clark, Ernest Foo, Gina Farrington, Gary Gaskell, Anne Hamburger, Elizabeth Hansford, Mark Looi, William Millan, Lauren Nielsen, Christine Orme, Selwyn Russell, Leonie Simpson, Alan Tickle, Melanie Wark and Jeremy Zellers.

A special thanks must go out to my wife Kellie who has supported me continually, and also for my parents, brothers, extended family and friends for always being there. Finally thanks to my cycling partner Kevin Golding for distracting me from work each weekend.

Preface

Recent years have seen an exponential growth in the number of available computing resources and the dependency of the global economy on these computers. These computers are connected together via different kinds of networks. In this way resources can be shared and it is possible for people to interact. Because of the extreme importance of the data residing on these computers or transmitted over the communication lines, the need for security has become a vital issue.

The number of computer security related incidents has reached an all time high. Although it is almost impossible to get an exact idea of the number of computer related crimes. Most companies that are subject to these attacks are either not aware of them, or do not report them to the appropriate authorities. The general idea behind this being that the financial loss resulting from negative publicity for the company far outweighs the costs caused by the successful computer hacker. Moreover, some of these companies even pay off these *criminals* to keep silent about their activities. The costs for affected computer systems go even further, because it takes significant resources to ensure that the intruder can get no further access to the system (e.g., eliminating the possibility of hidden backdoors).

In 1994 there was a famous incident involving a Russian computer hacker Vladimir Levin who managed to break into the American Citibank's mainframe in New York. He was able to transfer more than 10 million dollars into foreign accounts. Levin was only the frontman as the break-in was an idea of the Russian Mafia. They were only caught because of the simplistic way in which they tried to launder the money through Russian banks. This incident clearly shows that the potential gain for criminals is usually big enough to take a gamble. In this case the hacker masqueraded as a regular user in order to access the computer and to make the money transfers.

In 1995 Nick Leeson proved that the 80's are alive and well, offering hope to renegade financiers everywhere and providing good newspaper copy for days. He managed to bankrupt Britain's venerable Barings Bank with a mountain of bad debts while working as a derivatives trader on the Singapore International Monetary Exchange. The problem in this case was not that Nick Leeson had not been identified properly to the bank's computer, but that he should not have been *authorized* to make transactions that could have such disastrous effects.

Although banks and the military environment are the major sectors that need security, they are far from alone in their quest for a practical solution to the security problem. Many others are becoming increasingly aware that their privacy might be in danger. Sensitive medical data is stored on computers, and sent over computer networks. In Belgium people will be required to have a *social identity card* in 1998. This will be a Smart Card that stores medical and related personal information. The need for an enforceable security scheme in this environment cannot be more evident.

Corporate espionage is another topic that needs to be discussed. More and more international companies are hooking up their networks to the Internet to exchange information. For a trained computer user it is usually not hard to listen in on these messages, which can be of vital importance to the future of the company.

The aim of this book is to highlight how unauthorized access to computers is accomplished, and to describe a broad range of the solutions for this problem. The book is written for network administrators and managers who want up-to-date information on solutions for protecting their information resources. One of the primary goals of this book is to assimilate the masses of research literature and try to present it in a simple and complete way. This should then allow the reader to form their own opinion on what sort of technology is suitable for their environment.

Network security solutions can be approached from two different angles:

1. How to secure specific applications.

2. How to build a security architecture to secure the whole network.

In this book both approaches are represented. On the one hand a range of solutions that are application specific is examined. That is these solutions are complete applications that have security built into them and are available as stand-alone products. Electronic mail and remote-login programs are the most common examples of these type of solutions. On the other hand the security architectures are also investigated. These architectures tackle the network security problem from a different approach. They provide an infrastructure of security components that can then be used by application developers to secure their own applications. In some cases there are applications that have already been secured to work with the architecture and these might also be available to the public.

This book is organized into three parts. The first part titled **Network Security Concepts** gives the reader the necessary background information in cryptography, networking and network security. It includes a description of the most common attack methods used by intruders to gain unauthorized access to computers. The aim of this part is to ensure that all readers have a reasonable understanding of the problems and concepts before tackling the rest of the book.

The second part of the book titled **Kerberos and SESAME** gives a description of the Kerberos and SESAME architectures. Kerberos is the well known authentication architecture, with widespread acceptance in industry. SESAME is a newer architecture based on Kerberos, with additions such as the use of public-key cryptography and an access control service based on role based access control. A significant portion of this part of the book is devoted to SESAME, including descriptions of how SESAME was used to secure telnet, the BSD rtools, the Remote Procedure Call. This is to assist application developers in securing their own applications, highlighting the problems that were faced and how these were solved.

The third part of the book titled **Other Security Solutions** completes the picture with a description of the wide range of security technologies available. It begins with a description of more security architectures. The differences with the Kerberos and SESAME architectures are outlined. The book then describes a number of other security solutions that are also commonly being used in the industry to provide security. A comparison concludes the third part of the book.

In addition to the three parts, three appendices are included: the first explains the acronyms used in this book, the second gives instructions on using the included CD-ROM, and the third is the licence agreement.

The book has been written so it can be read from front to back. For some readers this will be the best way to complete the book. Other readers may be interested in particular sections of the book only (for example information on the SESAME architecture), and the book has been written with enough detail to allow the reader to do this comfortably.

The CD-ROM that accompanies this book contains SESAME V4 sources (both system and applications) as well as comprehensive installation and configuration guides. Before installing and using this software it is important to carefully read and agree to the enclosed license agreement. The sources and documents were up to date at the time of printing of this book. However SESAME and its associated applications are continually evolving. We therefore refer the reader to the SESAME home page for the latest updates at **https://www.cosic.esat.kuleuven.ac.be/sesame**.

We are always interested in receiving feedback from the readers of this book. If you have any comments, criticisms or you just want to ask a question, please email us at **sesame@esat.kuleuven.ac.be**. We will try to reply to all correspondence.

PAUL AND MARK

I Network Security Concepts

1 SECURITY SERVICES AND CRYPTOGRAPHY

1.1 INTRODUCTION

The origin of the word *cryptology* lies in ancient Greek. The word cryptology is made up of two components: KRYPTOS, which means hidden and LOGOS, which means word. Cryptology is as old as writing itself, and has been used for thousands of years to safeguard military and diplomatic communications. For example, the famous Roman emperor Julius Caesar used a cipher to protect the messages to his troops. Within the field of cryptology one can see two separate divisions: *cryptography* and *cryptanalysis*. The cryptographer seeks methods to ensure the safety and security of data communications while the cryptanalyst tries to undo the former's work by breaking these systems.

The main services offered by modern cryptography are:

1. Entity authentication;

2. Data authentication:

   - Data integrity;
   - Data origin authentication;

3. Non-repudiation;

4. Data confidentiality.

In the following sections these services are elaborated. A related topic is the problem of adding authorization to data or a computer that needs to be protected. Therefore it is explained how these services can be realized using cryptographic and other primitives. In the latter sections some issues that arise in real-life situations are descibed: key escrow and recovery, export regulations and public-key certificates.

For more details the interested reader is referred to the excellent *Handbook of Applied Cryptography* by Menezes, van Oorschot and Vanstone [181].

1.2 CRYPTOGRAPHIC SERVICES

In general the scenario shown in Figure 1.1 is used as the model. Alice sends a message to Bob and enemy Eve taps the line between them.

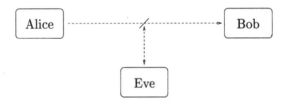

Figure 1.1. Communication between Alice and Bob

Wire-tapping is only a matter of cost: tapping a telephone line is obviously easier than tapping a coaxial cable or a micro-wave. Active wiretaps (modifying and then relaying the messages) are also more difficult than passive wiretaps (listening in on the messages). Computer networks are however easier to listen into than the common telecommunication (phone, fax) networks [42].

1.2.1 Entity Authentication

If you log on to a computer system there must (or at least should) be some way that you can convince it of your identity. Once it knows your identity, it can verify whether you are entitled to enter the system. The same principle applies when one person tries to communicate with another person: as a first step you want to verify that you are communicating with the right person. Therefore there must be some way in which you can prove your identity. This process is called *entity authentication*. In the case of human entities this is defined as *user authentication* or *identification*. There are several ways to obtain user authentication.

One possibility is to give to the computer something that is known only to a particular entity: a password, a (pre-designed) user-id, a pin code, etc. Another way is to use specific items to prove your identity: a magnetic strip card, a smartcard (a hand-held computer the size of a credit card), a token. Finally it is possible to make use of biometric properties; it is a well-known fact that fingerprints, the shape of the hand and retinal pattern of a person are good decision criteria. More information about entity authentication can be found in Chapter 2 of this book.

It can also be required that the computer authenticates itself to the person logging on. If both parties are authenticated to each other, the term *mutual authentication* is used.

1.2.2 Data Authentication

Data authentication consists of two components: the fact that data has not been modified (data integrity) and the fact that you know who the sender is (data origin authentication).

1.2.2.1 Data Integrity.

A *data integrity* service guarantees that the content of the data or the message, that was sent, has not been tampered with. Data integrity by itself is not necessarily meaningful: it does not help to know that the data received has not been modified, unless it has been sent directly and by the right person. Therefore it should always be combined with *data origin authentication.*

One should always be alert for possible intruders in the network or in the communication system. The most renowned network is the Internet, which connects universities, companies and homes world-wide. Electronic mail over the Internet does not offer any security. As a consequence, an educated computer user can tap into the messages that are being transmitted over the line or even change them with the use of some hardware equipment.

Referring to Figure 1.1, if data integrity is not provided, Eve can change the message and then relay it to Bob. Bob does not see that the message has been tampered with and assumes Alice really intended it the way he got it.

1.2.2.2 Data Origin Authentication.

In this case, the goal is to make sure that the person who is claiming to be the sender of the message really is the one from whom it originates. Referring to Figure 1.1, if Alice sends a message to Bob but Eve intercepts it, and sends it to Bob claiming that Alice has sent it, how can Bob be sure of the real origin of this data? A variation on this theme is: Eve could send a message to Bob claiming that Alice is the originator.

1.2.3 Non-repudiation

Non-repudiation protects against denial by one of the entities involved in a communication of having participated in all or part of the communication. Four kinds of non-repudiation services have been defined by ISO [124]:

1. *Non-repudiation of origin* protects against any attempts by the sender to repudiate having sent a message.

   An example illustrates the importance of non-repudiation of origin. Suppose Bob is the owner of a mail-order company and he decides to let his customers order through electronic mail. For him it is really important that he can show to an arbitrator (judge) that Alice really ordered the goods he claims she did. Otherwise it would be easy for a customer to deny the purchase. In a paper and pencil world, non-repudiation of origin is provided by a handwritten or manual signature.

2. *Non-repudiation of submission* gives the sender of a message a proof that the message has been submitted. In the traditional postal services, this is realized by *certified mail.* In the world of the Internet, this service could be provided by the ISP (Internet Service Provider).

3. *Non-repudiation of delivery* protects against any attempt by the recipient to deny, falsely, having received a message. Again this relates to *registered mail* in the real world, where the sender of a letter receives a card from the postal services proving that a letter has been accepted by the correspondent. It does NOT say anything about the content of the letter. To this end the next form of non-repudiation is needed.

4. *Non-repudiation of receipt* provides the originator of the message with a proof that a message has been received correctly by the intended receiver. In the example of electronic commerce this gives the customers a proof so that the merchant cannot later deny having received their order, or claim to have received it at a different time.

1.2.4   Data Confidentiality

This aspect of data security certainly is the oldest and best known. The fact that confidentiality was considered to be much more important than authentication of both sender and data, and non-repudiation, can be explained as follows. The latter services have been provided implicitly by the physical properties of the channel: a letter was written in a recognizable handwriting, with a seal and a signature.

With data confidentiality, the goal is to protect against an unauthorized disclosure of the message. Referring to Figure 1.1, if Alice sends a message to Bob, but Eve intercepts it, Alice wants to make sure that Eve never understands the content of this message. Confidentiality protection is very important in the military, the medical world and also in the banking sector. World-wide there are several million transactions each day and all of these have to be passed from one financial institution to another. If there were no way to achieve confidentiality, everybody would be able to see who had purchased what, who has made what kind of withdrawal, etc.

1.3   ACCESS CONTROL AND AUTHORIZATION

While authentication can verify the identity of an entity, the *authorization* determines what the entity is allowed to do. Authorization is thus the act of granting rights and/or privileges to users, permitting them access to an object.

Access control is a means of enforcing this authorization model. Usually a successful authentication is a must before the authorization of an action can be decided. In modern computer networks (e.g., the Internet) it is necessary to control the access to the various computers.

When controlling the access, three goals are primarily targeted:

1. Confidentiality: data should not be disclosed to unauthorized people.

2. Integrity: data should not be modified by unauthorized people.

3. Accountability: all users should be accountable for all their actions.

1.3.1 Access Control Lists (ACLs)

B. Lampson has done some outstanding work in the field of access control [71, 162]. Referring to his terminology, the state of the system can be described with a triplet: subjects, objects and an access matrix. Subjects are active entities that perform actions. Objects are entities that are accessed in some way. Subjects can be computer processes running on behalf of a specific user. They can also be objects at the same time: e.g., to halt (kill) a person's specific process. On these subjects and objects can be defined generic rights. They allow to specify what subject is permitted to do what action on a certain object. The access matrix basically is a cartesian product of the subjects and objects. An access is permitted if the right is in the matrix. Referring to Table 1.1, subject S1 has the right to read/write object 1, subject S2 has the right to read/write object 2, etc.

Table 1.1.   A Lampson access matrix (r = read, w = write, k = kill, - = none)

Subject	Object 1	Object 2	Subject S1	Subject S2
S1 (vdwauver)	rw	-	k	-
S2 (vdwalle)	-	rw	k	k

Each column in this matrix is an *access control list* (ACL). It holds a list of (subjects, rights) pairs. The authorization rules are kept with the accessed objects. Each entry in the ACL specifies the subject and the allowed action with respect to the object.

Another possible approach is the use of *capabilities*. One can compare capabilities to electronic keys: holding the key permits you to do something. Each row in the access matrix above, is a capability. Each subject has the permission to do things to certain objects.

1.3.2 Delegation

Sometimes it is very helpful to have a server act on a client's behalf. This is the case when a user U is logged into a server A and then needs to access files on a different server B. In order for this to work, machine A needs to inherit some of user U's privileges to be able to access the files on machine B. A classical example is when a user asks a print-server to print out a file and this file is located on a different file-server. This process is called delegation.

There are several ways to achieve delegation. One possibility is to forward the user's password to the server that needs to access another server. This mechanism is only secure if the user changes password every time so it is not a practical scenario. Another way is by adding every system explicitly to every access control list (Section 1.3.1) and delete these entries when the operation has finalized. Again this is too inconvenient to use in day-to-day operation.

In Chapter 6, it is shown how SESAME has solved the delegation problem in a more elegant way.

1.4   CRYPTOGRAPHIC PRIMITIVES

The cryptographic services, that were described in the previous section, can be realized by several cryptographic primitives. It is possible to distinguish between primitives for encryption and primitives for authentication. Encryption primitives can be used to provide confidentiality, authentication primitives can be used to provide data authentication.

1.4.1   Encryption Primitives

In cryptography encryption is a basic tool. Referring to Figure 1.2, the cleartext (or plaintext) P is transformed into ciphertext C with the encryption function. To get back to the original text, the inverse transformation, called the decryption function, needs to be applied. Usually these transformations themselves are public. This makes it possible to analyze these algorithms and to develop efficient implementations. However they use a secret parameter: the *key K*. This key K is known only by the sender and/or the receiver. The key is the only information needed to apply the encryption or decryption function. This means that it is very important to manage these cryptographic keys and keep them secret when necessary.

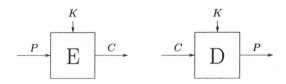

Figure 1.2.   Encryption and decryption

Every primitive that is described in the following sections can be attacked by a cryptanalyst. These attacks are classified according to the access that the cryptanalyst has (see Rijmen [206]). If the attacker mounts an attack using only the value of some ciphertexts, the attack is a *ciphertext-only attack*. If a primitive can be broken with a ciphertext-only attack, it should not be used in practice. An example of this attack is an exhaustive key search, in which a cryptanalyst tries every possible key.

A second approach is where the cryptanalyst has obtained the knowledge of some ciphertext with their corresponding plaintexts. This is called a *known plaintext attack*. If the attacker has even more access and can choose the plaintext, the attack is a *chosen plaintext attack*. The number of practical situations where this last attack can be mounted is very limited.

Parallel to these attacks (and this applies to any primitive, not just encryption functions) some schemes suffer from *certificational weaknesses*. This means that there is a reliable indication that there is something wrong. It is not an actual attack but usually cryptographers do not recommend to use primitives of which a certificational weakness has been discovered.

Two types of encryption primitives are discussed, *symmetric* or conventional ciphers and *asymmetric* or public-key ciphers.

1.4.1.1 Symmetric Ciphers.   There are two kinds of encryption schemes. The oldest ones and most used are the symmetric ciphers. In these schemes, the key used to decrypt the ciphertext is equal to the one used to encrypt the plaintext or is easy to compute from this key.

The best known cipher in this category is the Data Encryption Standard (DES), that was adopted in 1977 by the American National Bureau of Standards (NBS) as a Federal Information Processing Standard (FIPS) [92]. Since then it has been used all over the world and no major flaws have yet been discovered.

During the last years, Biham and Shamir [24], Davies and Murphy [67], and Matsui [173] have published attacks which break DES in the academic sense (i.e., their attacks require significantly less computer time than exhaustive key search). They are no threat to the DES in practice, since they require huge amounts of chosen or known plaintexts which means that part of these attacks needs to be performed on-line (in contrary to exhaustive key search which can be done completely off-line).

The DES makes use of a 56-bit key which is unfortunately short. Researchers [237] have estimated that exhaustively searching for all possible values of this key in one day requires an investment of about U.S.$ 200,000 (this requires only a few pairs of plaintext and corresponding ciphertext). In 1997, the DES key challenge, initiated by RSA Data Security, obtained the key in less than 6 months using spare computer cycles on machines connected to the Internet. In 1998 the DES search machine was actually built by the Electronic Frontier foundation [98].

Better security can be achieved using a cipher with a longer key such as the 2-key triple-DES (see Figure 1.3). The triple-DES uses the DES as a black box and encrypts the message (P_i) with a certain key K_1, then decrypts the result with another key K_2 and finally encrypts again with K_1. In this way a key of 112 bits is obtained, which is sufficiently large to prevent exhaustive search. At the same time, one is protected against further improvements in academic attacks on the DES. The reasoning behind using only two different keys was that chips implementing 2-key triple-DES could also be used to implement single round DES by choosing K_1 equal to K_2.

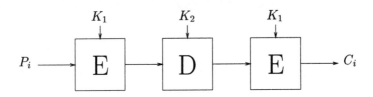

Figure 1.3.   2-key triple DES

The DES and triple-DES are both *block ciphers*. This means that they split the message into blocks of equal length P_i (64 bits in the case of DES and triple-DES), and then apply the encryption function to this message block (resulting in C_i).

It is not sufficient to choose a secure cipher. It is also important to specify a secure mode of operation (see Figure 1.4). Depending on the nature of the communication channel or storage space, one chooses between Cipher-Block-Chaining (CBC), Cipher-Feedback (CFB), and Output-Feedback (OFB) (as specified in FIPS 81 [93]). Encryption block by block (or Electronic Code Book (ECB) mode) should only be used for encryption of keys. The CBC mode adds the result of the previous encryption to the input block, in order to make the ciphertext blocks dependent on the previous blocks: $C_i = E(P_i \oplus C_{i-1})$. In the CFB mode the last r bits of the ciphertext block are fed back to the r-bit shift register. The ciphertext is the result of the exor of the leftmost r bits of the DES output with the r-bit plaintext block: $C_i = P_i \oplus (S_i >> (n - r))$. The difference between the CFB and OFB mode is that in the OFB mode the intermediate result S_i is fed back to the input register of the DES encryption.

Looking a few years ahead, the short key is not the only problem with systems as the DES. It is widely known (e.g., Maurer in [175], Knudsen in [152]) that the 64 bit block length is also problematic. Let us illustrate this with the example of the DES in CBC mode. If one looks at the output (C_i), then after 2^{32} outputs one expects a match: $C_i = C_j$. Going back to the input of the DES, this means that: $C_{i-1} \oplus P_i = C_{j-1} \oplus P_j$. Reordering this gives us: $P_i \oplus P_j = C_{i-1} \oplus C_{j-1}$. Thus information about the plaintext is gathered. Therefore, newer algorithms such as SQUARE [66] and RC-5 [208] use blocks of 128 bits.

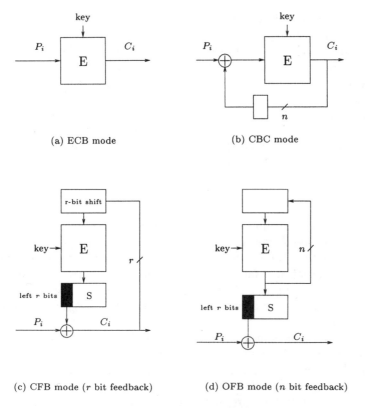

(a) ECB mode

(b) CBC mode

(c) CFB mode (r bit feedback)

(d) OFB mode (n bit feedback)

Figure 1.4.   Modes of block ciphers.

An important subclass of the symmetric key ciphers is formed by the *stream ciphers*. These can be defined as ciphers where the encryption scheme can change for each symbol of the plaintext. Some possible advantages of stream ciphers are (according to Maurer [175]):

- They can be used when the data needs to be processed one symbol at a time (memory-less systems).

- They can be made self-synchronizing and thus have no error propagation (in case of transmission errors).

- They usually have a very high through-put which makes them suitable for high speed applications.

In recent years, many new ciphers have been proposed. An excellent overview for block ciphers can be found in [153]. Most of them have been analyzed by cryptographers [181, 206]. The future must reveal which algorithms withstand the test of time.

1.4.1.2   Asymmetric Ciphers.   The asymmetric or public-key ciphers are the more recent cryptographic tools [75]. In contrast to the symmetric systems, the key used to encipher and the key used to decrypt are different. Each entity in the system thus has two keys. One key is kept private and the other is made publicly available. A necessary condition for security is that it should be hard to find the private key from the public key.

If a user Alice wants to send a message M to Bob, she only needs to encrypt the message with Bob's public key (P_B). Since Bob is the only one who has access to the corresponding private key (S_B), Bob is the only one who can decrypt the message and read the content.

$$S_B(P_B(M)) = M.$$

The most popular public-key cipher is the RSA system (RSA stands for Rivest, Shamir and Adleman, the names of the three people usually credited with its invention). The security of this scheme is thought to be related to the mathematical problem of factorization. It is easy to generate two large primes and to multiply them, but given a large number that is the product of two primes, it is believed that a huge amount of computation is required to find the two prime factors.

At the moment of writing of this text, the biggest number that has been factorized is about 430 bits long and attacks on numbers of 512 bits have been announced. Therefore the absolute minimum length of the key in the RSA system has to be set at 640 bits. 768 or 1024 bits are required for any system that requires security for more than a few months.

In the last years elliptic curve cryptography (ECC) [180] has appeared to open up many new opportunities. The main advantage of ECC is that shorter key lengths are expected to be sufficient: 1024-bit RSA is reported to be equivalent to 180-bit ECC. A possible disadvantage of these systems is that they require the generation of a random key for each encryption process. This results in an extra overhead and vulnerability.

For a comparison of the various public-key techniques the reader is referred to the excellent analysis by Wiener [236].

1.4.1.3   Symmetric versus Asymmetric Ciphers.   The biggest drawback of the asymmetric systems up until now has been the relatively low performance of the asymmetric technology. For example, the implementation of DES on a Pentium/90 based PC can achieve a 17 Mbit/s encryption rate, while the RSA (768 bits full length modular exponentiation) implementation on the same PC achieve only a 6 Kbits/s rate. Thus symmetric systems are typically 1000 times faster than their asymmetric counterparts. An overview of typical speeds of the best known ciphers can be found in Tables 1.2 and 1.3. For more details the reader is referred to [201].

Public-key systems provide significant benefits in terms of key management. If every user generates his own key, only an authentic channel is required, eliminating (expensive) secret channels as couriers.

Table 1.2.   Performance of block ciphers (Pentium 90 MHz)

Algorithm	Block (bits)	Key (bits)	Performance (Mbit/s)
Blowfish	64	32-448	36.50
DES	64	56	16.90
3DES	64	112	6.20
IDEA	64	128	9.75
RC5-32/16	64	$8s$ ($s < 256$)	28.90
RC5-64/24	128	$8s$ ($s < 256$)	13.90
SAFER SK	64	40, 64, 128	17.00
SHARK	64	128	9.85
SQUARE	128	128	47.20

Table 1.3.   Performance of RSA (full length modular exponentiation - Pentium 90 MHz)

Length (bits)	Speed (Kbit/s) C language	Assembly
512	1.800	13.40
768	0.845	5.80
1024	0.490	3.40
2048	0.128	0.89

In systems without a central trusted server, the number of keys can be reduced. Indeed suppose a network of N users exists, every one of which wants to communicate with every other. Since each communication requires a secret key, the total number of keys required equals $N * (N - 1)/2$.

In a public-key system each user only needs a personal public/private key pair, yielding a total of only $2N$ keys. If N equals 1000 this would mean 2000 versus 499500. In systems with a central management system, both approaches require the same number of keys. However, the central system can be off-line in the case of public-key technology, which reduces the cost and minimizes the security risks, and the system based on public-key technology is scalable.

In practice one often encounters hybrid systems in which one uses a public-key system for the distribution of the symmetric keys and a symmetric cipher for the bulk encryption of data.

1.4.2   Authentication Primitives

1.4.2.1   One-way Functions and Hash Codes.   A *one-way function* is defined to be a function f such that for every x in the domain of f, $f(x)$ is easy to compute; but for a random y in the range of f, it is computationally infeasible to find an x such that $y = f(x)$.

One-way functions can be used to protect passwords: one stores a one-way image of the password in the computer rather than the password itself. One then applies the one-way function to the input of the user and verifies whether the outcome agrees with the value stored in the table.

A *hash function* is a function which maps an input of arbitrary length into a fixed number of output bits. It is possible to distinguish two types of hash functions:

1. A MAC (Message Authentication Code) uses a secret key.

2. A MDC (Manipulation Detection Code) works without a key.

In order to be useful for cryptographic applications, a hash function has to satisfy some additional requirements. For a MAC one requires that it should be impossible to compute the MAC without knowledge of the secret key. For an MDC one requires that it is a one-way function, collision-free (it should be hard to find two arguments hashing to the same result), and it should be hard to find a second pre-image: given an x and the corresponding value of $f(x)$, it should be hard to find an x' different from x which has the same image under f.

Hash functions can be used to protect the authenticity of large quantities of data with a short secret key (MAC), or to protect the authenticity with a short string (MDC). Sometimes an MDC is used in combination with encryption, which can yield both data confidentiality and data authenticity.

There are several schemes which have been proposed for use as hash functions. Several MDCs have been constructed based on the DES, but other dedicated designs such as SHA-1 (Secure Hash Algorithm or FIPS 180 [94]), and RIPEMD-160 [78], have also been adopted by the International Standards Organization (ISO/IEC) [129]. These hash functions typically achieve a very high throughput (Mbit/s), even in software implementations (see Table 1.4).

1.4.2.2   MAC Construction and Security.   MACs can be constructed in many ways. Some of the MACs that are in use today are based on MDCs. The reason for this is the excellent performance of these primitives (Table 1.4). Table 1.5 gives an overview of different MDC-based MAC constructions.

Several attacks on MACs have been described in the literature. The terminology from Menezes, van Oorschot and Vanstone [181] is used to describe them. If the attacker obtains the secret key, he can produce a MAC for any data. This is defined as a *key recovery* attack. *MAC forgery* implies that an attacker can produce another data/MAC pair with a valid MAC (without necessarily knowing the secret key). Two kinds of forgery exist. In an *existential*

Table 1.4.   Performance of hash functions (Pentium 90 MHz)

Algorithm	Block (bits)	Hash (bits)	Performance (Mbit/s)
MD5 [207]	512	128	136.2
RIPEMD-128	512	128	77.6
RIPEMD-160	512	160	45.3
SHA-1	512	160	54.9

Table 1.5.   MDC based MACs

Name	Construction
secret prefix	$MDC(key\|data)$
secret suffix	$MDC(data\|key)$
envelope	$MDC(key\|data\|key)$
HMAC	$MDC(key \oplus opad\|MDC(key \oplus ipad\|data))$
MDx-MAC	see [202]

forgery, the attacker can find another data/MAC pair, but there is no control over the content of the data. In a *selective forgery*, the attacker cannot only find another data/MAC pair, it is also possible to choose (part of) the content of the data. The forgery is *verifiable* when the attacker can verify whether the produced MAC is valid.

The simplest MDC based MACs involve one MDC and a secret key. This key can be inserted in three different ways: prefix, suffix and envelope. Unfortunately these types of MACs are not secure as Preneel and van Oorschot have proven that these three types show a certificational weakness [202, 203].

A secure construction is the HMAC by Krawczyk, Bellare and Canetti [16, 158]. It is constructed by invoking the MDC function twice. The *data* used as input of the outer MDC function, is not known to the attacker, as it is the output of the internal MDC function to which the original data and the secret key is supplied. The HMAC was originally designed using concatenations instead of exors and this version is also still used (see Section 9.5). Another construction is the MDx-MAC by Preneel and van Oorschot. The interested reader is referred to [202] for more information.

1.4.2.3   Digital Signature. Public-key techniques can also be used for other purposes than for encrypting information. In the case of RSA, if Alice adds some redundancy (RED) to her message M and transforms the result using her private key (S_A), anyone who knows Alice's public key (P_A) can verify that this message was sent by Alice (by verifying the redundancy). In this way one can create a digital signature with message recovery, which is the equivalent of the hand-written signature on a document.

$$P_A(S_A(RED(M))) = RED(M)$$

Since the digital signature is not physically connected to the signed data or the originator, it must depend on this data and on the private key of the originator. Several signature schemes have been proposed by ISO/IEC [127]. In general it is possible to distinguish between two signature schemes: schemes offering message recovery and schemes without message recovery.

The RSA public-key cryptosystem [211] is an example of a primitive which can be used for both encrypting data and applying digital signatures. Schemes which can only be used for digital signature purposes are e.g., the Digital Signature Algorithm (DSA) [96] and the Fiat-Shamir scheme [91].

Note that it is possible to produce a digital signature based on conventional ciphers like the DES. However, these schemes are less efficient in terms of memory and computations. Other constructions use a conventional cipher in combination with tamper resistant hardware [127].

Assume Bob has received from Alice a digitally signed message. If Alice subsequently denies having sent the message, Bob can go to a third party (e.g., a judge), who is able to obtain Alice's public key. Subsequently they can verify the validity of the signature. In this way a digital signature can provide non-repudiation of origin. It is easy to see that it provides in addition entity authentication and data authentication, i.e., data integrity and data origin authentication.

1.4.2.4 Hash Functions and Digital Signatures. Hash functions can only be used in a situation where the parties mutually trust one another. They cannot be used to resolve a dispute.

As in the case of encryption, hash functions tend to be three orders of magnitude faster than digital signatures. This explains why one first computes the hash code of the message with a fast hash function and subsequently applies the digital signature to this short hash code. The hash code is padded (PAD) to counter attacks on the signature scheme [127]:

$$P_A(S_A(PAD|h(m))) = PAD|h(m).$$

This provides digital signatures which are not only faster and shorter, but also more secure (on the condition that the hash function used is secure).

1.4.3 Hybrid systems

In practice one often encounters hybrid systems in which a public-key system is used for the distribution of the symmetric keys and a symmetric cipher for the bulk encryption of the data. An interesting case study is securing electronic mail (e-mail). The cryptographic services (Section 1.2), that a secure e-mail environment usually offers, consist of:

- Confidentiality of the message (data confidentiality);

- Authenticity of the sender of the message (data origin authentication);

- Authenticity of the intended receiver of the message;

- Integrity of the message (data integrity);

- Non-repudiation of origin (and receipt) of the message.

The properties of secret key cryptography and public-key cryptography have been explained in the previous sections. In this real world situation both are combined in a hybrid system to take advantage of their respective benefits. The secure e-mail scenario is the one illustrated in Figure 1.5. Two entities take part in the protocol, the sender (A) of the message and the receiver (B).

To protect against an intruder listening in on the e-mail, the message is encrypted using a symmetric key algorithm. Performance is the primary factor in deciding to opt for symmetric systems. The key that is used in this way is called the *Data Encrypting Key* (DEK). To avoid all of these DEKs having to be distributed off-line, a public-key system is used to send the DEK along with the message.

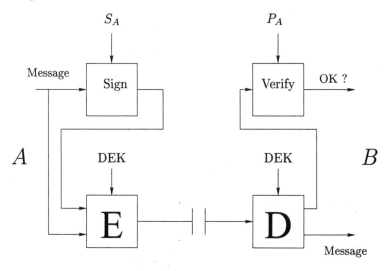

Figure 1.5.   Secure e-mail

Referring to Figure 1.6, when A (Alice) sends a secure message to B (Bob), B's public key P_B is used to encrypt the DEK. When B receives the message he is able to decrypt the encrypted DEK because he knows the corresponding private key (S_B). The process of encrypting the message with the DEK and then transmitting this DEK by encrypting it with a public-key system, is defined as *enveloping the data*.

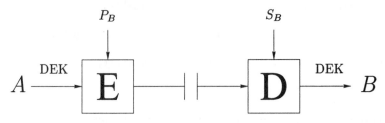

Figure 1.6.   Transmission of the DEK

B is also the only one who knows S_B and this means that nobody but B can read the message (authenticity of the receiver). A digital signature [127] is also applied to the message (see Figure 1.5) by the sender using his private key (S_A) before it is encrypted.

The digital signature mechanism that is used should be one without message recovery (e.g., applying a hash function to the data before it is signed) because this enhances the overall performance (see Section 1.4.2.3). The receiver of the message then verifies the signature on the message using A's public key (P_A). At this moment B is convinced that :

- Nobody has changed the message (integrity);

- Sender A is the real sender (data origin authentication) because A signed the actual (plaintext) message;

- He can prove to an outsider (e.g., a judge) that A really did send this message (non-repudiation of origin).

From an academic point of view the standards should be open. This means that the actual algorithms that are used to implement this model should be as diverse as possible.

1.5   KEY ESCROW AND KEY RECOVERY

The notion of *Key Escrow* was invented to counteract in part the issues mentioned in Section 1.6. The goal of the system is to provide the actually used symmetric keys to properly authorized parties (read information agencies). These organizations are only supposed to make the keys available under very special circumstances.

The first well-known example of key escrow was the Clipper system proposed by the Clinton administration. In this proposal a LEAF (Law Enforcement Access Field) would be sent with each message. This LEAF contains a copy of the session key encrypted by a key K_U. To generate this key, two independent key escrow agents need to work together. Whenever the authorities would need access to an encrypted message, they would file for a court-order and with this order they could obtain K_U from the two escrowing agents. More details of the system can be found in [83].

The Clipper proposal has finally not been approved because of the reaction of the American public that is very sensitive to the subject of free speech and related topics. A general disadvantage of key escrow systems is the fact that you are labeled as a criminal even before you have done something wrong (you have to send the LEAFs with your session keys). To counteract this issue and to answer the demand of companies for being able to decrypt files that were encrypted by employees that had been dismissed or where the password used to encrypt the file had just been forgotten, the system of *Key Recovery* was suggested.

The difference between key escrow and key recovery is that in key recovery schemes the agents don't need to be governmental agencies and that one can use as many agents as required. Also this form of key recovery would not be mandated by law but enforced by company regulations. An example of this system is IBM's SecureWay solution [120].

1.6   EXPORT REGULATIONS

When discussing implementations of cryptography, it is also often necessary to mention some legal concepts. Some countries (U.S., France, U.K.) have a specific policy regarding import and, especially, export of cryptographically enhanced products. This section is restricted to the U.S. policy as it has serious implications on the level of security that can be obtained with the most popular WWW browsers and servers.

Until January 1997, the best cryptography that U.S. companies were allowed to export was limited to a 40-bit security level. Thus the Netscape Navigator's and Internet Explorer's (the two most popular browsers) international versions were limited to this level of security. Whenever an algorithm was used that needed a longer key, the excess amount of bits would be sent in the clear or would be disguised in a more obscure way, but the end result was always 40-bit security. As already explained in Section 1.4.1.1 this scheme does not provide a sufficient level of security.

The maximum level of security that can be exported since January '97 is 56-bit although certain restrictions still apply. The export of 56-bit is only allowed if the vendor commits to implementing key recovery by January 1, 1999, and a governmental approval is needed for each customer the product is transferred to. An example of this is the Netscape Mail application, that is a part of the current Netscape Communicator distribution. It offers the Secure Multipurpose Internet Mail Extension (S/MIME) (Section 9.4) protocol with an implementation of the DES with a key length of 56 bits.

Netscape Communications is also able to offer full security (128 bits or more) to international companies, when they can demonstrate that it is essential (e.g., banks and other financial institutions). The international version of Netscape Communicator contains an implementation of algorithms with full key length. The standard level is still limited because the access to these implementations is supposed to be controlled by the use of digital certificates. However in July '97, McKay [176] published a program with which all versions of the Netscape browser could be patched to a version with strong cryptography support. As it turned out, it was only necessary to change a few bytes of the Netscape executable to achieve this.

1.7   PUBLIC KEY INFRASTRUCTURE

As seen in Section 1.4.3, public-key systems can be used for key management purposes. Basically the problem is solved by a little shift. Instead of having to distribute secret keys in a secure way, one has to find a way to distribute the public key of each entity in an authentic way. The public key infrastructure based on X.509 is one way to achieve this.

1.7.1   X.509

The X.509 standard [131] was issued by ITU-T (International Telegraph Union - Telecommunications), and has also been adopted by ISO/IEC [126]. It contains many guidelines, e.g., the authentication protocol discussed in Section 2.5.3.3. Trusted Third Parties (TTPs) called Certification Authorities (CAs) , that issue certificates, are introduced.

Basically, a certificate contains a digital signature of the CA on an entity (e.g., a human user) and its public key, thus binding them together. In this way the CA guarantees that a particular public key belongs to a particular user. If the user can now prove that they know the corresponding private key (e.g. by signing a challenge), they are authenticated to their correspondent. The certificate can be seen as a token to prove one's identity just as a driver's license or a passport. Many well known Internet security tools such as the Secure Sockets Layer (SSL) (section 9.5) use these certificates. There are now a number of commercial CAs on the market : Verisign, AT&T, Thawte, ...

Up to now there have been three major releases of the X.509 standard. Version 1 was issued in 1988, version 2 in 1993 and version 3 was published in 1995.

A version 1 certificate has the following components:

- *Version*: version number.

- *Serial number*: A unique number attributed by the CA.

- *Signature algorithm*: Information about the algorithm used to sign the certificate (e.g., RSA or Digital Signature Standard (DSS)).

- *Issuer name*: The unique name (also known as *distinguished name*) of the CA. A distinguished name is an identifier that uniquely identifies an entity, e.g., CN=be;O=kuleuven;OU=cosic;CN=vdwauver

- *Validity period*: Specifies the start and end times of the validity of the certificate. This is based on universal time to avoid confusion about time zones.

- *Subject name*: All details about the owner of the public key that is being certified.

- *Subject public key information*: The actual public key that is being certified.

- SK_{CA}: This is the signature of the CA generated by using the CA's private key. The public key of the CA is needed to verify it.

Version 2 added two fields (*Issuer unique identifier* and *Subject unique identifier*) to make implementation of directory access control possible. The latest release (V3) has made the biggest change by introducing cross-certification and the Extensions field.

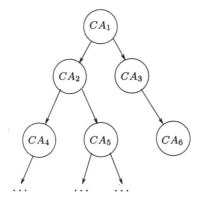

Figure 1.7.   Hierarchy of X.509 based CAs

Certification authorities are organized in a strictly hierarchical way (see Figure 1.7). In order to verify a certificate that is generated by a lower level CA, it is necessary to reconstruct the certificate chain back to the root CA. Before cross-certification there only existed one root CA. This model thus implied an unconditional trust in this root CA. Because of the success of the Internet, it became clear that this model would not suffice for the millions of Internet users. Therefore, cross-certification was introduced. There are now multiple root CAs that can cross-certify each other. Example: the root CA of domain B has cross-certified the root from domain A. When a certificate issued by one of the CAs in domain A needs to be verified by a user in domain B, the only certificates that are needed are the certificate chain back to the root CA in domain A and the cross-certificate by domain B's root on domain A's root.

The extensions have been defined to improve the functionality and to answer some specific requests of people using X.509 certificates. These extensions contain a criticality flag indicating whether a non-compliance means that a certificate is rejected or not. Specific extensions can be defined in future standards or by user communities. Some of the possible extensions include:

- Alternative naming so that the certificates can be used on the Internet.

- More information about the key: e.g., whether the key can be used for key management, verification of a digital signature, encryption of data.

- Other identification data such as the e-mail address of the person concerned.

- Where the Certificate Revocation List (CRL) can be obtained. The CRL is the list of the certificates that are not valid anymore. Reasons for an invalid certificate include:

  - The user has increased the bit-length of its modulus and has switched to a new public key;

  - The user has left the organization thus rendering the certificate futile;

  - The private key of a user has been broken or divulged (worst case scenario).

Because the X.509 certificate is more or less a digital passport, it is very important to know when this passport has lost its validity. The service offering this CRL must be on-line as it needs to be contacted every time an entity wishes to check whether a certificate is still valid.

A solution based on X.509 certificates usually contains the following components:

- The *Registration Authority*: this is responsible for identifying the individual that wants his/her public key certified.

- The *Certification Authority*: this issues the actual certificate.

- *Directory Services*: to make the certificates available on request.

- A *Key Backup/Recovery* facility: this is usually a business requirement and not so much a demand from the government.

1.7.2 SDSI

X.509 has many advantages but it is claimed to also have some disadvantages. The main problem is that X.509 is too complicated and it does not match the real world. An X.509 certificate ties a distinguished name to a public key. In order to get someone's public key, their distinguished name needs to be known, so that the correct X.500 directory can be found with the correct certificate.
There are two flaws in this scheme:

1. The model does not scale: it assumes that the distinguished name is common knowledge.

2. The global X.500 directory will *never* happen. It is unthinkable that companies publish a list with the names of their employees (i.e., at least in the

Table 1.6.   SDSI certificate

Issuer	name of the issuer
Subject	name of the entity that is being certified
Delegate	whether these rights can be delegated
Permit	what rights are issued
Validity	validity period of the rights

U.S.), so they surely will not publish an X.500 directory with this kind of information.

Confronted with these issues, Rivest and Lampson proposed the Simple Distributed Security Infrastructure (SDSI) [210]. The main ideas behind their proposal are:

- There is no longer a global namespace.

- Each key is a principal, can be used to sign keys, and has its own namespace. E.g., Bob is known to Alice as Red, because he has red hair. These can be compared to mail aliases.

- The link from the alias to the public key is the SDSI certificate.

- There are a number of rules to link private namespaces into groups.

SDSI also allows for an implementation of access control. Because it acknowledges that there can be no global name space, it allows the ACL author to define a local namespace. Also since it defines groups, it makes it easier to manage the access control (see Section 6.5.1). There are no certificate chains in SDSI, only certificate loops (Figure 1.8). Each certificate consists of a 5-tuple signed by the issuer (Table 1.6). In a certification loop, the rules from Table 1.7 apply for the reduction of SDSI certificates.

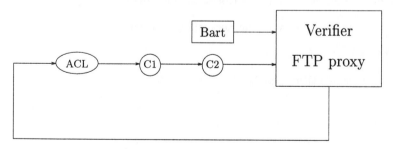

Figure 1.8.   Loop of SDSI certificates

Table 1.7.   Rules for reducing a SDSI certificate loop

R1	I1, S1, D1, A1, V1
R2	I2, S2, D2, A2, V2
R1 + R2	I1, S2, D2, A1 ∩ A2, V1 ∩ V2 if S1=I2 and D1=true

Table 1.8.   Example of a SDSI certificate loop

ACL	ftp-proxy, sys-admin, true, ftp until 12/31/1998
C1	sys-admin, Bob, true,ftp://foo.com RW, forever
C2	Bob, Bart, false, ftp://foo.com/Bob R, until 7/1/1998
R	ftp-proxy, Bart, false, ftp://foo.com/Bob R, until 7/1/1998

In the example of Table 1.8 the ftp-proxy gives the system administrator all ftp privileges until December 31, 1998. The system administrator can now delegate part of this authorization to Bob, who inherits read-write access to *foo.com*. Bob in turn wants his colleague Bart to have read access to the directory *Bob* on this ftp-server until July 1, 1998. Here is where the chain ends because Bob has decided not to give the option to Bart of delegating this right. When Bart wants access to the directory *Bob* on the ftp-server *foo.com*, he signs a challenge to authenticate the channel to the ftp-proxy. The result is that Bart gets read access, if he tries this before July 1, 1998, and the signature on the challenge verifies.

The status of the Simple Public Key Infrastructure (SPKI) working group is that SDSI 2.0 has been issued as an Internet Draft [88]. They identify the following advantages to SDSI (over X.509):

- Permits multiple trust paths (for fault tolerance);

- Answers more directly to the need of the verifier;

- Permits trust refinement;

- Has firmer identities than allowed by X.500.

2 AUTHENTICATION AND KEY MANAGEMENT

2.1 INTRODUCTION

In this Chapter the issues concerning user/entity authentication and the problem of key management are discussed in depth. In Section 1.2.1 the user/data authentication paradigm was introduced. In order to be able to enforce any security scheme it is necessary that every entity in the network is always convinced of the identity of the other parties it is communicating with.

In Chapter 1 the basics of modern cryptography have been illustrated. It was shown that it is possible to reduce the problem of safe-guarding information of indefinite length to keeping a short key secret. The key management is essential to the system. It is therefore important to find a way to distribute these keys in a safe and secure way.

2.2 UNIX AUTHENTICATION

The UNIX system solves the user authentication problem with the mechanism of passwords. In order to prove their identity, a user or entity sends a mutually shared secret to the system. Typically the secret consists of a letter word, where a letter can be any 7-bit character and the maximum number of letters is eight. UNIX typically stores the password information in the */etc/passwd* file. This file contains the name of the user, a salt (one of 4096 possible values) and the result of a one-way function applied to the password. In standard UNIX the one-way function is constructed from the Data Encryption Standard

25

(DES), where the expansion is altered based on the user's salt. The final 64-bit result is obtained by applying the modified DES repeatedly (25 iterations) to an initial value of zero, using the user's password as the key for the DES [186]. The salt is used to prevent an attacker from generating a look-up table containing the encrypted versions of the most popular passwords, thus giving the attacker a swift access to the system.

Personal Identification Numbers (PINs) work in the same way as passwords. They usually consist of a secret 4-6 digit code that needs to be typed in using a key-pad. The classical example is the use of a PIN to let a bank identify a customer who wants to withdraw money using their ATM (Automatic Teller Machine) card.

The password or PIN technique are vulnerable to several attacks as shown by Karn and Feldmeirer [140] and Leong and Tham [163]:

1. *Password stealing*: because of the Local Area Network's (LAN) inherent features, it is easy to listen in on a communication. With the help of some dedicated software (usually called a sniffer or LAN analyzer), it is possible to eavesdrop on the login session of a user. The password obtained in this way can then be used to get access to the system.

2. *Password guessing*: although the password is not stored in cleartext, it is still possible to guess a user's password. Users are usually unaware of the security issues and often choose passwords which are easy to guess. Also, the password file must be readable by all users (because the password file stores other information about the user such as User ID and Group ID, it must be readable by non-root programs) and thus it can be copied and attacked off-line. This kind of attack is called a *dictionary attack*. The algorithm is straightforward:

    (a) Pick a user.

    (b) Guess this user's password.

    (c) Look up the user's salt.

    (d) Apply the one-way function corresponding to this salt to this password.

    (e) Compare the result to the value stored in the password file.

The performance of this process can be enhanced by using computers in parallel. Each of these computers can look for the passwords of a number of users. On average it is possible to obtain 20 to 40% of the passwords in this way as is shown by Klein in [151]. Therefore, it constitutes a big security hole in the system. Password crackers (as these programs are called most of the time) can be located within a couple of minutes on the Internet. The most popular is the Crack (v50a) package. We recommend that system administrators run this software at regular intervals and take appropriate action.

3. *Password replay*: the UNIX password protection is static. This means that the same password is used every time a user attempts to log into the system (although it should be common practice to have users change their password regularly). With any static authentication mechanism, an intruder in the system can just replay the access token to gain access. This is called a *replay attack*.

4. *Social engineering*: even with the best possible security scenario, the human factor cannot be avoided. In many cases, the easiest way for an attacker to enter a secure system is just to call an authorized user, claiming to be the system administrator, and claim to temporarily need their password for some maintenance of their account. Other tricks include bribing people (selling passwords), intimidating users, etc. Users are also known to write down their password on a piece of paper and keep it close to their computer.

Table 2.1.   Number of passwords guessed at our site

	users	passwords found	percentage
1994	397	99	25
1995	504	101	20
1996	610	26	4
1997	702	15	2

Table 2.1 presents the result of a search for passwords at our site. Our findings were quite devastating the first time we ran the password cracker. This motivated us to send our users a series of guidelines on how to choose their passwords, accompanied by a letter from management to support our case. This only led to a small decrease in the relative number of bad passwords. Our conclusion was that human users, when left to their own devices, would continue to choose easily guessed passwords. During 1996, we obtained the source code of a *passwd* program, with which users are able to change their password, and changed it so that it also checked for bad passwords. After all users had been forced to choose a new password, the improvement was remarkable. Now only 2-4% can be found and only after about a month's work on a workstation (HP 715/80). An alternative to changing the *passwd* program is an automatic password generator such as the one specified in FIPS 181 [95]. However, the passwords generated by these tools are often not easy to remember and this causes them to be written down on notes next to the computer terminal.

Other methods to reduce a site's vulnerability to a password guessing attack include the use of *shadow password* files [105], or the password aging tool. With shadow password files, the password file is not readable by regular users, preventing it from being copied and attacked off-line. Password aging forces users to change passwords at regular intervals (e.g., each month) and keeps a history file with the users' previous passwords (to avoid them re-using old passwords).

As an example, here are the guidelines that were distributed to the users. Bad passwords include:

- Words that appear in a dictionary. Even if the word is supposed to be obscure, it is not suitable. This includes words from foreign dictionaries (it is a good idea to check for these if your site has many foreign users).

- Any password which can be derived from a person's name, department, or other personal information. Classical examples from this category: name of girlfriend, dog, license plate of a car, hostname of a computer, etc.

- A password that can be derived from the user's personal information in the password file (normally called the GECOS field). E.g., office number, phone number, etc.

- Something related to the username. Some people try to fool the attacker by reversing their username, capitalizing some letters and use this as their password.

- Place names (New York), or any other proper noun, fictitious persons (e.g., gandalf is always a good try when guessing a user's password).

Good passwords can be obtained following some basic rules. Their goal is to force the attacker to have to search the global 2^{56} bits space:

- Combine capital and small letters.

- Use non-alphabetic characters ($,%,&, ...) and/or numbers.

- The password must remain easy to remember, to prevent users from writing them down.

- The password should use the full allotted length (8 characters in most UNIX variants).

As an example of a good password, one can take two short words (ball and eye) and combine them with a %, resulting in eye%ball. Alternatively use acronyms – With a faery hand in hand–, and append a number (Wafhih56). Of course, now that these passwords have been published, they should not be used anymore!

2.3 BIOMETRICS

Instead of using a password to identify the user, it is possible to exploit the user's biometrical characteristics. It is a well-known fact that these usually form excellent decision criteria. Their biggest advantage is that they represent something that cannot be easily forged, stolen or forgotten. However they also have some disadvantages, such as requiring specialized equipment and thus a large investment. Also these biometric systems are not perfect. Some legitimate users inevitably fail the identification and some intruders are accepted as genuine. Therefore, the FAR (False Acception Rate — the probability of an imposter being accepted as a genuine user) and the FRR (False Rejection Rate — the probability of a genuine user being rejected) must be kept to a minimum.

The biometric concept is not a recent invention. The ancient Egyptians are reported to have measured people for identification purposes. Today's technology of course offers many more possibilities for capturing human characteristics to distinguish one individual from another. These systems have the greatest appeal in government or military applications, where extra security is often required and extra cost is not a deciding factor.

Because the FAR and FRR are never equal to zero, these systems are usually combined with other authentication mechanisms such as passwords, PINs or hardware tokens. Tokens are described in Section 2.4.

An overview of some of the most frequently used techniques is presented in the next sections.

2.3.1   Fingerprints

For general security fingerprints are gaining popularity. The probability of two people, even twins, having the same print is very low (in the order of 1 in a billion). Drawbacks of this system are the negative impression caused by the widespread use of fingerprints by the police to identify criminals and the risk of somebody cutting your finger of to obtain your access privileges.

2.3.2   Hand Geometry

At the Atlanta Olympics in '96 this technology was used to identify the Olympic athletes. When they first arrived in Atlanta, they were asked to put their hand into a little box. This box, a hand geometry reader, created a biometric template that was stored on a microchip inside the athlete's ID badge. This badge also contained a photo of the individual. When a person wanted to access a certain venue, they were asked to put their hand into a reader. If the result matched the value stored in the badge, access was granted. All of this may sound complicated, but the average verification procedure was executed in 2-3 seconds. Advantages of this system include:

- Low memory requirements (a template can be stored in as little as 9 bytes);

- Very low FAR and FRR (in the order of 1-2%);

- Acceptance by the general public.

2.3.3 Retina

A person's retina is unique and can be used to build very reliable identification systems. A major problem with this system is that people tend to display a natural fear about damaging their eyes, and they are thus anxious that the device reading their retina might not be safe. Also these scanning devices tend to be very expensive. As a result, these techniques are only used in high security military applications or banks.

2.3.4 Voice and Face Recognition

A significant amount of research has been performed to improve automatic speech recognition. While most research did not have security in mind (in contrast, most systems are trained to not distinguish at all between different voices), the results can be used to implement an authentication mechanism. In comparison with the retina techniques, they are cheaper and more readily accepted by the general public, but they suffer from a higher FAR and FRR.

The same that has been said about voice recognition applies to facial recognition. New techniques have reduced the FAR and FRR considerably, even distinguishing between someone holding a photo before the camera and an actual person sitting in front of the camera.

2.3.5 Writing

Although handwriting skills are rarely used now, they are still used to identify a human being. Usually these techniques involve signature verification but they could also be applied to regular writing. Until recently this method's success was minimal as it was considered to be unreliable. New techniques have resulted in much lower FAR and FRR.

This can be illustrated with two recent examples: the first one is the SMART-PEN developed at the IMEC institute in Belgium. The SMARTPEN [62] contains a micro-chip and modem that allows it to correspond with desktop stations and to verify the signature inside the pen. Instead of just comparing the signature of the user to a stored copy, it also measures the force with which the pen is put onto the paper, the three-dimensional angles in which the pen is held, the three-dimensional accelerations during the signing process, the moments of rest, etc.

The second one is the user identification system using a signature written with a mouse by Syukri, Okamoto and Mambo [224]. The main advantage of their system is that they only need a mouse and no additional equipment. They obtain a system where the FRR and FAR are approximately 10%.

2.3.6 Typing Speed

Similarly to the signature recognition, typing speed is a biometric technology based on behavioral activity. It is usually hidden from the end user as it is incorporated into a standard password system (e.g., by De Ru and Eloff in

```
81:  truf gruw red firt ghiu
82:  hju gerg kjil gewg gege
83:  fred anne mary ghuy erg
84:  jenn wary dor jean tram
85:  mari ghok lkiu mki mkki
86:  zaxc fgij klo kjnb hjws
87:  dit isnt good pass word
88:  hoe lang will this last
89:  isth isra ndom nopo yes
90:  ikbe idfr rats sind gis
91:  erty kjuu juik ikl opkj
92:  diti smoe iend buit wer
93:  wert zijn yes ghjs njgh
94:  mano wert jnu ghas qwer
95:  asdf oikm hdf qwer vnbh
96:  plqa oke rijk retg wern
97:  afwe erkg erg gker lqqq
98:  fjwh fwe werf lkvx xcvp
99:  xvxc rrre wer plfr wkmg
```

Figure 2.1.   S/Key print-out

[69]), and applies an extra test based on the typing speed of the user, to achieve a higher level of authentication.

2.4 DYNAMIC AUTHENTICATION

Even the very sophisticated techniques, discussed in Section 2.3, are not foolproof if it remains possible to replay the authentication information. Therefore, a good solution is to use one-time passwords. These passwords are automatically changed after every login and thus eliminate the value of an eavesdropped or lost password.

Several kinds of dynamic authentication schemes can be distinguished, but as a common denominator most of them use hardware devices. These devices are called *tokens* and they vary from a plain piece of paper to Smart Cards implementing a whole computer on a handheld credit card.

It is important to note that the procedures outlined below do not authenticate the user, but rather the device. In order to increase the security, the user should be forced to authenticate with respect to the device, using for example a PIN. This makes the device harder to use if it is stolen.

To increase the security it is recommended to use a combination of techniques as discussed below. The cryptographic protocols that are used in these systems are explained in Section 2.5.

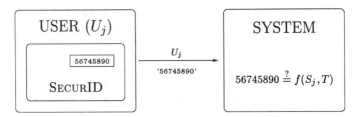

Figure 2.2.   SecurID principle

2.4.1   Code Book

This is the simplest form of one-time passwords. The first system was developed by Lamport [161]. Using an adequate mathematical algorithm (e.g., a one-way function), one can generate a sequence of passwords.

$$h(PW_i) = PW_{i+1}$$

The user can either run this algorithm on a portable computer, or it could be run by the system administrator and then transferred to the user on a piece of paper (see Figure 2.1). The passwords are written down in reverse order. When the user logs in with PW_i, the central server looks up the previous password that was used by this user (PW_{i+1}) and checks whether the above formula applies.

Each time the user logs in, a password is removed. When the passwords run out, the whole procedure can be repeated. A variant of this system, called S/KEY, was developed at Bellcore and has now been incorporated into an Internet standard [111]. The advantage is that it is very cheap and that the system does not have to store a secret value; the disadvantage is that if the synchronization between the user and the system is lost, it becomes impossible for the user to log on. Because the system is not authenticated to the user, an attacker could set up a fake server and collect a number of valid passwords, which could then be used to access the real server (as pointed out by Mitchell and Chen in [183]). However as explained above the regular user should notice this and trigger appropriate actions.

2.4.2   Time Based

If the user possesses a device which can perform simple computations, the security can be increased significantly. In the time based solution, the device calculates the current password, based on the current time (T) and a shared secret (S_j) with the system. The procedure is outlined in Figure 2.2.

The best known example of this technology is the SECURID token. This generates a new password every 60 seconds. There exist several versions of it:

- With a keypad: before releasing the current password, the user must first type in a PIN.

- Without a keypad: this requires the additional use of a traditional password (which is vulnerable to password eavesdropping).

2.4.3 Challenge-Response Based

When the authentication procedure is initiated, the system generates a random challenge and sends it to the person or to their device. In case of a token (a mini-calculator), the user has to enter the challenge on the keyboard. The device then computes the corresponding response, using secret information which has been assigned to it, or using public-key cryptography (using e.g., the protocol outlined in 2.5.3.3). This response is then sent back to the system, which verifies it.

2.5 CRYPTOGRAPHIC PROTOCOLS

In the following paragraphs some examples of cryptographic protocols are given and it is shown how they can be used to achieve entity authentication, key establishment, or a combination of both. This list is not comprehensive as they have been chosen based on their historical importance, clearness, and practical implementations (e.g., in the Kerberos or SESAME system).

The basic scenario is the same for all of these protocols, although some of them involve an extra entity. Basically there are two players A and B. In some cases they use a Trusted Third Party (TTP) P with whom they share long term keys.

The protocols use both symmetric encryption techniques and public-key cryptography. Table 2.2 gives an overview of the symbols that are used in the description of the protocols.

2.5.1 Glossary and Definitions

The following classification and terms as they have been introduced by Rueppel and van Oorschot in [213] is used. It is important to note that there exist several alternative definitions for these terms as pointed out by Gollman in [109] but for the sake of clarity the following definitions are used:

1. A *protocol* is a multi-party algorithm, defined by a sequence of steps precisely specifying the actions required of two or more parties in order to achieve a specific objective.

2. These objectives consist of:

   - *Entity authentication*: the process whereby one party is assured of the identity of another party involved in the protocol and that this party has actually participated in the protocol.

   - *Key establishment*: the process whereby a shared secret (usually a cryptographic key) becomes available to two or more parties.

Table 2.2.   Notation for the protocols.

A	user Alice
B	user Bob
K_{ij}	long term key shared between i and j
k_{ij}	session key to use by i and j
$MAC(K)(m)$	MAC on message m calculated with key K
$ENC(K)(m)$	message m encrypted with the symmetric key K
PK_A	public key of A
PK_A^{-1}	private key of A
$CA(PK)$	a certificate for PK (see Section 1.7.1)
$ENC(PK_A)(m)$	message m encrypted with public key PK_A
$SIGN(PK_A^{-1})(m)$	message m signed with private key PK_A^{-1}
N_i	nonce chosen by party i
T_i	timestamp from i's clock

The entity authentication protocol is *strong* if a possible attacker cannot gain anything useful from listening to the messages sent during a run of the protocol.

Key establishment protocols result in a shared secret. This secret is usually called a *session key*. A session key is a cryptographic key that has a limited lifetime and is used to cryptographically enhance the subsequent messages. There are several reasons for using session keys instead of long term keys:

- Session keys limit the amount of data that is encrypted with the same key.

- In case a session key gets divulged, the time during which the session can be compromised is limited.

- It is possible to avoid long-term storage for an abundance of keys.

If a compromise of the long-term keys does not lead to a compromise of the past session keys, the protocol has *perfect forward secrecy*.

Key establishment protocols can further be divided into *key agreement* and *key transport* protocols. In a key transport protocol, one of the parties generates (or obtains) the key and transfers this securely to the other party. With key agreement protocols neither of the participating parties uniquely determines the ultimate key as it is derived from information that is exchanged or generated during the run of the protocol.

The word *authentication* is used throughout this book and should be interpreted differently according to the context. In Table 2.3 an overview is given of the types of authentication that are distinguished. The top two have been defined previously but the bottom three need some more explanation. *Key authentication* is the property whereby a party is assured that no other party (aside from a specified second party) can know a particular secret key. Because key authentication is independent of whether this key is actually known to any of the parties, it is also referred to as *implicit key authentication*. *Key confirmation* is the process whereby a party is assured of the fact that the other party knows a particular key. *Explicit key authentication* is obtained when both implicit key authentication and key confirmation hold.

Table 2.3.   Summary of the meanings of authentication

Authentication	Focuses on
Entity authentication	Identity of a party
Data origin authentication	Identity of the source of data (Section 1.2.2.2)
(Implicit) key authentication	Identity of party which may share the key
Key confirmation	Evidence that the key is known by a party
Explicit key authentication	Evidence that an identified party knows the key

2.5.2   The Use of Timestamps and Nonces

In order to prevent replay, man-in-the-middle and interleaving attacks (outlined in [181]), the parties involved in a cryptographic protocol need to know that the messages they have received are recent, fresh, unique and timely. To obtain this goal several mechanisms can be used separately or concurrently.

2.5.2.1   Timestamps.   A timestamp can be seen as the obvious way to achieve the goals outlined above. When a receiving party receives a message they have to check that the timestamp contained in it is valid. This is done by verifying:

1. The current time is within a certain margin of the time indicated by the timestamp;

2. No message has been received with an identical timestamp previously.

    The timestamp mechanism has several drawbacks:

- The clocks of all parties concerned need to be synchronized;

- The system clock becomes a security critical element that must be well protected;

- All parties need to store a certain amount of the recent messages.

2.5.2.2 Nonces. A nonce is usually defined as a number that is used *never more than once*. Sometimes the term nonce and random number are viewed as synonyms but this is not always valid. Nonces may have a certain degree of randomness but they do not always need to be random to fulfill their purpose in the protocols. A *sequence number* can be used, for example, to prevent replay. When both communicating parties keep track of the sequence number they can easily check whether a new message they receive is a replay of an old message or not. Most of the time it is sufficient to generate the nonces by a good pseudo-random number generator. The basic scenario of using a nonce between two parties A and B is the following:

1. Party A generates a nonce N_A and sends it to B.

2. B uses this nonce N_A in a cryptographic function and returns this result to A.

3. A now validates this response to see whether it contains N_A. A then is convinced that this response from B is recent, unique and timely.

From this scenario it is clear that the nonce mechanism (except for the sequence numbers) has the drawback of needing at least two messages (if B would have used a timestamp, the same result could have been obtained in one step).

2.5.3 Entity Authentication

2.5.3.1 ISO/IEC 9798-2. In ISO/IEC 9798-2 [128], several mechanisms have been standardized to authenticate communicating parties to each other. In this scenario, both A and B share a long term symmetric key K_{AB}.

1. One-way authentication, based on timestamps.

   $$A \to B : ENC(K_{AB})(T_A, B)$$

   When B receives this message, he verifies whether the timestamp is recent and whether the target identified inside the message is indeed himself. While the timestamp protects against a replay attack, the inclusion of B prevents an outsider from reusing this message to try to impersonate B to A.

2. Mutual authentication, based on nonces.

   $$A \gets B : N_B$$
   $$A \to B : ENC(K_{AB})(N_A, N_B, B)$$
   $$A \gets B : ENC(K_{AB})(N_B, N_A)$$

   Upon receipt of the second message, B extracts A's nonce N_A, verifies that the nonce N_B he sent in the first message is included, and that his name is identified as the target of the message. B then sends back both nonces (in reverse order) encrypted with K_{AB}, to A. A then checks if both received nonces match the one she received before and the one she generated herself.

Analysis: These protocols are very simple and straightforward but they rely on a prior established long term key K_{AB}. In the case of the Internet, this is not a viable solution. If the encryption function would be the Vernam scheme [234] or an additive stream cipher, this scheme could be trivially broken.

It is possible to adapt these protocols to make use of MACs instead of symmetric ciphers. How this can be realized is described in [128]. A possible advantage of using MACs is that this software is usually less bound to export regulations, in contrast to data confidentiality providing software (Section 1.6).

2.5.3.2   ISO 9798-3. The ISO 9798-3 standard [128] describes a simple set of protocols to achieve authentication using public-key cryptography.

1. One-way authentication using timestamps:

$$A \to B : CA(PK_A), T_A, B, SIGN(PK_A^{-1})(T_A, B)$$

When B receives this message, he checks whether the timestamp T_A is recent, and then verifies A's certificate to obtain PK_A. With this public key, he verifies A's signature on the timestamp and B's identifier. Because entity A is the only person who knows the key needed to create the signature, A has been authenticated to B upon successful completion of the procedure.

2. Mutual authentication using random nonces:

$$A \leftarrow B : N_B$$
$$A \to B : CA(PK_A), N_A, B, SIGN(PK_A^{-1})(N_A, N_B, B)$$
$$A \leftarrow B : CA(PK_B), A, SIGN(PK_B^{-1})(N_B, N_A, A)$$

After receiving the second message, B checks whether the correct identifier (B) has been used, verifies A's certificate and extracts PK_A from it, to finally verify A's signature on the two random nonces (N_A and N_B) and B's identifier.

Upon reception of the third message, A performs the same checks (verifying the certificate, pulling out PK_B, and verifying B's signature). For the same reason as mentioned in the protocol above, both participants have been mutually authenticated at the end of a successful protocol.

2.5.3.3   X.509. The International Telegraph Union - Telecommunication's (ITU-T, formerly known as CCITT) recommendation X.509 contains two authentication protocols. The certificates and certification authority structure, that are defined in this guideline, are detailed in Section 1.7.1.

1. Strong two-way authentication protocol:

$$A \to B : CA(PK_A), T_A, N_A, B, data$$
$$\qquad\quad SIGN(PK_A^{-1})(T_A, N_A, B, data)$$
$$A \leftarrow B : CA(PK_B), T_B, N_B, A, N_A, data'$$
$$\qquad\quad SIGN(PK_B^{-1})(T_B, N_B, A, N_A, data')$$

A generates the timestamp T_A (this is an indication for how long this message is valid and it also allows to detect a forced delay) and the nonce N_A. This information together with B's identifier and some optional data (containing e.g., an encrypted session key $ENC(PK_B)(k_{AB})$), is then signed by A and sent to B.

B processes the first message by checking the validity of the certificate, the timestamp and A's digital signature. If all checks are successful, A is authenticated to B. In the reply to A, B includes the nonce N_A together with another nonce N_B, timestamp T_B and A's identifier (again the $data'$ could be an encrypted session key). B then signs this information to authenticate to A.

When A receives the second message, she proceeds in the same way as B did in the second stage. The checks include the verification whether the received N_A is equal to the one A has sent in the first message. Upon successful completion of all checks, B has authenticated to A.

If the $data$ field contains an encrypted session key, B decrypts this field with the private key PK_B^{-1}. Because A has signed the data field, B learns that A knows the encrypted session key. The same checks can be performed by A and mutual entity authentication is obtained with key transport and mutual key authentication.

2. Strong three-way authentication protocol:

$A \rightarrow B : CA(PK_A), N_A, B, data, SIGN(PK_A^{-1})(N_A, B, data)$
$A \leftarrow B : CA(PK_B), N_B, A, N_A, data', SIGN(PK_B^{-1})(N_B, A, N_A, data')$
$A \rightarrow B : N_B, B, SIGN(PK_A^{-1})(N_B, B)$

The difference between this and the previous protocol is, that in the three-way setup there is no need for timestamps. Instead the security of the protocol relies on the nonces N_A and N_B. In step 2, A checks that the received N_A is equal to the one she sent before. After the third message, B has to verify that N_B and B's identifier are correct.

2.5.4   Key Establishment

2.5.4.1   Diffie-Hellman.   The Diffie-Hellman protocol [75] is an example of a key agreement scheme. Although it has a number of weaknesses and should not be used in its simplest form, it has been very important in the development of public-key technology.

Both parties A and B previously agree on a generator g and a prime number p. It is important to choose a prime p of the form $p - 1 = 2p'$ with p' a smaller prime as shown by van Oorschot and Wiener in [229].

1. $A \rightarrow B : g^a \bmod p$

   A picks a random secret number a, and calculates the public key $p_A = g^a \bmod p$ and forwards this to B.

2. $A \leftarrow B : g^b \bmod p$

   B picks a random secret number b, calculates the public key $p_B = g^b \bmod p$ and returns it to A.

3. $K = (p_B)^a \bmod p = (g^b)^a \bmod p = g^{ab} \bmod p$

   $K = (p_A)^b \bmod p = (g^a)^b \bmod p = g^{ab} \bmod p$

   Both A and B can now calculate the shared secret key. A obtains the key by raising B's public key p_B to the secret value a. B performs a similar calculation but using A's public key p_A and the secret b.

Analysis: The Diffie-Hellman scheme provides no entity authentication, key authentication or key confirmation. In practice it is therefore essential to use modern variants as the Station-to-Station protocol explained in Section 2.5.5.4. One big advantage of the Diffie-Hellman protocol though is that it offers perfect forward secrecy if the exponentials (public keys of both parties involved in the protocol) are based on short-term keys.

2.5.5   Entity Authentication and Key Establishment

2.5.5.1   Needham-Schroeder. The Needham-Schroeder protocol [189] is very important for historical reasons. Most of the modern systems, such as Kerberos (Chapter 5) and SESAME (Chapter 6) are based on it. In this protocol there is no long term symmetric key shared between A and B. However, there is a Trusted Third Party P with whom both parties share long term keys. Needham-Schroeder (and its derivatives) are also used to establish keys to protect the communication between A and B.

1. $A \rightarrow P : A, B, N_A$

   A generates a nonce N_A and sends this, together with her name and the name of the party she wants to authenticate to, in her message to the TTP P.

2. $A \leftarrow P : ENC(K_{AP})(N_A, B, k_{AB}, ENC(K_{BP})(k_{AB}, A))$

   In his response to A, the TTP P includes a freshly generated session key k_{AB} and a ticket $ENC(K_{BP})(k_{AB}, A)$. This information inside this ticket can then be used by A to authenticate herself to B. The message, that is sent back to A, is encrypted with the long term key K_{AP} so that A should be convinced that the originator of this message is the TTP P.

3. $A \rightarrow B : ENC(K_{BP})(k_{AB}, A)$

   A decrypts the message from P and verifies that the nonce N_A is equal to the one she sent in her first message. A then forwards the ticket to B.

4. $A \leftarrow B : ENC(k_{AB})(N_B)$

   Party B decrypts the ticket. From this, he obtains the session key k_{AB} and the name of the party that wants to authenticate to him (A). He then generates a new nonce N_B and encrypts this with the session key k_{AB} and returns this to A.

5. $A \rightarrow B : ENC(k_{AB})(N_B - 1)$

A decrypts the message from B with the current session key k_{AB} and reveals the nonce N_B (if there is any redundancy in this nonce B has authenticated to A). She then subtracts one from this nonce and sends the result, encrypted with the session key k_{AB}, back to B. When B processes this message, A is authenticated to him. Indeed, A is the only party that should know the session key k_{AB} (except for the TTP and B) and in returning the message in step 5, she proves to B that she knows the correct session key k_{AB}.

Analysis: The Needham-Schroeder protocol provides mutual entity authentication (under the condition outlined above), key transport and mutual key confirmation. It however has some serious weaknesses as pointed out by Denning and Sacco in [72]. In step 2 of the above protocol, the ticket is unnecessarily double encrypted. This introduces an unnecessary overhead. Moreover an attacker obtains a large number of known plaintexts which he can use to attack the encryption algorithm that is used and thus break the protocol. B also has no proof that the session key is fresh (recent), thus if any session key ever gets compromised, it would be possible to impersonate A to B. Therefore, Denning and Sacco suggest to use timestamps.

Finally it is remarked that using an encryption primitive to provide authentication is not recommended. As noted in Section 2.5.3.1 this prohibits the use of algorithms as the Vernam scheme or an additive stream cipher.

2.5.5.2   Authenticated Key Exchange Protocol (AKEP).   This protocol was designed by Bellare and Rogaway [17]. Three messages are exchanged to set up a session key k_{AB}. It achieves mutual entity authentication and implicit key authentication of k_{AB}.

Before the protocol starts there are two long term symmetric keys K_{AB} and $K_{AB}^{(1)}$ ($K_{AB} \neq K_{AB}^{(1)}$) shared by parties A and B. The function $HASH$ is a keyed one-way function that is used to derive the session key k_{AB}. The nonces that are used should be pseudo-random and cannot be sequence numbers.

1. $A \rightarrow B : N_A$

A picks a random number N_A and forwards it to B.

2. $A \leftarrow B : (B, A, N_A, N_B), MAC(K_{AB})(B, A, N_A, N_B)$

B also picks a random number N_B and sends the message B, A, N_A, N_B to A together with a MAC of this message. A then checks the identities inside the message, verifies whether N_A received is equal to the one sent in the first step and verifies the MAC with the shared key K_{AB}. If the MAC is correct, party B is authenticated to A.

3. $A \rightarrow B : A, N_B, MAC(K_{AB})(A, N_B)$

A sends to B the values A, N_B and a MAC on them. B then needs to verify whether the N_B received and the MAC are correct. Doing so authenticates A to B.

Both parties A and B now generate the session key as:

$$k_{AB} = HASH(K_{AB}^{(1)})(N_B)$$

Analysis: Shown above is the AKEP-2 variant of the protocol. There also exists a AKEP-1 protocol that uses probabilistic encryption techniques. In [17] Bellare and Rogaway provide a model and formal definitions for secure symmetric-key two-party mutual authentication and key establishment protocols. They *prove* that AKEP-1 and AKEP-2 are secure relative to this model under certain assumptions (pseudo-random character of the MAC and $HASH$ functions).

2.5.5.3 Modified Needham-Schroeder. To achieve mutual entity authentication, key transport, and mutual implicit key authentication, public-key cryptography is used.

1. $A \rightarrow B : ENC(PK_B)(N_A, A)$

Party A picks a random nonce N_A and encrypts this along with the identifier A with the public key of the party B she wants to authenticate to.

2. $A \leftarrow B : ENC(PK_A)(N_A, N_B)$

B decrypts the incoming message with his private key PK_B^{-1} and retrieves the random nonce N_A and checks who is trying to set up the identification procedure. In this case, it is party A, thus he retrieves her public key PK_A and uses this to encrypt N_A and a self-chosen random number N_B.

3. $A \rightarrow B : ENC(PK_B)(N_B)$

When A decrypts the incoming message with her private key PK_A^{-1}, she obtains N_A and this authenticates party B, since B is the only entity that has the key needed to decrypt the message A sent in step 1. She then sends back the random nonce N_B to B encrypted with his public key PK_B. Upon receipt of this message, A has been authenticated to B because A is the only one to possess the key necessary to decrypt the message in step 2. The session key can be obtained from $k_{AB} = f(N_A, N_B)$, where f is a one-way function.

Analysis: As pointed out by Lowe in [171], B cannot be sure that the final message came from A. Lowe fixes the problem by adding B's identifier in the second message $(ENC(PK_A)(N_A, N_B, B))$. However, Boyd shows [35] that even with this change it is necessary that the public-key primitive used has strong properties, such as "non-malleability", to prevent an attacker changing the message values.

2.5.5.4   Station-to-Station Protocol.   This variant [76] of the Diffie-Hellman protocol (Section 2.5.4.1) adds mutual entity authentication and mutual explicit key authentication.

Both parties agree on a suitable prime p and a generator g. They also have a public/private key pair that is used for applying a digital signature. Hereto the RSA algorithm (Section 1.4.1.2) is used.

1. $A \rightarrow B : g^a \bmod p$

   Like in regular Diffie-Hellman, party A generates a secret a and sends B the above message.

2. $A \leftarrow B : g^b \bmod p, ENC(k_{AB})(SIGN(PK_B^{-1})(g^b, g^a))$

   B also generates a secret b and immediately calculates the shared key $k_{AB} = g^{ab} \bmod p$. B then signs the concatenation of the exponentials (using RSA) and encrypts the result with the shared key k_{AB}. B then sends this together with his exponential to A.

3. $A \rightarrow B : ENC(k_{AB})(SIGN(PK_A^{-1})(g^a, g^b))$

   A computes the shared key k_{AB} and decrypts the second part of the message sent by B in step 2. A then uses B's public key to verify the signature. If this is successful, A learns that B also knows the key k_{AB} and B has been authenticated (because of the digital signature).

   A then sends a similar message to B but it uses the exponentials in reverse order. When B has performed similar checks on this message, A has authenticated and has shown that it knows the shared key k_{AB}.

Analysis: the STS protocol has until now not shown any major flaws. Lowe describes an attack in [172] but it only proves that entity authentication according to the definition in [35] is not achieved.

2.5.6   Overview

Table 2.4 provides a summary of the discussed cryptographic protocols and the services they provide. Again these examples are only a very limited subset of the available protocols and have been shown here because of their importance and relation to the Kerberos and SESAME protocols outlined in Chapter 5 and 6. The interested reader is referred to [181] for a more elaborate and thorough analysis of the current state of the art.

Table 2.4. Overview of protocols (the second column indicates the kind of entity authentication, the third and fourth specify whether the protocol offers key transport or key agreement, and the last three detail if the protocol provides implicit key authentication, key confirmation or explicit key authentication. M stands for mutual authentication and U stands for unilateral authentication from A to B.)

Services	Entity	Trans	Agree	Impl	Conf	Expl
ISO/IEC 9798-2 (1)	U					
ISO/IEC 9798-2 (2)	M					
ISO/IEC 9798-3 (1)	U					
ISO/IEC 9798-3 (2)	M					
X.509	M	X		M		
Diffie-Hellman			X			
Needham-Schroeder	U	X			M	
AKEP-2	M	X		M		
Modified N-S	M	X		M		
STS	M		X			M

3 COMPUTER NETWORKS

3.1 INTRODUCTION

This chapter aims at providing an overview of computer networking. It begins by introducing concepts in computer networks: circuit and packet switched technologies, LANs and WANs, and hardware addressing. It then describes the two most popular layered protocol architectures: the Open System Interconnection (OSI) and the Transmission Control Protocol/Internet Protocol (TCP/IP). It follows with a description of the Internet, the largest of all networks, including a description of the Internet standardization bodies. The chapter finishes with a description of firewall technology, perhaps the most popular of all security technologies for computer networks.

3.2 COMPUTER NETWORKING CONCEPTS

There are essentially two approaches used for building computer networks [64]:

- *Circuit Switched*: A dedicated connection is established between sender and receiver before the communication of payload data begins. All data is transferred over the same path. This type of network is often called *connection oriented* and the most common example is the telephone system.

- *Packet Switched*: No connection is established between sender and receiver. Data is broken up into small pieces called *datagrams* or *packets*. Each separate datagram can travel a different route to reach the destination. Hence each datagram has an identifier of the destination so that it can be correctly routed through the network. This type of network is often called *connectionless* and most data networks use this type of technology.

Circuit switched networks can guarantee bandwidth to the sender, but are notoriously inefficient (if the sender isn't sending data the bandwidth is wasted). Packet switched networks do not guarantee bandwidth for the sender but are more efficient as the underlying networking infrastructure is shared.

Circuit switched networks traditionally have been the most popular, mainly because of the widespread use of telephone networks. However today packet switched networked are rivalling circuit switched networks in popularity, and it has been suggested that in time even telephone networks will become packet switched.

Networks that span large geographic distances are called *Wide Area Networks* (WANs) and those that span shorter distances are called *Local Area Networks* (LANs). In general WAN technology is much slower than LAN technology. WANs typically have speeds ranging from the kilobit per second range to the megabit per second range, whereas LANs have speeds ranging from the megabit per second range to as high as the gigabit per second range.

All packet switched hardware technology defines a unique addressing mechanism. Each datagram carries a destination hardware address which is used to identify the receiver. Each hardware technology has a unique standard describing the number of bits used, format of the address, and the location in the datagram. Hardware addressing schemes in general are incompatible between different technologies.

3.3   LAYERED PROTOCOL ARCHITECTURES

Modern computer networks have layered protocol architectures. They have been designed this way for maximum flexibility, i.e., to accommodate a wide variety of applications and networking technologies. A benefit of layering is that the networking problem is divided into discrete subproblems, as each layer can be researched separately (each layer functions independent of any other layer).

The two most famous layered protocol architectures are the OSI Reference Model and the TCP/IP Model. Other architectures do exist, however they are becoming less common each year. By far the most popular architecture is TCP/IP. This is perhaps because it was adopted for the Internet and the 7-layer OSI architecture is often considered too unwieldly and cumbersome for widespread use. The OSI Reference Model today is viewed as a theoretical base standard to compare other models.

3.3.1   OSI Reference Model

The OSI reference model [123, 124] consists of seven layers (see Figure 3.1). These layers can be indicated by their names or their number N (N=1, ... ,

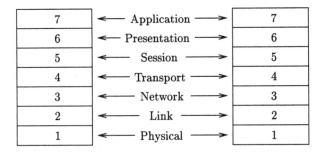

Figure 3.1.   OSI reference model

7). Each layer performs a well defined function in the communication between two or more computers.

The functions of the different layers:

1. The *physical* layer transforms the information (represented in bits) to actual signals which can be transported by the physical transmission medium.

2. The *link* layer provides the network layer with a reliable transfer facility. It is responsible for error detection, transmission errors, possible retransmissions.

3. The *network* layer establishes network wide connections, and includes facilities such as network routing.

4. The *transport* layer provides the session layer with a data transfer facility that is independent of the type of network actually used.

5. The *session* layer establishes and synchronizes the communications between applications.

6. The *presentation* layer converts from an abstract syntax to a concrete syntax (e.g. ASCII) and vice versa.

7. The *application* layer enables applications to get access to distributed information services. For example an application could get access to a remote computer and download files from it.

Each of the layers communicate with the equivalent layer on a different network node. The idea is that each layer uses the services of the layer below, adds functionality, and provides a service to the layer above.

In practice an application generates data at the application layer, and passes it down through the layers, with each layer adding its own header and data. The packet is transferred across the network, and at the receiving node the data passes up the layers from physical to application layer with each layer processing its header and data. Eventually it reaches the application of the receiving node.

3.3.1.1 Security in the OSI Reference Model. Although the original OSI Reference Model was comprehensive, it did not outline security functionality. This was developed separately as the OSI Security Architecture [124]. It is not an implementable standard, but contains:

- Formal definitions of terminology to be used in writing other security standards;

- Description of security services required by the OSI Reference Model, for example Authentication, Access Control, Data Confidentiality, Data Integrity, and Non-Repudiation. It also describes the mechanisms that can be used to implement these services. Some examples include encryption, digital signatures and access control;

- Most importantly, a description as to the appropriate layer placement of security services.

3.3.2 TCP/IP

The OSI Reference Model has not been adopted by the Internet. Instead the simplified model from Figure 3.2 has been used [38]. In contrast with the OSI-model, only four layers have been implemented:

Figure 3.2.   TCP/IP model

1. The *Host-to-network* layer connects the host to the network using some kind of protocol. It contains several sublayers. The MAC (Medium Access Control) sublayer is an example of such a sublayer and it is used to determine what packet is sent next on a multi-access channel.

2. The *Internet* layer is essential in the model. Its goal is to permit hosts to send packets into any network and make sure that these packets travel to the correct destination. These packets may arrive in a different order than they were sent but it is up to the higher layers to re-arrange them if necessary.

   The Internet layer defines the Internet Protocol (IP). The Internet layer transfers packets between different hosts and is thus similar to the network layer in the OSI model.

3. The *Transport* layer has been implemented with two different protocols:

- *TCP* is a reliable connection oriented protocol. This entails that a connection is established between the source and target machine. The Transmission Control Protocol (TCP) is very reliable and creates a two-way stream connection between two computers. Each TCP connection is attached at each end to a *port*. The well known `telnet` (port 23) and `ftp` (port 21) programs are implemented over TCP. The TCP protocol uses two special bits in the packet header, *SYN* and *ACK*. To open a connection a host sends a TCP packet with the SYN bit set but the ACK bit unset. In response to this, the target host sends a packet with both bits set. To finalize this *three-way handshake* the first host sends a packet with the SYN bit unset but the ACK bit set.

- *UDP* is an unreliable, connectionless protocol. In this case, there is no connection set-up between the originator and target machine. The originator sends out the packets without getting back an acknowledgement from the target machine. The User Datagram Protocol (UDP) provides a simple system for sending data between two computers, but the obtained service is unreliable. *Unreliable* means that there is no guarantee that all packets are sent and delivered or that they arrive in order. However on a LAN or any other fault-free network, UDP can attain 100% reliability. UDP needs less overheads than TCP and is used primarily for programs such as talk, rwho, etc.

4. The *Applications* layer contains the regular Internet services such as HTTP, SMTP, `ftp`, etc.

3.3.2.1   Security in the TCP/IP Model.   Similarly to the original OSI Reference Model, the TCP/IP model did not have any security designed into it (not completely true, the IP header had some service bits allocated that were intended to determine if packets were to be forwarded over insecure or secure networks, these unfortunately were rarely used).

  Unlike the OSI Reference Model however, TCP/IP has never had a security standard written for it. It is most likely the reason that security in TCP/IP has a number of problems:

- Security services are duplicated throughout the architecture;

- Incompatible security features are being used in different parts of the architecture;

- Uneconomical techniques are being used.

  The forthcoming IPv6 (the replacement to the current IP protocol) is designed to fix these problems with security built into the model (see Section 9.7).

3.4   THE INTERNET

Over the last couple of years, the Internet has become a real fact of life, in the same way as people are used to watching television. In its current form, it is a gigantic network across the globe, that connects more than 150,000 independent networks (LANs and WANs), and has more than 90 million users from more than 180 countries. The Internet has been growing exponentially and it is hard to make any predictions on future growth. In Figure 3.3, it is shown how the current Internet population is divided between the major countries and how the numbers are targeted to increase in the next few years. A first conclusion one can draw from this figure is that still more than 50% of the users are situated inside the U.S.

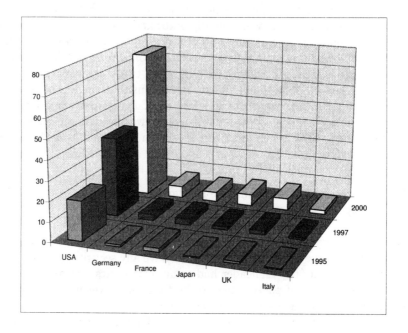

Figure 3.3.   Internet users

Historically, the Internet dates back to the late 60's when the U.S. Department of Defense (DoD) sponsored the building of the then called ARPANET in the context of their Defense Advanced Research Project Administration (DARPA) initiative. The ARPANET connected hundreds of universities and government departments using leased telephone lines. Later on, satellite and radio networks were added.

Also a shift in the applications that are offered can be seen. In the early days, the most successful programs were `telnet` (a program to remotely login on another computer), `ftp` (to execute file transfers), and electronic mail (still very popular). Nowadays the immense popularity of the World Wide

Web (WWW) has brought with it an abundance of opportunities: electronic commerce, information services, distance learning, etc.

The main design criterium of the Internet was to build a robust network. Therefore, a process called dynamic routing was applied. This means that the route between different hosts on the Internet is not static and it allows for packets to get to their destination via several ways. The main problem of the Internet (except for the limits in bandwidth that people are encountering more and more) is that security was not an issue when it was designed. It is thus not a surprise to see that there are many different ways to abuse the Internet to access local and remote computer resources. Recent studies suggest that there are 60,000 attacks per day aimed at computers connected to the Internet [89].

3.4.1   Internet Standards

Not unlike the rest of the world, the Internet community found a need for standardization. The procedures that are used are however very different from those used by regular standardization bodies such as ISO or ITU-T. The top organization is the Internet Architecture Board (IAB). The IAB has two sub-groups called IRTF (Internet Research Task Force) and IETF (Internet Engineering Task Force). The IRTF focuses more on the long-term research, while the IETF tries to solve the short-term engineering problems. The IETF is organized in several working groups. It is important to distinguish the different stages an idea has to go through in order to become an Internet standard. There are four major stages:

1. Internet Draft;

2. Proposed Standard;

3. Draft Standard;

4. Standard.

The first stage is an *Internet Draft*. Anyone on the Internet can create one. When there is sufficient interest in the community, the idea is explained in an *RFC* (Request For Comments) by one of the IETF working groups and it becomes a *Proposed Standard*. These RFCs form a set of rules with which product developers can build their products. To advance to the *Draft Standard* stage, there must be working implementations available and these must have been thoroughly tested for 4 months. Ultimately the IAB can decide to declare the RFC as an *Internet Standard*. In order to advance to this stage a lot of operational experience is required and the interoperability between different products must have been demonstrated. Examples of Internet Standards are IP and TCP/IP. All of these standards can be obtained from various Internet sources.

3.4.2   IETF Security Working Groups

Due to the emergence of electronic commerce and numerous reported incidents on the Internet [39], a large number of security working groups have been formed recently. At the time of writing of this text, they are:

- Authenticated Firewall Traversal (AFT);

- Common Authentication Technology (CAT);

- Domain Name Security (DNSSEC);

- IP Security Protocol (IPSEC);

- An Open Specification for Pretty Good Privacy (OPENPGP);

- One Time Password Authentication (OTP);

- Public Key Infrastructure based on X.509 (PKIX);

- Secure Shell (SECSH);

- S/MIME Mail Security (SMIME);

- Simple Public Key Infrastructure (SPKI);

- Transport Layer Security (TLS);

- Web Transaction Security (WTS).

3.5   FIREWALLS

Firewalls are a relatively recent phenomenon and are perhaps the most used of all security technologies. In their short history they have evolved tremendously: the first firewalls were simple packet filters for controlling access between networks. Now they are expected to provide numerous security functions [188]:

- Track and maintain state between multiple sessions;

- Support low overhead protocols for multimedia needs such as UDP, and broadcast protocols;

- Authenticate individual users using tokens or one-time passwords;

- Encrypt/decrypt traffic passing through the firewall;

- Create secure private tunnels and virtual networks through untrusted networks;

- Support IP address translation: to provide another layer of security by making the computers non-routable on the Internet (using private addresses), and to address the shortage of IP addresses;

- Protect against viruses, active-X and Java;

- Ensure its own security is not compromised.

It would not be practical in this section to discuss all of the possible firewall requirements (this is left to books devoted to firewalls). Instead this section focusses on the original and core service provided by firewalls: to operate between protected and unprotected networks, controlling and monitoring access between them.

3.5.1   Inter-network Access Control

A firewall is a component or set of components that primarily restricts access between a protected network and the Internet, or between other sets of networks [61]. The firewall system controls access based on configured rules, these rules are designed to enforce an organization's security policy.

Figure 3.4 shows a typical firewall system separating an organization's network from the Internet. The aim of this firewall system is to restrict and monitor access between the Internet and internal hosts. At a minimum, the organization requires a firewall system for each connection to the Internet.

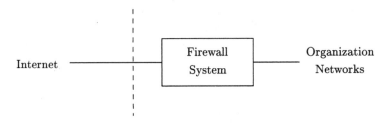

Figure 3.4.   Firewall system

The advantages of a firewall system are as follows:

- The organization can concentrate its security efforts at one point, and ensure the firewall system is as secure as possible (rather than trying to secure every system on the internal network).

- All traffic between the Internet and the internal network can be regulated and monitored to ensure it meets the organization's policy.

The first advantage is critical to understanding the benefit of a firewall system. It is impractical, and probably impossible (with current operating system technology) for system administrators to ensure the security of every internal host. For example, all hosts would have to be configured to ensure adequate authentication of users (no weak passwords, passwords changing often, use of tokens). System administrators must also ensure that no host applications provide access through misconfiguration or software bugs. Clearly these two objectives are very difficult to achieve. Hence, it is much more practical to concentrate the efforts at one point and rely (to some extent) on the firewall's security.

It should be noted however that no system (including a properly configured firewall system) is absolutely secure. Firewall systems are often very large and complex software and hardware configurations and it is unwise to rely completely on this system as they are usually built from untrusted components. Hence system administrators should still ensure at least reasonable efforts have been made to secure internal hosts.

3.5.2   Structure of a Firewall System

A firewall system should be designed with two goals in mind:

1. To protect itself from attack.

2. To protect the network behind the firewall system from attack.

To provide such protection firewall systems are normally designed with a *defense in depth* principal. That is, multiple mechanisms are used that back each other up. This principal is not new to security, for example a car usually has door locks, and an ignition lock.

There are numerous configurations for firewall systems implementing the defense in depth strategy. Figure 3.5 shows a popular implementation.

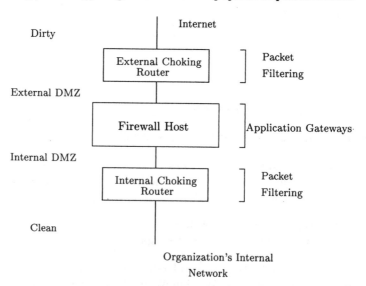

Figure 3.5.   Firewall configuration

Starting at the top of the figure, the Internet (marked as *dirty* on the figure), connects to the Organization through an external choking router. The router performs *packet filtering*, selecting which packets may pass through the router in each direction. This is the first line of defense. The router then connects to a host computer (normally termed the firewall host). The network between the external router and the firewall host is usually termed the *external demilitarized zone* (DMZ). The firewall host implements an *Application Gateway* (also called a proxy service) for applications that must traverse the firewall. The firewall host may also implement packet filtering. The firewall host connects to an internal choking router that again implements packet filtering, with the network between the firewall host and internal choking router termed the internal DMZ, and after the router the clean network.

The defense in depth principal can be seen in the implementation. For example the external router protects the firewall host from external attack, and the internal router is still providing some security even if the external router and firewall host are compromised.

3.5.3 Packet Filtering

In traditional routers, when a datagram arrives at an interface, the router consults its routing table to decide where to send the datagram. The decision is made based on the destination IP address of the datagram and what the routing table says to do with that destination IP address.

Routers and hosts that implement packet filtering [60] (the routers are commonly called choking routers) perform an additional check. They look at other information in the datagram to decide if the datagram should be routed or discarded (based on the requirements of the security policy).

The information available in the datagram is:

- IP source and destination addresses;

- TCP/UDP source and destination ports;

- Protocol Type (Internet Control Message Protocol (ICMP), TCP, ...);

- Other information.

The packet filtering systems make decisions based on the datagram information and also on the incoming and outgoing interfaces.

To create packet filtering rules, detailed knowledge of the protocols for each application is required. This knowledge is used to create the packet filter's rules. For example consider an SMTP service (SMTP is Simple Mail Transfer Protocol and is used for email) that needs to traverse a packet filtering router. The requirements for SMTP are:

- SMTP is TCP based;

- SMTP servers use port 25;

- SMTP clients use ports above 1023.

Table 3.1.   SMTP packet filtering rules

Direction Mail	Direction Packets	Source IP	Dest IP	Protocol	Source Port	Dest Port	ACK Bit
Incoming Mail	In	External	Internal	TCP	>1023	25	–
	Out	Internal	External	TCP	25	>1023	Yes
Outgoing Mail	Out	Internal	External	TCP	>1023	25	–
	In	External	Internal	TCP	25	>1023	Yes

Possible rules to allow SMTP traffic are shown in Table 3.1. Note that the rule set is quite sophisticated in that IP addresses, protocol types, port addresses and ACK bits are all used to control access (as well as the direction of the traffic). Not all packet filters provide this functionality.

Chapman [60] discusses a number of problems with packet filtering:

- Complexity of packet filtering specifications: it can be very difficult to set up packet filtering rules.

- Reliance on accurate IP source address: IP source addresses can be easily faked so packet filters should watch for strange addresses (for example a valid internal address coming in from outside the firewall).

- Dangers of IP source routing: IP source routing lets the sender determine the route to take. In most IP filtering situations this should be disallowed.

- Testing and monitoring filtering is difficult: tools are required to allow system administrators an opportunity to test their configurations before going live.

Chapman lists other problems too and the reader is referred to [60].

Depending on the security policy of the Organization, a number of applications may need to be configured in the choking routers, some examples are:

- Terminal Service: `telnet`;

- File Transfer: File Transfer Protocol(`ftp`), Trivial ftp (`tftp`), File Service Protocol (FSP), Unix to Unix Copy (UUCP);

- Electronic Mail: Simple Mail Transfer Protocol (SMTP), Post Office Protocol (POP);

- BSD rcommands: rlogin, rsh, rcp;

- News: Network News Transfer Protocol (NNTP);

- Information Resources: Gopher, WAIS, Archie, finger, whois, talk;

- Administration: Domain Name Service (DNS), Simple Network Management Protocol (SNMP), Internet Control Message Protocol (ICMP);

- WWW: Hyper-Text Transfer Protocol (HTTP).

Because of their inability to examine the data content of the packet (application payload), and to analyze and maintain state information about the application and user, packet filters themselves are inadequate for firewalls.

3.5.4   Application Gateways

A firewall host should provide application gateway services to all (or at least as many as possible) of the applications that need to communicate through the firewall. Application gateway services are specialized cut-down versions of programs that take requests and forward them as appropriate to the actual programs (which is why they are called proxy services).

For example an `ftp` application gateway can receive `ftp` requests from the internal network, and forward the request to the appropriate `ftp` server on the Internet. The application gateway can be transparent in which case client software is modified to forward all requests to the application gateway automatically, or can require users to change procedures to specifically use the proxies.

Application gateways have a number of advantages:

- They protect server programs from direct connection thus reducing the chance that an attacker can exploit a weakness in the program. The application gateway servers have been written to be minimal versions of the programs to reduce the opportunity for vulnerability.

- They allow for access restrictions, in that the application gateways can be configured to control access to services (for example you may be only able to `ftp` files from the Internet to the internal network, and the application gateway may stop you sending files out through the firewall).

Firewall hosts provide application gateway services for a range of applications, some examples are:

- Terminal Services (`telnet`, Rlogin);

- File Transfer (`ftp`);

- Electronic Mail (SMTP,POP3);

- World Wide Web (HTTP);

- Gopher;

- X Window System (X11);

- Printer;

- Remote Execution (Rsh);

- Sybase SQL;

- Real Audio;

- Active X;

- Java.

  There are a number disadvantages to application gateways:

- They impose limitations on the the applications that are supported because the firewall manufacturer must write an application gateway program for each application.

- In many cases transparency is lost because the user is required to know about the application gateway and connect first to it before connecting to the final server.

- There is huge-overhead for the firewall as it has to copy and process all application data.

3.5.5   Stateful Inspection

Stateful inspection is a new firewall paradigm, designed to combine the merits of both packet filter and application gateway techologies, but without their drawbacks. It provides transparent connectivity for an application, yet it is application and user aware.

Stateful inspection works by examining all layers in the communication, analyzing and processing them, and maintaining state information about the specifics of the application and user. The system also has the security policy configured within it, so that it can decide to accept or reject, or possibly to encrypt the data.

To enable inspection of all layers, stateful inspection is placed at the network level on the host or inside the router. This module is programmed with the security policy rules, which instructs the module how to extract and process information.

The major benefits and advantages of stateful inspection are [188]:

- Flexibility to support any existing protocol and application and to instantly adapt to new ones.

- High performance (it is placed in the host kernel or in special hardware).

- Absolute transparency to authorized users and applications.

- Protecting the firewall host (by blocking network traffic as soon as it enters the host).

3.5.6   Firewall System Configuration

There are other concerns when configuring a firewall system:

- Logging: All devices in the firewall system should perform logging. Typically this can occur with the choking routers forwarding logging information to the firewall host, and the firewall host writes this information and also its own logs to write-once media.

- Strong Authentication: The choking routers and firewall host should be configured to require strong authentication of users that want to access them. In most cases this means that hardware tokens should be used.

- Minimal Configuration: The choking routers and firewall host should provide a minimal configuration. In the case of the choking routers remote configuration programs (such as Trivial `ftp`) should be disabled. On the firewall host all non-essential services should be disabled and more appropriately removed altogether.

- Firewall Host Operating System: Firewall hosts come in two varieties: those with a single operating system/firewall product, and those that are a firewall product loaded onto a standard operating system. In the second case the administrator must be sure of the integrity of the operating system before using it.

4 TAXONOMY OF VARIOUS ATTACKS

4.1 INTRODUCTION

The aim of this chapter is to describe the various attacks used to gain unauthorized, and often illegal, access to computers. These attacks can occur remotely through computer networks and also through actual physical access. The chapter begins by describing the motives behind the attacks and gives some publicly available statistics which indicate the frequency of the attacks. It then describes a number of vulnerabilities that in general allow attackers unauthorized access to computers. Finally it describes vulnerabilities in the Internet Protocol suite that gives attackers many opportunities for a malicious attack on Internet connected computers. The reader should be aware that new attacks are appearing every day, and therefore the reader is referred to [39] for information on the most recent attacks.

4.2 MOTIVES FOR ATTACKS

Our society is increasingly dependent on the use of computers and computer networks in business, education, government and personal use. Unfortunately there has been a corresponding increase in unauthorized exploitation of these computer systems. Computer attacks can be classified by their motive according to Icove, Seger and VonStorch [73]:

61

- Government and Military: Trying to access information of national strategic importance.

- Business: Obtaining information with regards to competitiveness such as design information and source code.

- Financial: Trying to gain with direct financial return. For example stealing of credit card details, or transferring money from accounts.

- Terrorist: These groups are realizing that more damage can be done through attacks on computers rather than through traditional means.

- Grudge: Personal reasons dictate destruction of computing resources (for example being fired from a position).

- Fun: Wanting to gain access more for enjoyment or enhancement of reputation than any potential profit.

4.3 DOCUMENTED ATTACKS

Getting a clear indication of the nature and extent of computer attacks is very difficult. Most organizations do not publish information about their experiences because of the fear of losing reputation in the community. One way to get an indication of the types and frequency of attacks that are occurring is to look at public advisories. One such advisory group is the Computer Emergency Response Team (CERT) Coordination Center [39] at the Carnegie Mellon University. This center publishes discovered vulnerabilities as well as solutions for a wide range of computer systems.

Table 4.1.   Number of CERT advisories

Year	Number of Advisories
1998	10
1997	28
1996	26
1995	18
1994	15
1993	19
1992	21
1991	23
1990	12
1989	7
1988	1

Table 4.1 shows the number of CERT advisories from 1988 to 1998. An advisory lists a newly discovered vulnerability and solution. One interesting point to note is that the number of advisories each year is not decreasing.

Table 4.2.   Vulnerabilities listed in the CERT advisories

Year	Physical	Software	Poor Config	Communications
1998 (10)	-	9	-	1
1997 (28)	-	27	1	-
1996 (26)	-	23	2	2
1995 (18)	-	13	2	1
1994 (15)	-	13	2	1
1993 (19)	1	15	2	-
1992 (21)	-	16	2	-
1991 (23)	-	18	3	-
1990 (12)	-	8	3	-
1989 (7)	-	1	5	-
1988 (1)	-	1	1	-

Table 4.2 shows the four main types of vulnerabilities and the number that appear in the advisories. These are described in some detail in the next section and are physical access (Physical), software flaws (Software), poor configurations (Poor Config) and communication vulnerabilities (Communications). The table indicates that the main source of vulnerability is software flaws.

Table 4.3 shows what access is achieved as listed in the advisories. The advisories list unauthorized access to resources as the most common impact of a vulnerability. Note that some vulnerabilities allow both unauthorized access and denial-of-service.

4.4 GENERAL VULNERABILITIES

This section outlines the general vulnerabilities in computer systems and computer networking that allow attackers to gain access.

4.4.1 Physical Access

If a computer can be physically accessed, gaining control of it is usually very straightforward. For example, most Unix systems allow a user to reboot the computer into single user mode, even without requiring a password. Even when this function is disabled, the computer can be broken into. A method that works most of the time (except when the disk is encrypted) is to take the system disk out of the computer, mount it on another computer and edit the password file. The aim of this attack is to gain access to a privileged account which in

Table 4.3.   Access achieved in the CERT advisories

Year	Unauthorized Access	Denial-of-service
1998 (10)	9	4
1997 (28)	26	2
1996 (26)	23	3
1995 (18)	16	-
1994 (15)	14	-
1993 (19)	17	1
1992 (21)	18	-
1991 (23)	21	-
1990 (12)	11	-
1989 (7)	7	-
1988 (1)	1	-

most cases gives the attacker full access to the computer system. Depending on the operating system, there are other ways to achieve the same result. In Linux for example, booting with a floppy disk usually permits you to change the password file without actually having to physically open the computer.

These are only a couple of examples. There are numerous others. For these reasons and also because of theft and vandalism, computers with high security needs must be kept in a physically secure environment. Particularly those computers that are part of the security infrastructure such as Certification Authorities and Security Servers (used e.g., by Kerberos and SESAME). Moreover, Certification Authorities do not need to be connected to the network at all.

4.4.2   Software Flaws

Software flaws or bugs are errors discovered within software applications, typically after they have been released. In most cases these flaws are due to programming errors. A flaw typically results in unexpected and unpredictable behavior. They can also compromise security in the following way:

- If a program requires elevated privileges to perform its task, and this program has a bug, this bug is executed with these extended privileges. Sometimes this bug can be used to pass these privileges to an attacker. An example of this is using a buffer overflow attack (discussed below) on programs that run with higher than normal privileges.

- Attackers often look for software bugs that may simply bring the system (or a service on the system) down to cause a denial-of-service attack. Examples of this are:

- The WINS port 42 attack for Windows NT V3.51 and V4.0: The Windows Internet Name Service (WINS) listens for connections on TCP port 42. By opening a telnet session to this port and feeding the connection garbage data, an error is written to the event log. Depending on the configuration, this flaw can cause a server to slow down, or even use all of the hard drive resources causing the system to fail.

- Land IP Stack Attack: Some implementations of TCP/IP are vulnerable to SYN packets in which the source address and port are the same as the destination [55]. This attack has been successful against a variety of Unix and Windows systems, and results in the TCP/IP protocol stack locking up and in some cases bringing the whole system down.

To exploit a bug the attacker examines the compiled code or the actual source code (if it is available) and determines whether it is possible to interact with the program to obtain a desired effect. In some cases the vulnerabilities are discovered by accident.

Software flaws can occur in the operating system, or in application programs. Even applications whose primary purpose is to add security to the system, can introduce a vulnerability unintentionally. An example of this is the advisory relating to the SSH program [57] which describes a vulnerability introduced by the SSH client program.

4.4.2.1 Buffer Overflows. Buffer overflows to date have been the most common software flaw. A buffer overflow occurs when data is written past the end of a memory buffer (probably because the author of the program did not check the length of the data before writing into the buffer). In its most simple form a buffer overflow causes data corruption which could lead to a service or system crash. Alternatively when the buffer is a local array and the overflow extendss far enough to corrupt the execution stack, it is possible to execute the attacker's code, e.g. to spawn a privileged shell.

The execution stack contains the address of the next command in the parent function. If the data written to the buffer is user data, the user could thus modify this pointer to make the program return to a routine that was put in memory (somewhere further in the buffer overflow). This code could start a shell (it is usually called shell-code), and if the program is being run with super-user rights, the shell inherits these rights.

A typical example of an exploitable bug is a buffer overflow in a program that is executed as a privileged user. For example, Unix systems have programs that can be run by a user but they actually run with the security level of the system administrator (root). They are called *Set-User-ID* (SUID) programs and can be used to perform system functions like changing passwords. If a user can run these applications and supply invalid data to cause a buffer overflow then unexpected results could happen. These range from application or system crashes to a raising in privileges for the user running the program.

Programs to abuse buffer overflow in SUID root programs and daemon processes, as well as shellcode can be found freely on the Internet. Buffer overflow attacks have been reported on a regular basis, some examples are [48, 49, 50, 51, 53, 58].

4.4.2.2   Out-of-Band Data.   Another variety of the software flaw is commonly called the *Out-of-Band* (OOB) attack. In communication protocols, OOB data is characterized by data that is not part of the communicating parties normal transmission. For example if one of the communicating parties is receiving data too quickly, or is receiving data in error, an OOB signal may be sent to the sending party to notify the sender of the problem.

OOB attacks are not so clearly defined and generally refer to two types of attacks:

- Attacks based on using actual OOB data to cause unexpected results. These attacks may be exploiting a buffer overflow or some other problem. An example of this:

  - WinNuke [112]: An attacker sends OOB data to the destination's NETBIOS port (139) by the setting the URGENT bit flag in the TCP header. The receiver uses the URGENT POINTER to determine where in the segment the urgent data ends. This can be exploited on some Windows NT systems to bring the system down.

- Attacks based on producing specific **valid data** that maybe outside of the normal data scope. However, instead of being for a useful purpose, this data is used to cause software to behave unexpectedly. Examples of this are:

  - With Kerberized telnet it is possible for an attacker to spoof a packet that sets the "do encryption" option to off.

  - FTP Bounce [54]: By using the `port` command in active FTP mode, an attacker may be able to establish connections to arbitrary ports on machines other than the originating client. This behavior is RFC compliant but it is also potentially a source of security problems for some sites.

  - Smurf [56]: In this attack ICMP echo requests are directed to IP broadcast addresses from remote locations to generate an avalanche of messages. This results in denial-of-service. Network addresses with all zeroes in the host portion can also produce a broadcast response.

OOB programs are becoming more prevalent as attackers search for new attack mechanisms.

4.4.2.3   CGI Coding.   A Common Gateway Interface (CGI) program is a program that is executed by a Web Server, primarily for the processing of user data entered through a web page, and for producing a web page as output. In many cases the CGI program accesses some type of database, and generates queries based on the user's data.

Some CGI scripts have a problem that allows an attacker to execute arbitrary commands on a Web Server under the effective user-id of the server process [52]. The cause of the problem is not the CGI scripting language (such as Perl or C). Rather the problem lies in how an individual writes a script. In many cases, the author of the script has not sufficiently checked user supplied input, and unintentionally may give an attacker an opportunity for access. For example, some CGI scripts pass commands entered by the user to the local shell, and an attacker may use this to delete files, or mail a password file to the attacker's account.

4.4.3 Insecure Operating Systems

Some operating systems are inherently insecure. For example, DOS and Windows 3.x environments do not provide any kind of security as they were targeted to address single user environments. Users can impersonate one another and read/write everyone's data. These problems are especially prevalent in terminal rooms. Anyone can usually enter them, and circumventing traditional computer authentication is usually not very difficult.

It should be noted that there are no CERT advisories (see Table 4.2) describing the vulnerabilities of these types of operating systems. This is probably a result of the fact that these operating systems work in the way they were designed, and the lack of security is a feature of these systems rather than a discovered vulnerability.

These operating systems however can be used in a very secure way. That is, when they are used as single-user, personal, closed systems (without network access) and you can lock them physically.

4.4.4 Poor Configurations

Poor software configurations can cause many vulnerabilities. This can occur in software configurations for the operating system or in application programs. It can also occur in network devices such as routers and firewalls. There are many examples of poor configurations:

- Password-less accounts.

- Wrong permissions on files and directories.

- World exportable file systems.

- Allowing mounted floppy disks with SUID programs.

Often systems are shipped from the manufacturer with a poor configuration, and unless the administrator is organized in checking for known problems, vulnerabilities can exist.

The BSD rtools are a particularly important example of how a poor configuration can give unwanted access. The rtools use a *trusted host* and *trusted user* philosophy. The trusted host philosophy is that if one host trusts another host, then any user that has the same user name on both hosts can login from the trusted host to the other computer without typing a password. The trusted user is slightly more restrictive in that a specific user from a trusted host is allowed to login without a password. The `rtools` are quite powerful providing such services as remote login `rlogin`, remote shell `rsh` (for executing commands on another computer) and remote copy `rcp` (for copying files from one computer to another). Problems can occur due to misconfigurations. For example, if a home directory is world-writable (this is not uncommon), it may be possible to replace the trusted user configuration file (usually named `.rhosts`) with a file created by an attacker to allow unauthorized access. The problems with the `rtools` are further discussed in Chapter 7, including how the security was strengthened with SESAME.

4.4.5   Communication Vulnerabilities

Computer communication is often a target for attack and this is due to the lack of security in most current protocols. There are numerous examples:

- Entities involved in the protocol are rarely authenticated and even if they are, typically the authentication is very weak.

- Most protocols do not use cryptographic protection of data so are vulnerable to attack.

- Protocols make false assumptions about trusted information, e.g., source addresses and port numbers. These are in general easy to fake.

Even if the protocols are provided with some cryptographic protection often there are weak points in the protocol that still allow an attack. Examples of this are replay attacks where legitimate communicated data is retransmitted for illegitimate purposes [97], or man-in-the-middle attacks where a third party takes part in the communication protocol without the knowledge of the legitimate parties [181].

4.4.6   Access to Intermediate Computers

Attackers rarely attack their target computer directly. In most cases attackers use intermediate computers as stepping stones to the final computer. There are two main reasons for this:

- The attackers can hide their trail by making access from legitimate accounts, leaving these account footprints behind. Also it is easier to cover a trail on a less secure computer.

- It is often difficult to attack the target computer, so the attacker uses other computers to obtain user accounts, and for loading attack tools, that may enhance the chance of accessing the target.

Like a virus, this kind of infiltration compromises accounts exponentially. The process is as follows:

1. Get advanced privileges on a system.

2. Try to get as much access with these privileges to remote systems.

3. For each system you get access to, repeat the previous steps.

In the next paragraphs some examples of this procedure are illustrated:

- Trusted IP-address: many systems use tools such as the `rtools` (discussed above) or TCP-Wrappers, that control access based on the source IP address of the data. Because IP addresses can be masqueraded so easily, this may allow initial access to the host.

- Eavesdrop the network segment [42]: on broadcast networks, e.g., Ethernet, network devices are listening to all packets. If the destination address of a packet corresponds to the local address, it is forwarded to the operating system. Besides the fact that some Ethernet interfaces have the feature that their Ethernet address can be changed by software, a much bigger problem is the existence of *promiscuous* mode. In this mode the network device forwards all the packets that are transmitted on the segment to the operating system, regardless of their destination address. While this option is regularly used as a debugging tool, an attacker can nevertheless use it to listen to all packets that appear on the network segment. Data from or to some ports (`telnet`, `ftp`, POP, ...) can then systematically be filtered out to catch cleartext passwords. On heavily-loaded segments this attack has the potential to compromise many accounts in a very short period of time. Software to perform these attacks is freely available. These programs are called sniffers, or network analyzers and often come free with the operating system.

- Hijack tty's [43]: this is a very powerful attack e.g., in the Unix environment. It can defeat most security systems that are put in place, and is technically very easy to achieve. On multi-user systems the super-user can read from and write to all the users' terminals. The user can for instance send a command to be executed in a shell to a user's tty. In the worst case, when the super-user completely takes control of the user's terminal, this is called *tty hijacking*. If a user made a "secure" connection to a remote host, and the network stream is encrypted, the communication is still vulnerable to a hijacking attack from the super-user. The encryption is indeed always performed at a lower level than the tty level. Programs to perform this attack are called tty-snoopers or tty-watchers.

4.5 INTERNET PROTOCOL ATTACKS

The Internet is by far the largest installed network, and it is not surprising that most attacks are on Internet connected computers. For this reason the rest of this chapter is dedicated to outlining attacks specific to the Internet protocol suite (or TCP/IP suite).

4.5.1 Scanning the Address Space

As a precursor to attack, an attacker tries to determine which hosts exist on a target network. This is typically done by attempting to ping (based on ICMP messages) every machine in the target network range. If a ping response is returned then the host is alive and is a possible target. Other methods for determining if a host exists is to examine routing, address resolution protocol (ARP) and simple network management protocol (SNMP) information. ICMP should be disabled to ensure that the address space cannot be scanned, and other requests such as for SNMP data should not be replied to.

If an attacker cannot determine if a host exists then a probe is often attempted next. In a probe, the attacker tries a *TCP connect* to a particular port. It receives a response from the port if it is in the *listen* state. This type of scanning is potentially easier to detect by the target site. Often a host is scanned on multiple ports to determine which services are operating. More sophisticated attacks exist (half-open connection, and the most recent *TCP Port Stealth Scanning*) that are more difficult to detect.

4.5.2 Attacks on Internet Services

On the Internet, services are provided to remote hosts. An Internet service listens to a specific port and answers all incoming requests. An example is the mail program, that handles the Simple Mail Transfer Protocol (SMTP) on port 25 to give users the ability to send electronic mail. This service is available on most hosts on the Internet.

Sendmail (the electronic mail program on Unix) is, for historical reasons, a good example of an insecure program. To deliver incoming mail, sendmail has to be run as a daemon process that has super-user rights. It is such a complex system, allowing for the processing of hundreds of mail options, that it is not surprising that security holes are still found in its latest releases [47]. The oldest security bug in sendmail is still famous. It is a backdoor which spawns a root shell without any authentication. Any user on the Internet could thus become root on a system simply by connecting to the SMTP port. The authors of the first sendmail version added a WIZ (wizard) command, which, followed by a SHELL command returns a shell with super-user rights [41]. Fortunately, this option was removed several years ago from most of the currently installed sendmail programs.

Leaving backdoors in Internet services is an easy way for an attacker to get into the system even after the break-in has been discovered [40]. DEBUG is another option [40]. Other bugs allow remote Unix root or user access, for instance by entering a shell pipe in the From: header.

Electronic mail is not the only vulnerable service. Other services (telnet, FTP, finger, NFS, DNS, RPC, X) can also be very dangerous. An overview of many services and their security-related problems can be found in [105]. Bellovin [19] describes an original way of detecting intrusions through Internet services and also provides some statistics.

The most famous example of an attack based on Internet services was the Internet Worm. This worm relied on bugs in the Sendmail and finger services to gain root access to systems. It then tried to crack passwords and access other hosts via trusted host authentication (rtools). The only thing the worm did was copy itself to other systems. Because of several bugs, probably present because the worm was prematurely and/or accidentally released, it ran several times on the same hosts. Therefore it quickly overloaded the systems, bringing them to a halt. This happened on November 2nd, 1988, and paralyzed 1% of the 60,000 hosts grouped by the Internet. Many studies have reverse engineered the worm and their findings are described in [84, 197, 205, 215, 217].

4.5.3 Attacks on Network Communications

These attacks use features of the underlying transport, network or physical layer. With Ethernet and TCP/IP (v4), it is possible to listen to all the network traffic, send packets with a fake IP source address, and set or unset any of their TCP flags.

4.5.3.1 Denial-of-service attacks. These attacks are usually very easy to perform (especially on a LAN). For instance users usually do not need any special privileges and a simple program, that can be acquired from the Internet, may either bring a whole network down, or target specific computers. An example of this is the Avarice program published in [5]. This program listens to SYN requests on a LAN and answers these requests by an RST packet (masquerading the source IP), which immediately shuts down the connection. If this reply is sent before the target's kernel can react to the SYN request, the target's connections is refused. A simple way to find the host which is denying service to the whole LAN is to find the RST packet's source MAC address and to locate the Ethernet device with that address.

The Ping floods, also known as ICMP Echo floods, are another example of denial-of-service attacks. In this the attacker broadcasts a bundle of ping commands and does not wait one second between each command (as they should). If the size of the ping command is big enough this has the potential to make the network unusable. A variant of this is the famous Ping of Death [46], where the attacker uses extra large datagrams (more than 64 KB) to bring down target systems. Another variant is the smurf attack [56] which uses ICMP echo request packets directed to IP broadcast addresses. This results in an avalanche of responses causing a denial-of-service attack on the network.

TCP SYN flooding [45] is a popular denial-of-service attack. In order to make a host unable to reply to packets sent to one of its ports, it fills up the queue on the host of incoming TCP requests. Normally, the host gets a SYN request, answers it with a SYN/ACK and waits for an ACK packet. By sending a bundle of SYN requests whose source addresses are set to a routable but unreachable host on the Internet, the destination host's queue is filled with pending connections. When the queue limit is reached, TCP silently drops all new incoming requests until a time-out is reached, which is the desired effect of this attack. This technique is usually just a part of the attack. It can be a way to make the trusted host unable to answer the server requests in an *IP-spoofing* attack.

The Universal Datagram Protocol (UDP) is a connectionless protocol. It is very easy to send packets with invalid originator addresses. As part of a typical TCP/IP protocol stack simple services are often provided. These include echo, discard, daytime and other services. Often simple UDP services exist, like a UDP echo. A UDP echo generates a UDP packet to be sent back to the originator. A denial-of-service attack exists where a forged UDP packet is sent to the echo port of a machine with an originators address of another host with a UDP echo port open [44]. This generates a perpetual cycle of echoing between ports, effectively causing bandwidth to be consumed. This type of attack is thwarted by disabling simple services and through proper filtering.

4.5.3.2   Sequence Number Guessing. Sequence number guessing attacks (also known as blind *IP Spoofing*) were described in 1985 by Morris [185] as a simple technique that allows an attacker to execute commands remotely on a host providing IP-based authentication. This is possible without even having to intercept any packets (blind attack), making it in theory possible to attack any host offering these services. The attack relies on a weakness in the 4.2BSD TCP/IP implementation. In 4.2BSD the sequence number can be guessed with a reasonable computational effort. If an attacker can guess the server's sequence number at the moment the first packet arrives at the server side, it is possible to establish a TCP session without receiving any packets from the server.

The procedure consists of:

1. Guess the server's sequence number. Guesses are based on previous connections between attacker and server, the time of day and round-trip of a packet.

2. Send a SYN packet to the server's `rsh` port, with the trusted host (client) as IP source, requesting the establishment of a TCP session.

3. The server replies with a SYN/ACK containing a sequence number, but to the real client. It is not necessary for the attacker to be able to read this packet's contents.

4. If the client is able to reply to the server, the client sends a RST packet bringing the attack to an end. But if the client is down, or has to deal with a denial-of-service attack, the server's packet is dropped.

5. In the mean time the attacker sends another fake packet, containing an ACK of the server's presumed sequence number and still masquerading as the client.

6. If the sequence number is correct, a TCP session is established.

7. By following the protocol specifications, the attacker can continue to send packets blindly to the server, and eventually execute a command.

4.5.3.3 TCP Hijacking. TCP hijacking is described by Joncheray [134] as a simple attack against TCP. The attacker has to be able to listen to the exchanged packets, so it is no longer a blind attack. Once a TCP session is established, an attacker can quite easily desynchronize the session (sequence number at the server side is different from the acknowledgment number at the client side and vice-versa). Once this is done, the attacker can act as a `man-in-the-middle`, i.e., listen to packets from the client (these are not acknowledged by the server as the connection with the client is desynchronized) and forward them to the server (the attacker is able to spoof the client as the attacker knows the server's sequence number). The attacker can do the same for packets coming from the server. The session goes on, without the user noticing anything. An attacker can also introduce new packets to the server, and filter the server's reaction to these packets out of the communication. For a `telnet` session, this means an attacker can send a command to the server, without the user's consent or knowledge.

4.5.3.4 Routing Attacks. Routing attacks try to alter the route a packet follows to reach its destination. Several methods to alter routing tables are described by Bellovin in [18]. When an attacker can redirect traffic it is possible to listen, intercept and emit packets. This can be a way to make `man-in-the-middle` attacks possible.

Source routing is the ability to stipulate an explicit path the packet must take from data in the IP protocol header. The initial intention of source routing was to be able to bypass faulty devices like routers and bypass situations where routing rules may have become corrupt. This concept has been used to impersonate hosts on remote networks. It may also be used to divert traffic to a hostile network for monitoring or tampering. Source routing is a well-known problem and most network device manufacturers provide the ability to drop source-routed packets.

The Routing Information Protocol (RIP) [64] provides a means for dynamically specifying routes to different networks. RIP is an insecure protocol, and as such, may be easily tampered with. It is possible for a malicious host to send fake routing information to routers and hosts. An attack of this nature has the potential to redirect all local traffic through a hostile network or tamper with data as well as impersonate as a trusted host. RIP is extensively used by many sites attached to the Internet, mainly because it allows easy route propagation. The Open Shortest Path First (OSPF) protocol [64] is a possible replacement to RIP with the advantage of security within its protocol.

4.5.3.5 Tunneling. Tunneling tools exist that allow an attacker to establish secure tunnels between their computer and a compromised server. This could be a simple TCP based terminal service. It is now possible for attackers to use UDP or ICMP as transports. In some cases the channel is compressed and encrypted to avoid detection. ICMP is passed by many routers and even some firewalls, and as such provides an easy path to the outside world that is virtually undetectable. These programs also have the ability to hop between protocols and ports so detection is practically impossible by analyzing network traffic.

4.6   OTHER INTERNET PROTOCOL ATTACKS

There are many other attacks possible due to the inherent insecurity of the Internet protocol. A number of them are mentioned below to give the reader an understanding of the broadness of the problem:

- Trivial FTP [64]: Standard FTP requires authentication of users before file transfer. The Trivial FTP service requires no authentication and may provide an opportunity for attack. This is especially true for low level devices such as routers that are typically configured using the service.

- Simple Network Management Protocol (SNMP): The service is defined to aid in network management. It consists of a distributed database. Often write and read requests to these databases are configured with no authentication.

- Finger Service: This service displays useful information about users such as names and phone numbers. Running this service at all poses the risk that valuable user information is supplied to an attacker.

- Electronic Mail: Most electronic mail services provide no authentication of sender. It is easy to fake email from: addresses and users should be aware of the possibility for abuse. Email is also a good method to pass viruses to a target network.

- Portmapper: The portmapper allows servers to register themselves. The clients communicate with the portmapper to find out server port addresses. The portmapper protocol is insecure so it is vulnerable to eavesdropping and denial-of-service attacks (unregistering a service).

- Domain Name Service (DNS): DNS provides two services, lookups and zone transfers. Neither service is protected and both therefore are prone to abuse. DNS also provides the same vulnerability as the finger service if the "HINFO" field contains the operating system information. This provides useful information to an attacker.

- Network Time Protocol (NTP): The NTP allows the clocks on systems to be set very accurately. Knowing the exact time is very important to some protocols (that use timestamps). If an attacker can impersonate the NTP service, there is a possibility for successful attack (such as a replay attack where tickets become valid again).

There are many other attacks to the Internet protocol, too many to be listed in this chapter.

II Kerberos and SESAME

5 KERBEROS

5.1 INTRODUCTION

Over the last decade, many organizations have shifted their computing facilities from central mainframes — accessed from simple terminals via serial lines — to servers accessed from personal computers via a local area network (LAN). The switch to LANs removed some old problems, but at the same time also introduced new problems. Many of the new problems are not particularly related to security. For example, backup and recovery from equipment failures require a different approach in a client-server architecture.

In the literature a number of proposed solutions are found to add security to these networks that are also called Intranets. Kerberos is certainly the technology which has had the most success and is widely used today. Kerberos was developed at the Massachusetts Institute of Technology (MIT) [150] in the mid 80's to try to enhance the security of their Athena computer system [59]. This network had both public and private workstations that were connected through various types of LANs to a campus backbone. Only a few of the servers could be considered as being in a physically secure location. Versions 1 through 3 of Kerberos were internal versions, with Version 4 [220] considered the original Kerberos. The latest version, Version 5 [155] is an enhanced version.

The name Kerberos comes from Greek mythology, where Cerberos is the name of the three-headed dog that guards the entrance to Hades.

This Chapter begins with a description of the design goals. This is followed by an overview of the architectural components, explaining the functionality of each of them. The two available releases of Kerberos are analyzed in the next two sections. It should be noted that because of the known limitations of Version 4 it is not recommended for use anymore. The Chapter ends with some extensions to Kerberos that have been developed to increase the overall functionality and security.

5.2   GOALS

The primary goal of Kerberos was to provide a secure network authentication service. Traditional computing environments relied on username and password to authenticate users. This system was quite suitable for single mainframe environments where users typically had one account and communication of user information was along controlled channels.

Modern environments however are quite different. Users need to access a number of computers across a WAN or LAN, user information is passed across these networks, and eavesdropping is very easy. The risks that were considered by the Kerberos designers were unauthorized use of resources by unauthorized parties as well as violation of a person's privacy, e.g., by browsing through personal files.

Kerberos thus has two main goals [191]:

1. To allow a user a *single sign-on* to the network. This means that the user only has to type in their username once at the beginning of the session. For the remainder of the session Kerberos is in charge of authenticating the user to the different application servers.

2. To protect the authentication information so that masquerading is far more difficult.

5.3   OVERVIEW OF THE ARCHITECTURAL COMPONENTS

In order to understand the Kerberos technology, it is important to mention the assumptions that the designers of Kerberos made when they were developing the system (see also Sections 5.4.4 and 5.5.4) [220]:

- The time is trusted. The protocols rely completely on the fact that the timestamps created are correct;

- The user trusts its workstation completely;

- The security server is on-line;

- The servers are stateless;

- Because of existing patents on public-key cryptography, only symmetric key cryptography would be used;

- The time that the user's password is available on the client machine needs to be minimized.

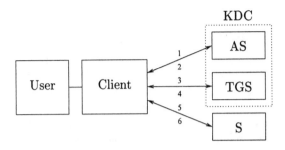

Figure 5.1.   Overview of Kerberos

Figure 5.1 shows the components of the Kerberos system: the *User*, their *Client* workstation, the *Authentication Server*, the *Ticket Granting Server* and the *Application Server*.

1. The *Client* workstation:

   The client machines are not considered to be secure as the user sitting at the console has full control over them. Therefore, the overall security of the system should not depend on them.

2. The *Authentication Server* (AS):

   The purpose of the authentication server is to define which users are entitled to log into the system and to provide these users with the possibility to authenticate to the system (more precisely the ticket granting server). The protocols that are used to obtain authentication are different in Version 4 and 5. They are explained in Section 5.4 and 5.5.

   The advantage of having a central authentication server is that the user only has to remember a single password, i.e, the password shared with this server. Since the authentication protocols (between client and server) used by Kerberos rely on a shared secret, it could be argued that the authentication server is present so that the user can exchange a weak secret (password) for a strong secret (a cryptographic key).

3. The *Ticket Granting Server* (TGS);

   In the course of a successful authentication procedure, the client obtains a *ticket granting ticket* (TGT). The ticket granting server generates the server application ticket for the client using the information obtained from the client's TGT (a ticket can be seen as a proof that one has been authenticated and that one is entitled to use a specific application). Since the clients use a TGT (more precisely the session key in it) to prove their identity to the ticket granting server, the user never has to re-enter a password. In this way, Kerberos provides a *single sign-on* service and there are only short term secrets in the client's cache (no passwords).

The ticket granting server also generates and distributes session keys so that the communications between clients and applications servers can be cryptographically protected.

The authentication server and ticket granting server are logically separated services but it is possible to run them both on the same physical machine or even in the same process. It is however very important that this machine is carefully protected and physically secure. If an attacker could make changes to the authentication server or ticket granting server, that would make it possible to subvert the security of the whole system.

The combination of the authentication server and the ticket granting server form the *security server* of the system and this combination is also known as the *Key Distribution Center* (KDC).

4. The *Application Server* (S).

An application server may provide a number of applications to the various client machines. After a successful logon the client authenticates to the server and optionally the server authenticates to the client (mutual authentication). Subsequent messages between them can be cryptographically protected (to obtain data confidentiality and data authentication).

5.4   KERBEROS V4

5.4.1   Notation

The protocols of Kerberos V4 are partly based on the Needham-Schroeder protocol described in Section 2.5.5.1.

Before the protocol starts, long term symmetric keys are shared between each user A and the authentication server (K_A), between the authentication server and ticket granting server (K_{AS-TGS}) and between the ticket granting server and an application server (K_{TGS-S}). K_A is derived from the user's password PW_A $(K_A = f(PW_A)$, where f is a one-way function). During a run of the protocol, new *session keys* (k_{i-j}) are generated by the authentication server and the ticket granting server. To protect against replay attacks, timestamps (T) are used (see Section 2.5.2.1).

5.4.2   Protocol of Kerberos V4

Referring to Figure 5.1 and to Table 5.1, the following messages are sent during the protocol. Steps 1 and 2 are only performed at the start of each user's login session. Messages 3 and 4 are exchanged whenever the client needs a new ticket or when it needs to contact an application server for which it doesn't already have a ticket. Therefore, the Kerberos protocols do not constitute a big overhead to the normal client-server interaction.

Table 5.1.   Notation used to describe the Kerberos protocols

A	User
C	Client
AS	Authentication server
TGS	Ticket granting server
S	(Application) Server
K_{i-j}	A long term key shared between i and j
K_i	A symmetric key, derived from the password of user i
k_{i-j}	A session key generated for use between i and j
$ENC(K_{i-j})(m)$	Message m encrypted under symmetric key K_{i-j}
$MAC(K_{i-j})(m)$	MAC calculated on message m with key K_{i-j}
$T_i^{(n)}$	$(n+1)$-th timestamp placed by i *
$N_i^{(n)}$	$(n+1)$-th nonce generated by i *
SN_{i-j}	Sequence number used by parties i and j
$RL_i^{(n)}$	$(n+1)$-th requested lifetime (of the ticket) by i *
L_i	Lifetime (of the ticket) granted to i

* For reasons of clarity n is omitted when it is equal to 0.

1. KRB-AS-REQ

   On behalf of the user A, the client C sends an authentication request to the authentication server AS (RL_C is the requested lifetime of the ticket granting ticket (TGT), where the lifetime determines the validity period of the TGT). As the designers of Kerberos V4 wanted to reduce the amount of time that the user's password would be available on the client machine, no part of this message is encrypted (with K_A):

$$A, TGS, T_C, RL_C$$

2. KRB-AS-REP

   The authentication server replies with the KRB-AS-REP, protected under K_A:

$$ENC(K_A)(k_{C-TGS}, T_C, ENC(K_{AS-TGS})(A, C, TGS, T_{AS}, L_C, k_{C-TGS}))$$

   The ticket granting ticket ($ENC(K_{AS-TGS})(A, C, TGS, T_{AS}, L_C, k_{C-TGS})$) is encrypted with K_{AS-TGS}. If the user A provides the correct password PW_A, the client C can generate K_A. C then decrypts the KRB-AS-REP to obtain the session key k_{C-TGS} and the ticket granting ticket, and also checks whether T_C is equal to the one sent in the first message (to counter a replay attack). In this way the authentication server AS is also authenticated to the client because it is assumed that only AS (and user A) know (or can otherwise obtain) K_A.

3. KRB-TGS-REQ

The client C applies for a ticket with the ticket granting server TGS, using the received ticket granting ticket and session key k_{C-TGS}:

$$S, T_C^{(1)}, ENC(K_{AS-TGS})(A, C, TGS, T_{AS}, L_C, k_{C-TGS})$$
$$ENC(k_{C-TGS})(C, T_C^{(1)})$$

$ENC(k_{C-TGS})(C, T_C^{(1)})$ is an authenticator. An authenticator is a record that can be shown to have been generated recently using a key known only to the two participants in an exchange. With this authenticator, the client C proves knowledge of the session key k_{C-TGS} and authenticates to the ticket granting server TGS.

4. KRB-TGS-REP

The ticket granting server TGS first decrypts the TGT offered with the long term key K_{AS-TGS}. TGS then uses the session key k_{C-TGS} obtained in this way to validate the authenticator. After checking whether the two timestamps are recent and the authenticator has not been used before, TGS generates a new session key k_{C-S} and a ticket so that the client C can prove its identity to the application server S.

The ticket granting server then sends the KRB-TGS-REP to the client C:

$$ENC(k_{C-TGS})(ENC(K_{TGS-S})(A, C, TGS, T_{TGS}, L_C, k_{C-S}), k_{C-S}, T_C^{(1)})$$

5. KRB-AP-REQ

The client C decrypts the KRB-TGS-REP, and obtains the new session key k_{C-S}, at the same time authenticating the ticket granting server in a way similar to the authentication of the authentication server by the client (it is assumed that there is redundancy in the session key k_{C-S} field in the KRB-TGS-REP as explained in Section 2.5.5.1).

C then forwards the ticket, received in the previous step, to the application server S and generates a new authenticator using k_{C-S}:

$$ENC(K_{TGS-S})(A, C, TGS, T_{TGS}, L_C, k_{C-S}), ENC(k_{C-S})(C, T_C^{(2)})$$

6. KRB-AP-REP

The application server S validates the authenticator, checks the timestamps and responds with KRB-AP-REP to authenticate to the client C (if mutual authentication was required):

$$ENC(k_{C-S})(T_C^{(2)} + 1)$$

7. KRB-PRIV and KRB-SAFE

The subsequent messages $m^{(i)}$ between client and server can be cryptograph-ically enhanced to obtain either one or both of the following services:

- Data confidentiality (KRB-PRIV): the messages and a timestamp (to counter replay attacks) are encrypted with the session key k_{C-S}:

$$ENC(k_{C-S})(m^{(i)}, T^{(i)})$$

- Data authentication (KRB-SAFE): A MAC is calculated on the message and a timestamp, using the session key k_{C-S} as the key input:

$$m^{(i)}, MAC(k_{C-S})(m^{(i)}, T^{(i)})$$

5.4.3   Inter-Realm Authentication

Up until now, it has been assumed that all parties involved (C, AS, TGS and S) belong to the same security domain (also called a *realm* in Kerberos). With Kerberos it is possible to divide the principals in the network into different realms. Each realm maintains its own key distribution center. This is done because in big networks it is usually hard (impossible) to find a single organi-zation that everyone trusts (as the key distribution center has all the user keys K_A it can impersonate any user A).

Kerberos V4 allows for inter-domain authentication if the ticket granting server from the local domain and the ticket granting server from the foreign domain share a symmetric key. This key is to be used as a key for the ticket-granting service. A client can obtain tickets for services from a foreign realm by first obtaining a ticket granting ticket for the foreign realm from its local ticket granting server, and then using that ticket granting ticket to obtain tickets for the foreign server from the foreign ticket granting server.

5.4.4   Limitations of Kerberos V4

Since Kerberos V4 was designed with a specific goal in mind (the project Athena), it is no surprise that the result had some shortcomings. They have been described by Bellovin and Merritt in [21], and Kohl, Neuman and Ts'o in [155, 191].

Their results are summarized here:

- Kerberos relies on the fact that the clocks are synchronized throughout the system (a small clock skew can be tolerated). Also it is necessary to store authenticators in order to prevent their re-use in the allowed clock-skew timeframe.

- The set-up of Kerberos V4 makes a password guessing attack straightfor-ward. An attacker only needs to send a KRB-AS-REQ with a fake identity to get back a token that is encrypted with the fake user's password. This token can then be cracked off-line.

- The clients must rely on the strength of the underlying operating system as the tickets and session keys need to be cached somewhere on the client workstation and thus may be accessible to all the concurrently logged in users.

  The situation is even worse when the clients are diskless workstations. They typically use a central file-server on which the session keys are stored in clear text. The same keys are also sent unencrypted from the client to the file-server and back.

- Tickets issued to one client cannot be forwarded for use by another client.

- Inter-realm authentication: the scheme explained in Section 5.4.3 does not scale well, because it requires $O(n^2)$ keys to interconnect n realms.

In addition to this, Kerberos V4 suffers from some legal and technical deficiencies:

- Kerberos V4 used the DES for encryption. DES could not be exported outside the U.S. and this prohibited a widespread use of Kerberos. Also as explained in Section 1.4.1.1 the keylength of the DES is too short.

- In the KRB-AS-REP message, the TGT is in fact encrypted twice. In general it is considered bad practice to encrypt the same thing twice as it generates no extra security, and increases the overhead. Moreover the nature of the Kerberos protocol provides the attacker with known plaintexts to launch a known plaintext attack on the underlying encryption algorithm (the TGT is sent encrypted once in the next message KRB-TGS-REQ).

- The maximum lifetime L that can be given to a TGT is 21 hours. This is too short for long batch jobs.

- Kerberos V4 uses a very specific encryption mode of the DES: the Propagating Cipher Block Chaining (PCBC) method [154]. This mode has the effect of making all subsequent blocks unreadable if one tampers with a ciphertext block. However it does NOT guarantee that the text has not changed. For example, if one interchanges two adjacent blocks the rest of the message still decrypts correctly.

- Kerberos V4 uses a proprietary checksum algorithm to authenticate the messages. This checksum has never been published. Until now there is no evidence of it being broken but it is bad practice to rely on these kind of assumptions for the security of a system.

5.5 KERBEROS V5

5.5.1 Differences with V4

In response to the above limitations and to include some new functionality, Kerberos V5 was released in 1991 [155, 156]. Some of the main changes are :

- To improve the modularity of Kerberos, the use of encryption has been separated into several modules. The PCBC mode of DES is replaced with the more standard DES in CBC mode.

- In Kerberos V5 a pre-authentication mechanism can be used to determine whether the user has entered the password correctly. There is however a disadvantage to using this mechanism as it still makes a password guessing attack possible.

- Kerberos V5 uses nonces and supports sequence numbers to avoid some of the problems associated with the synchronized clocks in V4.

- KRB-AS-REP has two parts in Kerberos V5 to avoid the double encryption of the ticket granting ticket.

- The lifetime L has been replaced with a starting time T_s and an expiration time T_e, resulting in an almost limitless lifetime. Also the client can ask for a specific lifetime RL_C.

- To improve the inter-realm authentication efficiency, the different realms are structured in a hierarchical way, thus limiting the number of secret keys needed (Section 5.5.3).

- Authentication forwarding has been provided in the following way: the original ticket granting ticket can be flagged so that if it is presented later to the ticket granting server, the ticket granting server replies with ticket granting tickets valid for other targets.

5.5.2 Protocol of Kerberos V5

The protocols as they are described here were obtained from RFC1510 [156] (see Figure 5.1 for the numbering of the messages).

1. **KRB-AS-REQ**

   A first difference with Kerberos V4 is that a nonce N_C is used instead of a timestamp. In addition an optional pre-authentication mechanism is implemented. This is realized encrypting a timestamp T_C with the key K_A, derived from the user's password PW_A. This is done so that the authentication server AS can determine whether the user has entered the correct password by checking that T_C is close to the current time:

   $$A, TGS, RL_C, N_C, ENC(K_A)(T_C)$$

2. **KRB-AS-REP**

   The authentication server replies to the client, with a session key (k_{C-TGS}) package and a ticket granting ticket for the ticket granting server TGS. The information that is relevant to the client has been separated from the information for the ticket granting server. The lifetime has been replaced by a starting time (T_s) and end time (T_e), thus providing greater flexibility:

$$A, ENC(K_{AS-TGS})(A, C, TGS, T_s, T_e, k_{C-TGS})$$
$$ENC(K_A)(k_{C-TGS}, T_s, T_e, N_C, TGS)$$

3. **KRB-TGS-REQ**

Upon reception of **KRB-AS-REP**, the client C decrypts the second part, retrieves the new session key k_{C-TGS}, and also verifies that the received nonce N_C is correct. To apply for a ticket to the application server, the client sends a nonce $N_C^{(1)}$, an authenticator, and the ticket granting ticket:

$$S, RL_C^{(1)}, N_C^{(1)}, ENC(k_{C-TGS})(C, T_C^{(1)})$$
$$ENC(K_{AS-TGS})(A, C, TGS, T_s, T_e, k_{C-TGS})$$

4. **KRB-TGS-REP**

The ticket granting server TGS validates the request from the client. TGS first decrypts the ticket granting ticket to obtain the session key k_{C-TGS}. With this session key, TGS verifies the authenticator. If all timing constraints are met (and the authenticator is not a replay), TGS forwards a ticket to the client and a package that contains the new session key k_{C-S}:

$$A, ENC(K_{TGS-S})(A, C, TGS, T_s^{(1)}, T_e^{(1)}, k_{C-S})$$
$$ENC(k_{C-TGS})(k_{C-S}, T_s^{(1)}, T_e^{(1)}, N_C^{(1)}, S)$$

5. **KRB-AP-REQ**

The client decrypts its part of **KRB-TGS-REP**, checks the nonce, and verifies whether the start and end time are sufficient. It then forwards the ticket to the application server together with a fresh authenticator.

In Kerberos V5, the client also has the option to send a sequence number SN_{C-S} in the authenticator. This sequence number can then be used to prevent replay attacks on the **KRB-SAFE** and **KRB-PRIV** messages:

$$ENC(K_{TGS-S})(A, C, TGS, T_s^{(1)}, T_e^{(1)}, k_{C-S})$$
$$ENC(k_{C-S})(C, T_C^{(2)}, SN_{C-S})$$

6. **KRB-AP-REP**

The application server decrypts the ticket, validates the authenticator and (optionally) replies with a message to authenticate itself to the client. Within this message the application server also returns a sequence number (if required) to be used in subsequent messages:

$$ENC(k_{C-S})(T_C^{(2)}, SN_{C-S})$$

7. **KRB-PRIV and KRB-SAFE**

The subsequent messages $m^{(i)}$ between client and server can be cryptographically enhanced to obtain:

- Data confidentiality (**KRB-PRIV**): the messages and a timestamp or a sequence number (to counter replay attacks) are encrypted with the session key k_{C-S}:

$$ENC(k_{C-S})(m^{(i)}, T^{(i)}) \text{ or } ENC(k_{C-S})(m^{(i)}, SN_{C-S})$$

- Data authentication (**KRB-SAFE**): a MAC is calculated on the message and a timestamp or sequence number, using the session key k_{C-S} as the key input:

$$m^{(i)}, MAC(k_{C-S})(m^{(i)}, T^{(i)}) \text{ or } m^{(i)}, MAC(k_{C-S})(m^{(i)}, SN_{C-S})$$

5.5.3   Inter-Realm Authentication

In Kerberos V5 different realms cooperate by establishing a hierarchy of realms (based on the name of the realm). Any realm can interoperate with any other realm in the hierarchy. Each realm exchanges a different inter-realm key with its parent node and each child node, and uses that key to obtain tickets for each successive realm. This arrangement reduces the number of key exchanges to a more manageable level.

When an application needs to contact a server in a foreign realm, it walks the tree toward the destination realm, contacting each realm's ticket granting server in turn. When a ticket for the end service is finally issued, it contains a list of all the realms consulted in the process of requesting the ticket. A server is permitted to reject authentication which passes through an untrusted realm.

5.5.4   Known Problems with Kerberos V5

- Kerberos V5 remains vulnerable to a password guessing attack. This can even be carried out off-line because a part of **KRB-AS-REP** is encrypted with the user's password. As noted in Section 2.2 users usually choose very easy to guess passwords. Several schemes have been proposed to counter this threat [22, 23, 110, 170].

- It is not completely secure against replay attacks. It has to rely partly on the capability of the server to store the recently used authenticators. This storage space however does not have to be large because the authenticators are small in size.

  Kerberos must also rely on the fact that the clocks are almost synchronized (a small clock skew can be tolerated). A nonce based solution that can solve this problem has been documented by Neuman and Stubblebine in [190].

- Kerberos is also dependent on the security of the client and in most cases clients are workstations that can be easily tampered with.

- Kerberos uses the same key k_{C-S} for both the KRB-SAFE and KRB-PRIV messages. In general it is not a good idea to have the same key both for providing data authentication and data confidentiality.

  Moreover if the Kerberos implementation uses the DES in CBC mode for confidentiality and the DES CBC-MAC for data authentication as suggested in RFC1510 [156], there is an attack as described by Preneel in [200].

  Muftic and Sloman [187] list some extra disadvantages :

- Since Kerberos is based on symmetric cryptography, it does not scale for large open distributed environments. For inter-realm interaction a public key solution using certificates would be better.

- Kerberos does not provide non-repudiation services.

McMahon [177] also recognizes that Kerberos supports only authentication and not access control. Each application must determine authorization solely on the basis of the user's identity carried in the ticket. This means that each application must be configured with the identity of each user permitted to use that specific service.

Finally it should be noted that it is not good practice to use encryption primitives for authentication purposes. Doing this poses a number of constraints on the encryption algorithms that can be used. In theory the Kerberos V5 technology was targeted to be algorithm independent. However if the Vernam one-time pad [234] is used as the encryption primitive, the Kerberos protocols are insecure.

5.5.5   The Kerberos Programming Interface

If a client-server application wants to be protected under the Kerberos system, then it must be *Kerberized*. This involves modifying the client and server code to add Kerberos specific calls to the application.

Early versions of Kerberos provided a non-standard interface to the Kerberos library. Since that time Kerberos has been standardized to use the GSS-API as its primary security interface. An Internet standard exists describing the Kerberos GSS-API interface [168]. Chapter 7 describes how this API can be used to secure existing applications.

5.6   EXTENSIONS

In this section an overview is given of systems that have been proposed as extensions to Kerberos. One of the most important proposals, a system called *Yaksha*, is covered in detail in Section 8.2 and hence is not covered in this section. It should become apparent to the reader that although Kerberos could be considered a mature technology, interest in updating it for current requirements has not diminished.

In general most proposals (but not all) for extending Kerberos are put to the IETF CAT Working Group [121].

5.6.1 Smart Card Kerberos

One of the limitations of Kerberos listed previously is related to the security of the client workstation. The workstation at some time must have access to the user's password. This leaves the workstation vulnerable to a *Trojan Horse* attack. An attacker could easily load software onto the workstation to record the user's secret. This is especially true since the client workstation is usually not physically protected and does not have a secure operating system.

To overcome this problem, Krajewski [157] suggests that Kerberos should be modified to support Smart Cards. A user would present a Smart Card containing the user's encryption key to a card reader attached to the workstation. The workstation login process would request a user's password and in combination with the key stored on the Smart Card could take part in the Kerberos authentication protocol. The encryption key on the Smart Card would be encrypted with the user's password and would never have to leave the Smart Card.

This system has a number of advantages over the current login process:

- It requires a user to provide both something the user possesses and something the user knows;

- The secret key shared between user and server could be truly random rather than derived from a limited keyspace, as is the case when using passwords;

- The data that is processed by the user workstation is always encrypted.

Warner, Trinkle and Gaskell [235] suggest various alternatives to Krajewski's Smart Card proposal based on the amount of trust. While Krajewski proposes to perform all the cryptographic operations on the card, they suggest it is probably better to decrypt the Kerberos ticket-granting ticket on the card but let the workstation perform the application related cryptographic operations.

5.6.2 Public Key Cryptography for Initial User Authentication

A proposal for incorporating public key cryptography into the initial user authentication scheme of Kerberos has been detailed in [227]. The proposal called PKINIT outlines the following changes to Kerberos:

- Users may authenticate using either conventional symmetric key cryptography, or using public key cryptography.

- If public key cryptography is used, public key data is sent in the initial messages to help establish identity.

- Users may optionally store private keys on the KDC for retrieval during the Kerberos initial authentication.

The proposal outlines three methods of using public key cryptography in the initial authentication phase and these are outlined below.

5.6.2.1   Method 1: Standard Public Key Authentication.   The first method called *standard public key authentication* works as follows (it is assumed all public key certificates are signed by a Certification Authority trusted by the KDC):

- The user sends a request to the KDC as before, except that if the user wants to authenticate using public key techniques, the user's certificate accompanies the initial request.

- The KDC verifies the certificate and issues a ticket granting ticket to the user. The message is encrypted with a randomly generated key (instead of the user's long term secret key). This random key is also sent encrypted with the user's public key, and also signed with the KDC's private key.

5.6.2.2   Method 2: Digital Signature.   The second method called *digital signature*, works as follows (note that in this case the client generates the random key and [227] warns that the client may not be able to generate a key to the same level of randomness as the KDC):

- The client sends a request for a ticket granting ticket as usual, except that the client generates a random key, encrypts it with the KDC's public key, and sends the encrypted random key with the request.

- The KDC generates its response as usual, except that it encrypts it with the client's generated random key rather than the user's long term secret key.

5.6.2.3   Method 3: Retrieving the User's Private Key from the KDC.   The aim of this method is to allow the KDC to store a protected version of the user's private key (protected in that the KDC cannot derive the user's private key from the protected version). The user can request the protected version of the private key from the KDC, and then derive the private key from it.

The KDC stores the following information:

- User's public key;

- Encrypted private key (encrypted using K_1);

- K_2 which is derived from a one-way hash function applied to the user's long term secret key K_1.

The user knows the long term secret key K_1 (usually derived from the password). The initial authentication request message contains the user's public key encrypted with K_2, to indicate to the KDC which protected private key is required.

5.6.3   Public-Key Cryptography for Cross-Realm Authentication

Using symmetric keys for cross-realm authentication means maintaining separate realm keys for each realm with which communication is permitted. Even if a hierarchy is established, other issues such as problems of trust mean that the system isn't always manageable.

A proposal called PKCROSS for incorporating public key cryptography into the cross-realm authentication scheme of Kerberos has been detailed in [228]. The proposal uses the PKINIT standard (outlined above) to allow inter-realm authentication using public-key cryptography.

The operation only requires changes to the Kerberos KDCs (and not to any client or server protocols) and works as follows:

- The client submits a request to the local KDC for credentials for the remote realm;

- The local KDC submits a PKINIT request to the remote KDC;

- The remote KDC responds as per PKINIT with a ticket called TGT(LR);

- The local KDC responds to the client with a ticket TGT(CR) which contains the cross-realm ticket TGT(LR);

- The client submits the request directly to the remote KDC.

5.6.4   Kerberos Change Password Protocol

Kerberos provides no means for a user to change their own secret keys. A proposal for adding an additional protocol to Kerberos to permit changing of a secret key is outlined in [117].

The protocol works as follows:

- When a user wishes to change their secret key, the user sends a change password request message to the KDC. The message contains the user's new secret key encrypted with the old secret key.

- The KDC sets the new value as specified if policy permits, and responds to the user.

5.6.5   Public Key Recovery of Kerberos

If a Kerberos KDC is ever compromised, then an attacker has access to all of the user's secret keys. When the compromise has been detected the Kerberos KDC has to be reinstalled, and each user must be given a new secret key. This can be a very slow and difficult process.

A proposal for using public key cryptography to overcome these problems is outlined in [226]. The scheme works as follows:

■ Instead of the KDC holding the user's secret keys, it holds a hash of the secret keys.

■ If the KDC's hashed secret key value is compromised, when the user next tries to authenticate to the KDC, the KDC sends an error message indicating it has been compromised. The KDC also sends a new salt value to the user, protected with public key techniques.

5.6.6   Other Proposals

Only a sample of proposals have been described in the previous sections. There are many others, some of which include (these ones are currently before the IETF CAT Working Group):

■ Anonymous credentials in Kerberos [179];

■ User to user authentication using the GSS-API [222];

■ Initial authentication with Kerberos and the GSS-API [221];

■ Multiple-path authentication of Kerberos [239];

■ Generating KDC referrals [223].

6 SESAME

6.1 INTRODUCTION

In the previous chapter it was shown that Kerberos has been a success in the field of network security. Unfortunately due to the governing export regulations in the U.S., this type of technology was not available on a large scale in Europe in the late 80's. It was possible to obtain the Kerberos distribution for the members of OSF through the DCE distribution but this was very costly and had numerous restrictions.

In the absence of a suitable product in Europe, many organizations chose to either do nothing at all or to buy an insurance policy against the almost inevitable disaster. It was this situation that the SESAME project set out to improve upon. The main SESAME project partners were Bull, ICL and Siemens, with partial funding from the European Commission. The main European computer manufacturers were thus a driving force behind the SESAME project.

It is important to differentiate between the original architecture and the actual implementation. Work on SESAME started in the early 80's (even before Kerberos was widely known), with the design of an architecture and then subsequent standardization by ECMA [81, 82]. This chapter does not describe the full architecture but focuses on the actually available implementation [216] which is a subset of the original architecture. The reader is referred to the

ECMA documents and also to a description of the SESAME development by Kaijser [136].

The name SESAME is both an acronym (A Secure European System for Applications in a Multi-vendor Environment) and alludes to the famous "Open SESAME" fairy tale.

In 1994 a beta release of the SESAME implementation was made available for testing. This release was called V2. Taking into account the comments from the various testers and adding more public key support, a new version was released half-way through 1995 (V3). By then it was clear there was only one thing standing in the way of making the code available to the general public: an approval by the U.S. government to use the Kerberos code, on which SESAME relied. It became clear that this might never be achieved so it was decided to rewrite the Kerberos part of SESAME, which resulted in V4. This version can now be downloaded [216] and tested.

This chapter begins with a discussion of the goals and decisions that were made by the implementers of the SESAME architecture [137]. For a good understanding of SESAME it is necessary to explain the functionality of the different architectural components. Since many benefits of SESAME are associated with the provision of the access control service, this is discussed in some detail. SESAME also offers a variety of protocols and some of them are explained. To finish the current SESAME implementation is analyzed and several improvements are suggested.

6.2 GOALS

The SESAME project started out with several objectives in mind:

1. The SESAME architecture was to be a solution for the European users that wanted to protect their network. The system thus had to be one which could be sold in Europe; that is, it needed to comply with whatever legislative requirements the various EU governments decided to impose.

2. In SESAME the communications between a client and a server would use separate data authentication and confidentiality keys. This provides a higher level of security as both services are offered independent of one another. If an attacker or a law enforcement agency can break the confidentiality of a message, this does not automatically lead to a breach in the data authentication (and vice versa).

3. Cryptographic technologies would be used in an optimal way. For example public-key cryptography would be supported. SESAME was not confronted with the patent on the RSA encryption technology as it was deemed not valid in Europe. Public-key cryptography opens up a lot of possibilities:

   - One of the main objections to Kerberos was that it relied on a password mechanism to authenticate the users. As shown in Chapter 2, this is not very strong and it is subject to a dictionary attack. In Section 6.6

it is shown how SESAME replaces this password based authentication with the X.509 authentication primitive (Section 2.5.3.3) using public-key cryptography.

- In Kerberos the security server must be trusted unconditionally. Indeed the Kerberos key distribution center can decrypt all the messages that are sent by a client to an application server because it generates the session keys, or can impersonate a user because it knows the user's secret key (see Section 5.5.4). SESAME prevents this by using public-key cryptography. The security server is not in possession of the user's private key and is thus unable to digitally sign a message pretending to originate from a user. Also in SESAME the client generates the session keys and transfers these to the server encrypted under its public key (when the public key method is used).

- To improve the scalability of the architecture, public-key cryptography would be adopted for inter-realm authentication purposes.

- By using public-key techniques it is possible to offer non-repudiation services.

4. All of the security services should be provided for a heterogenous environment. This means that the architecture should be implemented on a variety of different platforms, ranging from personal computers to powerful workstations and even mainframes. All of these computers use different operating systems so porting the software from one platform to another should be made as easy as possible.

5. An access control mechanism is the central goal of the system: as McMahon points out in [177], Kerberos does not really provide an authorization scheme (see Section 1.3). SESAME would give the user such a scheme. Because of the advantages explained in Section 6.5.1, the actual mechanism that was to be enforced was role based access control (RBAC). The way this was supposed to be enforced was through the use of *attribute certificates* (Section 6.5.2) defined in the ECMA-219 standard [81].

6. An extensive audit system would also be considered as very important: even with the best security in place things can go wrong. With this auditing system it would be possible for system administrators to locate the error and to react more rapidly to intruders.

7. A standard interface for program developers would be supported: through the adoption of the Internet standard *Generic Security Services Application Program Interface* (GSS-API) (then RFC1508 [165], now superseded by RFC2078 [169], see also Section 7.2), the work for application developers can be reduced considerably.

6.3   IMPLEMENTATION DESIGN DECISIONS

When trying to understand the SESAME implementation, it is important to take into account that the project started in 1992 and several decisions that were made by the designers then, should be re-evaluated in the current context.

Although the original SESAME architecture work began before Kerberos was widely known, by the time the implementation started Kerberos was already establishing itself successfully as an authentication service for networks. Thus the SESAME implementors decided to use Kerberos as the authentication system (rather than use their own protocol). It was hoped that a product based on Kerberos would inherit a lot of goodwill. Behind the scenes, the European companies were lobbying to have SESAME adopted by OSF into DCE. Therefore compatibility with Kerberos was unavoidable.

There were also a lot of good reasons to adopt Kerberos:

- Kerberos was a proven technology;

- Kerberos provided a solid network authentication service;

- Kerberos allowed for a single sign-on and was thus user-friendly.

An unfortunate consequence of the decision to adopt Kerberos is that the SESAME protocols (see Section 6.6) have not been designed from scratch and as a result are rather complex. Otherwise the implementation is based around a subset of the ECMA standards [80, 81, 81]. The benefits in following this architecture is that there is a clear separation in the building blocks. This should result in a system that is clear and modular (Figure 6.1).

Finally, the decision not to give cryptographic keys or other tokens to any components at the client end of the communication, was based on the assumption that these clients would have a single-user operating system (OS), such as MS/DOS or Windows. With these OS's it was assumed that an attacker could get access anyway to everything on the client workstation.

6.4   OVERVIEW OF THE ARCHITECTURAL COMPONENTS

Looking at Figure 6.1, the number of different components may be very confusing for the novice SESAME user. It is however possible to distinguish four boundaries (dotted lines) and this reduces the complexity to three entities:

- The SESAME security server;

- The client machine;

- The (application) server;

- The support components.

In the following sections the goal and functionality of each component is detailed and explained. The basic design philosophy is to separate as much as possible the different functions provided. This separation makes it possible to design and implement every entity independent of the other ones.

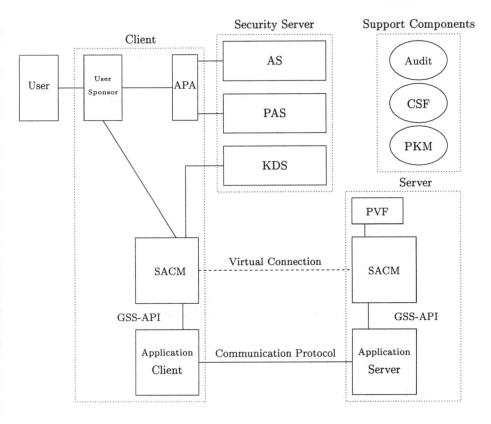

Figure 6.1.   Overview of the SESAME components

6.4.1 Security Server

Comparing the SESAME security server to the Kerberos one, the obvious difference is the presence of the privilege attribute server in SESAME. This server has been added to manage the access control mechanism that is implemented by SESAME. The function of the authentication server and key distribution server (ticket granting server in Kerberos) is basically the same: providing a single sign-on without storing the password in the local cache and managing the cryptographic keys.

6.4.1.1 Authentication Server. When discussing the function of the authentication server, it is essential to maintain a clear distinction between the *user* (the human being who is using the computer system) and the *user sponsor* (the computer program which enables the user to be authenticated) (see Section 6.4.2.1).

The goals of the authentication server are:

1. To enable the user sponsor to convince remote servers that it has permission to act on behalf of a particular user. That is, by typing commands into the computer on which the user sponsor runs, the user has given their consent for the user sponsor to act on their behalf and carry out these commands.

2. To convince the user sponsor that the person who is entering commands into the computer system is a user that is authorized to use the computer system.

The first goal is to protect remote servers against rogue user sponsors which have been created by people trying to attack the system. The second goal is to protect the computer on which the user sponsor runs from unauthorized use by attackers who walk up to the machine and attempt to use it.

In SESAME there are two authentication services.

- The first is based upon the Kerberos V5 technology and inherits all of its features and shortcomings.

- The second is based on the X.509 authentication mechanism (Section 6.6).

In addition to the services offered by the basic Kerberos authentication server, the second authentication server provides clients with the possibility of (mutual) strong authentication. If the client uses strong authentication, the authentication server knows whether the login has been successful. The mechanism of strong authentication also prevents the traditional dictionary attack. Mutual authentication (authenticating the authentication server to the user sponsor) defends users from malicious or fake servers who pretend to be the real authentication server.

6.4.1.2   Privilege Attribute Server. The privilege attribute server provides information about the privileges of users and user sponsors. These privileges are defined as privilege attributes (Section 6.5.2). They contain information about entities, that is used in making access control decisions.

The value of a privilege attribute may depend on factors such as the identity of the user, the nature of the user sponsor (e.g., which physical security mechanisms it employs), contextual information such as the physical location of the user sponsor (whether the login is performed from home or from work may be an important factor in making access decisions), and the time of day.

The privilege attribute server supplies this information to other entities in the form of *Privilege Attribute Certificates* (PACs) as specified in ECMA 219 [81]. A PAC contains the privilege attributes for a particular invocation of a user sponsor by a user. The PAC is described in detail in Section 6.5.2.

6.4.1.3   Key Distribution Server. The key distribution server (KDS) provides cryptographic keys for mutual authentication between the user and a remote application server (the target). Before the key distribution server can be used, the human user must have been authenticated by the authentication server, and the user sponsor must have passed on these tickets and keying material to the secure association context manager on the client machine.

Several authentication protocols are provided, depending on whether or not the target is in the same security domain as the user. If the user and the target are in the same security domain (the intra-domain case) the Kerberos V5 model is used. If the user and the target are from different security domains (inter-domain case), a protocol based on X.509 certificates is used, as described by McMahon in [177].

Note that if the application servers' PAC validation facility is equipped with a long term public/private key pair, the key distribution server can be bypassed and the session keys are generated by the user's secure association context manager. The result of this is that the security server is not able to listen in on the communication between the client machine and the application server.

6.4.2 Client

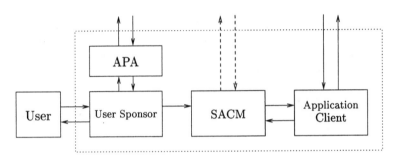

Figure 6.2.   The SESAME client

The interactions between the different SESAME entities on the client machine are illustrated in Figure 6.2. The user sponsor authenticates the user to the authentication server and obtains a PAC and keying material from the privilege attribute server, through the authentication privilege attribute (APA) client. This is then passed on to the secure association context manager. When an application client wants to set up a connection with an application server, the client sends the user's credentials using the secure association context manager. This also takes care of cryptographically enhancing the rest of the communication. Because of the design of SESAME, the secure association context manager cannot try to obtain new user credentials as it cannot access the authentication server or the privilege attribute server. This means that it is impossible that a user's credentials would be changed without the user realizing this.

6.4.2.1 User and User Sponsor. There is a clear difference between the user and the program that acts on her behalf (the user sponsor). The user cannot perform complex cryptographic operations, and cannot directly send data through the computer network. This can only be done by the user sponsor.

Before the user has logged in, the software running on the computer (including the user sponsor) is unable to act on behalf of that user. Furthermore, before the user has entered their username and password (or whatever is used for entity authentication), the user sponsor does not know who they are.

It can be seen as a weakness of the SESAME implementation that it does not provide any authentication mechanisms for the user sponsor (neither towards the user or towards the authentication server). This means that the system is vulnerable to the traditional *Trojan Horse* attack, in which an attacker replaces the login program on the client machine (i.e., the user sponsor in the SESAME scenario) with another version that enables the attacker to gain valuable information. However this is the result of a design decision as explained in Section 6.3. The original architecture caters for this. The proposed solution is similar to the one suggested in Section 6.7.

6.4.2.2   Authentication Privilege Attribute Client.   This entity is implemented as a set of function calls to the application program interface. The user sponsor can communicate through these calls with the authentication server and the privilege attribute server to have the user authenticated and obtain the necessary credentials.

Using these API calls it should also be easy for a programmer to write a user sponsor for a certain platform. This was done to satisfy the requirement to support heterogeneous environments (Section 6.2).

6.4.2.3   Secure Association Context Manager.   The SESAME *secure association context manager* (SACM) provides data authentication (data integrity and data origin authentication) and (optionally) data confidentiality for the communication between an application client and application server. It is implemented as a library of subroutines which can be incorporated into application-specific clients and servers.

The SESAME secure association context manager uses a protocol based on the ECMA Association Context Management protocol [80]. During this protocol the keys, that are used to provide the data authentication and confidentiality services, are generated by applying a one-way function to a basic session key that is either generated by the key distribution server and transferred in its ticket to the application server, or generated by the user's secure association context manager and sent in the first message to the application server (Section 6.6). This form of generating session keys is defined as *key offsetting* in ISO 11770-2 [130]. Its main advantages are that it prevents some forms of replay attacks (Section 4.4.5), and it reduces the amount of data that is encrypted using one single key (some block ciphers are known to be vulnerable to known plaintext attacks).

6.4.2.4   Application Client.   Every application client (e.g., TELNET) needs to be adapted to use SESAME. This procedure is illustrated in Chapter 7.

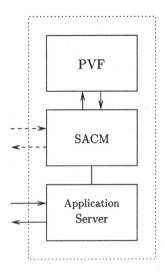

Figure 6.3.   The SESAME server

6.4.3 *Server*

Figure 6.3 illustrates the interactions at the server end of the communication. When the application server receives a message from an application client indicating that it wants to set up a secure connection, it forwards the client's credentials and keying material via the SACM to the PAC validation facility (PVF). This checks whether the client has the right to access the application. If this check is successful, it decrypts the keying material and forwards the dialogue integrity and confidentiality keys to the secure association context manager on the server machine. By obtaining these keys the client has been authenticated (mutual authentication of the application server to the client is also provided) and it enables the application server to secure the communication with the client.

6.4.3.1 PAC Validation Facility.   Application-specific servers are usually very large and complex programs. It is therefore often infeasible to check and test all of these programs with the thoroughness that is required for security-critical code.   The possibility exists that an application server accidentally reveals information it knows to an unauthorized entity, or that the server contains a bug that can be exploited by an attacker (Section 4.4.2). Hence it is desirable to locate the security critical parts of the server in a separate process. In SESAME, this separate process is called the *PAC validation facility* (PVF).

The SESAME architecture permits the PAC validation facility to be implemented either as a subroutine within an application server, or as a separate process which is protected from the rest of the application by the host's access control mechanisms. If the PAC validation facility and application are co-located, both must be validated to a degree that is appropriate for security-critical code. If the PAC validation facility is protected from the application, then only it needs to be validated to a high degree.

As the name implies, the PAC validation facility applies various checks to the PAC (Section 6.6). If one of the conditions is not met, the PAC validation facility does not accept the PAC, and does not reveal the PAC's contents (i.e., the session keys that are needed to provide the cryptographic services for the communication link) to the SACM. This prevents servers from accidentally using an invalid PAC (e.g., because a programmer forgot to implement one of the checks). This also prevents a server which has been subverted by an attacker from making unauthorized use of a PAC that was intended for a different server.

As well as validating PACs, the PAC validation facility also performs key management for application servers.

6.4.3.2   Secure Association Context Manager.   The ECMA-206 standard [80] defines also a secure association context manager at the server side of the communication. It has essentially the same functionality as the secure association context manager at the client end.

6.4.3.3   Application Server.   The application server (e.g., telnetd) also needs to be changed to introduce SESAME calls through the use of the GSS-API. How to do this is explained in Chapter 7.

6.4.4   Support Components

Several pieces of SESAME's functionality are required in a number of places within the SESAME architecture.

6.4.4.1   Public Key Management.   The public key management (PKM) is set of functions with which all the entities involved in the SESAME set up can manage their public and private keys. The way the keys are stored is similar to the PGP solution (see Section 9.3), using files (or key-rings) to contain the keys but the certificates are X.509 based (see Section 1.7.1). Also in contrary to the PGP system a passphrase or password is not needed to get access to the private key(s). The only protection is the standard Unix access control which is very limited. Therefore, it is recommended to use Smart Cards (see Section 6.7).

The public key management is used by the PAC validation facility on the target application server, by the privilege attribute server and the key distribution server in the client's domain.

6.4.4.2   Cryptographic Support Facility.   The cryptographic support facility (CSF) is responsible for providing all of the cryptographic primitives. Because of its modular structure it should be straightforward to replace the standard algorithms in SESAME by faster and/or more secure algorithms.

6.4.4.3   Audit Facility.   The audit facility records security relevant events and actions to log-files for future inspection. The main idea behind this is that no system can be considered as being a 100% secure. With the detailed audit information, it is possible to react more quickly and more efficiently to attempts to intrude the system.

In SESAME different meanings are assigned to the word 'identity'. Unlike the real world, in computer systems the term identity has multiple uses:

1. Authenticated Identity : the name the user offers to log on to the system.

2. Access Identity : the name upon which applications make access decisions.

3. Audit Identity : the name under which the user will be accountable.

4. Charging Identifier : if computer systems or other resources, that have to be paid for, are used then a billing address should be known.

6.5   ACCESS CONTROL

To address the authorization problem the SESAME consortium emphasized the concept of role based access control. In the next sections, this concept is explained. It is shown how SESAME uses attribute certificates to implement the authorization scheme and provide delegation at the same time. More information about this topic can be obtained from [230, 232].

6.5.1   Role Based Access Control (RBAC)

6.5.1.1   Problems with Regular ACLs.   In Section 1.3.1 the access control mechanism of access control lists (ACLs) has been explained. In practice there are some major problems that can be associated with this solution:

- It is resource oriented. The ACLs have to be managed at the resources and this is contrary to the need for a central management that is common in most commercial and non-classified governmental organizations.

- It is a costly solution. Each resource has to keep its ACL up-to-date and there are as many ACLs as there are resources in the system.

- It is difficult to scale. In distributed computer systems there are numerous subjects and objects involved and this renders these schemes unlikely to be implemented.

- It is situated at the wrong level of abstraction. To accommodate the ACL access control mechanism, it is usually necessary to translate the natural organizational view into another view.

6.5.1.2   What is RBAC.   In view of the problems identified with regular ACLs, SESAME supports role based access control. A trend towards role based access control has become apparent recently, as is shown by Ferraiolo and Kuhn in [90] and Sandhu, Coyne, Feinstein and Youman in [214].

Role based access control is defined by Ferraiolo and Kuhn as [90]: *A mechanism that allows and promotes an organization-specific access control policy based on roles.*

In comparison to regular ACLs, the subjects are replaced by roles and what subject is entitled to act in which role is defined separately. This means that access decisions are made based on the role of the user that is trying to run an application or access a resource. The result is a massive improvement in the management of the system if the number of required roles is smaller than the number of users.

Consider the following actual example. Since administrators only have to maintain a list of who is entitled to exercise which role, it easy for them to switch somebody from one department to another, or to add a user to the system. Access control at the application side is even more straightforward. The only thing one needs is to build an ACL (one per application) that specifies which roles are entitled to do what action. There is no need to care about who the user really is, only their role is important. This type of access control is also very user friendly. The user can log in with their rolename (e.g., secretary) instead of having to remember a username. They could even be granted a default rolename so that they can start working immediately upon entering the system. This does not imply that users are not accountable for their actions. This type of log-in is implemented in such a way that the audit identity contains the user's real identity.

Recent experiments have shown that there usually is a very nice mapping between the needs in the real world and RBAC (see Parker and Sundt [199]). Typically an organization with 400 workers can be modeled using 20 roles. This reduces the complexity of the system considerably.

Role based access control can thus provide a solution to the following problems:

- Distribution of privileges. When a user joins a company or changes jobs within the company, how can the access control mechanism be set up? How does the user get access to the resources and applications?

- Revocation of privileges. When a user leaves the company or changes jobs within the company, how can the access control mechanism be changed to instantly reflect this change? How do the users lose access to resources they previously had access to?

- Forwarding of privileges. In corporations, end users should not be able to pass on their access rights to other employees and definitely not to outsiders.

6.5.1.3   Formal Definition. The following formal representation from Ferraiolo and Kuhn [90] is used to explain the system of role based access control. For each subject, the active role is the role that the subject is actually using:

$AR(s : subject) =$ active role for subject s

Each subject may be authorized to act as one or more roles:

$RA(s : subject) =$ authorized roles for subject s

Each role may be authorized to execute one or more actions:

$AC(r : role) =$ actions authorized for role r

Subjects may perform action:

$exec(s : subject, a : action) = true \Leftrightarrow$ subject s can perform action a

Three basic rules can be defined:

1. *Role assignment*: before a subject s can perform an action a it has to be assigned a role.

$$\forall(s : subject, a : action) : exec(s, a) \Rightarrow AR(s) \neq \emptyset$$

The authentication procedure is not considered to be an action but all other user activities are conducted through actions. This implies that all active users must have an *active* role.

2. *Role authorization*: a subject's active role must be a role authorized for that subject.

$$\forall(s : subject) : AR(s) \subseteq RA(s)$$

Together with the first rule, this ensures that users can only take on roles for which they are authorized.

3. *Action authorization*: a subject s can perform the action a, only if the action a is authorized for the subject's active role.

$$\forall(s : subject, a : action) : exec(s, a) \Rightarrow a \in AC(AR(s))$$

These three rules guarantee that users are only able to perform actions for which they are authorized. As the conditional in rule 3 is "only if", this allows for the possibility that extra restrictions may be placed on the execution of an action.

6.5.1.4   Roles and Actions.   Referring to Figure 6.4, roles can be seen as a many-to-many relationship between individual users and their privileges. The privileges are associated with the corresponding roles. The users are granted membership to a role according to the ruling security policy. The roles then give the users the possibility to execute their privileges.

Some examples of roles in environments that role based access control is particularly suited for:

- University: student, lecturer, professor, dean, ...

- Hospital: secretary, nurse, pharmacist, doctor, physician, surgeon, ...

- Bank: teller, loan officer, manager, system analyst, auditor, ...

Related to the privileges, there also exists a many-to-many relationship (see Figure 6.5) between the objects and the actions. This relation can be defined as the authorized object for which the action a can be performed. All of these actions can be arbitrarily complex.

Examples in the case of the university:

- Everyone may publish a home-page;

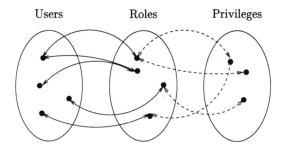

Figure 6.4.   Roles

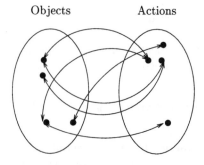

Figure 6.5.   Objects and actions

- A student may run the 'matlab' program to fulfill assignments;

- A professor may fill in the results of the examinations on a student's report;

- A lecturer can publish their notes on the internal web-page for their students to read.

Actions are non-discretionary relative to roles. This means that it should be impossible for a professor to give away their privileges to fill in the student's report card to a student.

6.5.1.5   Advantages of RBAC.   The system of role based access control provides many advantages:

- Role based access control provides a means of administering the access to data that is natural and consistent with the way most enterprises are organized and conduct business;

- the users can be granted membership to roles based on their competence and responsibility;

- user memberships can be revoked or re-established;

- the administrative functions can be applied centrally, locally or remotely;

- administrators can create roles and place constraints on role memberships;

- it is possible to define role hierarchies.

6.5.2   Attribute Certificate

Role based access control is implemented by SESAME using attribute certificates. Attribute certificates are tokens that contain the role(s) that users are allowed to act as. In this way they give the appropriate privileges to the user. This is why these attribute certificates have been defined as *privilege attribute certificates* (PACs) in SESAME (the major fields of the PAC are illustrated in Table 6.1). They are issued and managed by a central server (the privilege attribute server). To prevent these PACs from being forged by the user or by outside attackers, they are digitally signed with the privilege attribute server's private key.

It possible to distinguish two types of PAC:

1. *Non-delegatable*: these are bound to a particular identity. They are protected by the Primary Principal Identifier (PPID) method (Section 6.5.3.1). The security information inside the PAC gives more information about the particular session. Access control decisions may indeed need to take into account the relative security of the client computer the user is logging in from.

Table 6.1.   The privilege attribute certificate

Common Contents	Specific Contents	Signature
issuer domain	protection methods	value of the signature
issuer identity	privileges	algorithm identifier
serial number	miscellaneous	certificate information
creation time	time period	
validity		

2. *Delegatable*: these act like capabilities (Section 1.3.1). Thus it is possible to temporarily delegate some or all of a user's access rights to another user/server. It remains important to keep this user/server accountable for their actions. Therefore, each entity in the system has its own identity, and is always authenticated as that identity. To implement this delegation mechanism, the PV/CV mechanism is used (Section 6.5.3.2). In general it is good practice to make the rights that are conveyed as restricted as possible.

Both types of PAC are issued with short expiration times (the order of a few minutes) to limit the time a compromised key or capability can be used for. When an access control decision is presented with a PAC, the target (more precisely its PAC validation facility) checks that the PAC is currently valid. The time period during which a PAC is valid is intended to be short so that the user sponsor must periodically re-contact the privilege attribute server. This ensures that changes to a user's privilege attributes are guaranteed to take effect within a known, and short, period of time thus fulfilling the need for a possible revocation of the user's rights.

Delegatable PACs can be used to achieve pseudo-anonymity (the client is anonymous to the server but not to the system), provided that this is permitted by the security policy. A client that wishes to be anonymous obtains a delegatable PAC that does not contain its identity, and then delegates this PAC to a proxy server that acts on its behalf. The ultimate target of the access knows the identity of the proxy server but not the client behind it. The audit trails contain sufficient information to enable a security administrator to unmask an anonymous user if this should be required.

The PAC format is independent of the domain's security policy. The details of the security policy are contained in the system components that create or interpret PACs: the privilege attribute server and each application server's access control logic. The SESAME implementation assumes a particular form of role-based policy: for (and during) a particular session, each user takes on exactly one role; roles are enumerated and assigned identifiers; for each user, there is a list of the roles in which the user can act; the access rights of a user are determined by the role in which they act.

The SESAME PAC is based on a profile of the ECMA PAC. The ECMA PAC has been designed to conform to emerging ISO/IEC definitions of a security certificate, and in particular of an access control certificate [125]. A complete definition of the ECMA PAC can be found in ECMA 219 [81].

6.5.2.1   Online Pull-Push Model. SESAME employs an on-line *push* model to distribute the access rights to the remote servers. This means that the privileges are sent along by the client in their request to access an application. The other way to achieve this is the *pull* model, in which the remote server fetches the user's privileges from the central privilege server when a client tries to access it.

There are several advantages of using the online push model according to Kaijser, Parker, and Pinkas [137]:

- There is no need for extra communications as the access decision can be taken immediately.

- There is only one access to the privilege attribute server by each client, compared to the many accesses that would be needed by the target server.

- It is possible to access the server anonymously if the policy allows this. In the pull model, the server needs to know the client's identity to pull their privileges (this is actually not true as the same thing can be realized using pseudonyms known only to the privilege attribute server).

- It is possible to change the user's privileges according to the user's context (where did they log-in, which mechanism did they use to authenticate).

- The principle of least privilege: the client needs to provide to the server only the minimum of information that is needed to base an access control decision on (a system administrator can access a server without divulging their root privileges).

There is one disadvantage to using the online push model:

- The target server is unsure that the privileges are valid at that point in time and have not been altered or revoked.

SESAME has opted for the online push model and several provisions were included in the PAC to prevent its abuse.

6.5.3   Protection Methods

Since the digital signature on the PAC only provides data authentication, there have to be some other means to prevent an attacker from replaying a previously intercepted PAC in its data stream to obtain access to the resources associated with the role inside the PAC. In SESAME, three such mechanisms have been implemented:

- the primary principal identifier;

- the protection value/check value;

- the delegate target qualifier.

6.5.3.1   Primary Principal Identifier (PPID). In order to prevent a PAC from being used in an unauthorized manner, the concept of PAC ownership has been introduced. The protection method is known as the *PPID Protection* method. This method allows the PAC to be used securely from the original owner's workstation at more than one target, even though the targets concerned may not be trusted not to attempt to use the PAC as if they were its owner. Unless delegation is separately permitted (using the PV/CV method described in Section 6.5.3.2) none of the potential receiving targets can pretend to be its owner or act as delegate for its owner.

PPID stands for *Primary Principal's Identifier*. The term *Primary Principal* originates from the ECMA-219 standard [81] which distinguishes between the process in the workstation acting on behalf of the user, and the human user or application principal itself (known in ECMA as the *Secondary Principal*).

The PPID method controls the use of a PAC by putting an identifier (the PPID) for the primary principal initiating the request for the PAC in the PAC itself, and supplying the same information as part of the key establishment information. This enables a target application server to ensure that the requester of the PAC is the same entity as the one that obtained the keying information. This achieves the necessary protection and even if it is possible for a wire-tapper to intercept the PAC, any intercepted keying information cannot be sensibly used or forged.

In SESAME, all PACs are protected by at least this method. The exact mechanism that applies depends on the key establishment method:

- If the key establishment involves symmetric technology and the use of a key distribution server, it works as follows:

   1. When the user requests a PAC, the privilege attribute server generates the PPID for the user (as a random number). It includes this PPID into the PAC. Together with the PAC, the privilege attribute server returns a ticket-granting-ticket for the key distribution server that also contains the PPID.

   2. When an application client applies for a session key with the key distribution server, it uses the key distribution server's ticket. The key distribution server returns a ticket for the target application containing, among other things, the PPID value.

   3. The ticket for the target application and the PAC are sent to the server to be accessed. The PAC validation facility on the target then performs the necessary checks on the PAC.

4. If the ticket and the PAC contain the same PPID value, and if the security domain of the key distribution server creating the service ticket and the security domain of the privilege attribute server issuing the PAC are the same, then the sender of the PAC is the original requester of the PAC.

- If the method of basic key establishment uses public-key technology, and therefore does not require the use of a key distribution server, the value inserted into the PAC is the certificate identifier of the X.509 certificate (see Section 1.7.1) that is used by the initiator requesting the PAC. The subsequent protocol to establish the basic key between the application client and the application server involves the initiator signing the basic key package with its private key. The PAC validation facility then checks that the X.509 certificate validating this signature is the one identified in the PAC (see also Section 6.6).

6.5.3.2   Protection Value/Check Value (PV/CV).   The PV/CV protection method allows a PAC to be used by proxy: passed from the initiator to a delegate, and then from delegate to delegate or final target. Each delegate then has the capability of issuing new actions to the applications for which the PAC is valid.

In this method, valid initiators are linked to the PAC by means of a *Protection Value* (PV), inserted in the PAC. The PV has a corresponding randomly generated *Check Value* (CV). The protection value is the result of a one-way function applied to the check value. The only initiator that initially knows the CV is the original requester of the PAC.

$$PV = f(CV)$$

In SESAME, PV/CV pairs are generated by the privilege attribute server. The CV is returned to the initiator encrypted under the appropriate session key. The initiator, and subsequently its valid delegates, prove knowledge of the CV for a particular PV by passing it encrypted under the current session key. Each receiving target can then use the PAC by proxy (subject to the limitations imposed by the controls described in Section 6.5.3.3) since its PAC validation facility has now learned the corresponding CV.

Delegation can therefore be permitted and controlled without the original initiator needing to be aware of the precise identity of the final target application server or the route to it.

6.5.3.3   (Delegate) Target Qualifier (DTQ).   A SESAME PAC may contain one or more target and/or delegate-target application and/or *Trust Group* names specifying which targets or delegate-targets the PAC is valid for. A trust group name is simply the name of a group of applications, defined by the security administrator, that mutually trust one another not to spoof one another's identities. The control information is specified in a *Target Qualifier* or

Delegate/Target Qualifier protection method (referred to as the DTQ method in the text below) which may be used together with either the PPID or PV/CV protection method.

The presence of the DTQ method in the same group as the PPID or PV/CV method serves to limit the acceptability of the PPID check or PV/CV check to be only acceptable for the targets or delegate-targets identified by the DTQ method. If no DTQ method field is present, the PAC is acceptable by any PAC validation facility provided that it passes the other controls. If a DTQ method is present, a PAC validation facility checks this field against the identity of the application, or its Trust Group, on whose behalf the target is making the PAC validation request. The privilege attributes contained in the PAC are valid if one of the protection methods (PPID or PV/CV) is accepted and if the DTQ method also passes. There are two ways to pass the DTQ method controls:

1. There is no target qualifier;

2. The identity of the application or its trust group matches a DTQ method value.

In SESAME, there is a possible distinction between targets that are permitted also to be delegates, and targets that are not. For that purpose the DTQ method field may specify that the identities contained in it are the identities of targets only or of delegate-targets. An application that is only nominated as a target is not permitted to act as a delegate. Thus to be able to act as a delegate, an application must be nominated as a delegate-target. If a target is not permitted to be a delegate as well, the PAC validation facility does not return any received check value.

6.6   PROTOCOLS

In this section some examples of the protocols that have been implemented in SESAME are outlined. The differences with Kerberos are indicated. The interested reader is referred to the work of McMahon [177] and Vandenwauver [231, 233] for a more elaborate and detailed description of several other examples.

6.6.1   Notation

In the protocol, the messages can be cryptographically enhanced (see Tables 6.2, 6.3 and 6.4 for the notation):

1. A *sealed message* $SEAL(k_{AB})(m)$ is assumed to be the plaintext message m followed by a MAC computed using k_{AB} and m. In particular, the SESAME protocols rely on the assumption that the content of a sealed message can be recovered without knowing the key k_{AB}.

2. A *symmetric-key encrypted message* $ENC(k_{AB})(m)$ is assumed to have both data authentication and confidentiality protection. SESAME attempts to

achieve this by actually encrypting the concatenation of a one-way hash of m and m itself (actually this is not a good mechanism as explained in Section 6.7).

3. A *signed message* $SIGN(PK_A^{-1})(m)$ is understood to be the message m signed by party A (using its private key PK_A^{-1}) with a digital signature that provides message recovery.

4. A *public-key encrypted message* $ENC(PK_A)(m)$ is the message m encrypted with the public key (PK_A) of A. It is assumed that m contains redundancy or known information so that A can recognize it as a valid message m.

In order to increase the legibility of the protocol we define the following symbols:

1. $KeyPK_{i-j-k} = ENC(PK_j)(k_{jk}, T_s, T_e, data)$

   With this message, i transmits a new session key k_{jk} to the receiver j of this message. Entity j can then use this key in its communication with k. The timestamps T_s and T_e indicate the start and end time of the validity of this key. If i sends a ticket granting ticket along, then this ticket granting ticket contains the same key (k_{jk}), and the same start and end time (T_s, T_e).

Table 6.2.   Notation for entities involved in the SESAME protocol

A	The authentication server
P	The privilege attribute server
U	The user sponsor
R	The user
X	An application client
Y	An application server
Z	Another application server
V	The PAC validation facility of application server Y
W	The PAC validation facility of application server Z

Table 6.3.   Various cryptographic keys used in the SESAME protocol

K_{AB}	A long term key shared between A and B
k_{AB}	A session key shared between A and B
PK_A	The public key of A known by the other participants
PK_A^{-1}	The private key of A known only by A

Table 6.4.   Miscellaneous symbols used in the SESAME protocol

$ReqPriv_R$	Requested privileges by user R
	This value is sealed with the key k_{UP}
$Cert_i$	X.509 certificate for the public key PK_i of party i
RL_x	Requested lifetime for x
T_s, T_e	Start and end time
r_i	Nonce generated by i
n_i	Message sequence number
$h()$	A hash function

It is also possible for a key package to be transmitted from one party j to another party k. $KeyPK_{j-k} = ENC(PK_k)(k_{jk}, T_s, T_e, data)$ is used to denote this key package.

2. $AuthSK_{i-j} = ENC(k_{ij})(j, t_i, data)$

This is the authenticator that is also used by the Kerberos system. With this authenticator party i proves to party j that it knows the session key k_{ij}. The timestamp t_i is included to prove the freshness of the message.

3. $AuthPK_{i-j} = SIGN(PK_i^{-1})(j, t_i, data)$

This authenticator is based on public-key cryptography and is introduced by the SESAME architecture. It achieves the same goals as the previous authenticator and it adds non-repudiation. E.g., if the *data* field contains a key package $KeyPK_{i-j}$, the authenticator provides non-repudiation of origin to it. Actually it only provides this service to the encrypted key and not to the actual session key as the X.509 protocol does not provide key confirmation (Section 2.5.1). It is also possible to replace t_i in the authenticator with a nonce r_j (that i has received previously from j) (see Section 2.5.2.2).

In our example protocol there are two kinds of credentials that the user R obtains:

1. $TGT_R = ENC(K_{AP})(R, U, T_s, T_e, k_{UP})$

In the second step of the protocol, the user sponsor U receives a ticket granting ticket with which the user R can obtain a PAC from the privilege attribute server. The ticket granting ticket is encrypted with a long term symmetric key K_{AP} that is shared between the authentication server A and the privilege attribute server P. It contains the session key k_{UP}, the start and end time of the validity of the ticket granting ticket and the name of the parties that can use it (R and U).

2. $PAC_R = SIGN(PK_P^{-1})(attributes, PPID_R, PV_R, DTQ_R, data)$

The PAC for user R is digitally signed by the privilege attribute server P. It contains the attributes (role) for user R along with several protection methods $(PPID_R, PV_R, DTQ_R)$ and other data.

6.6.2   Outline

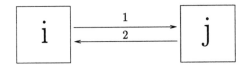

Figure 6.6.   Two party protocol

The goal of the SESAME protocol is to establish a symmetric key k_{ij} between two parties i and j and to have them mutually authenticated (Figure 6.6). This is achieved using two different techniques (timestamps and/or nonces are used to counter replay attacks):

- Using symmetric key technology (Kerberos):

    1. $i \rightarrow j : TGT_i, AuthSK_{i-j}$

       Party i has received a ticket or (ticket-granting) ticket (Section 5.5.2) from the security server in a previous message. This ticket (granting ticket) contains a fresh session key k_{i-j} and is encrypted with a long term symmetric key that is known to party j. In this way, party j can decrypt the (ticket granting) ticket TGT_i to obtain the new session key k_{i-j}. Party i sends the authenticator $AuthSK_{i-j}$ to prove to party j that they know the session key and at the same time i authenticates to j.

    2. $i \leftarrow j : AuthSK_{j-i}$

       Party j validates the authenticator $AuthSK_{i-j}$ with the session key k_{i-j}. Since SESAME targets mutual authentication, party j then generates and sends an authenticator $AuthSK_{j-i}$ to authenticate to i.

- Using public-key technology (X.509):

    1. $i \rightarrow j : KeyPK_{i-j}, AuthPK_{i-j}$

       In the public-key set-up, party i generates the fresh session key k_{i-j} and sends it to j encrypted with j's public key $(KeyPK_{i-j})$. To authenticate i digitally signs a message (containing a timestamp or nonce, the name(s) of the parties involved and in this case $KeyPK_{i-j}$) with their private key $(AuthPK_{i-j})$.

2. $i \leftarrow j : AuthPK_{j-i}$

j decrypts the incoming $KeyPK_{i-j}$ and verifies i's digital signature with i's public key. To authenticate to i, j signs a message and sends this to i.

In the SESAME protocol the above two techniques are sometimes mixed. It is possible that public-key cryptography is used for step 1 and that step 2 (the mutual authentication) is realized with symmetric key cryptography or vice versa.

6.6.3   Intra-Domain Protocol using X.509 and Delegation

Figure 6.7 illustrates the messages that are needed to set up a connection between the client and the server. In this example, the target application server (Y) may act as a delegate to access another server (Z). It is assumed that all entities reside in the same security domain. SESAME also provides protocols for inter-domain communication. This is also realized using the X.509 authentication protocol. For more details the reader is referred to [177, 231].

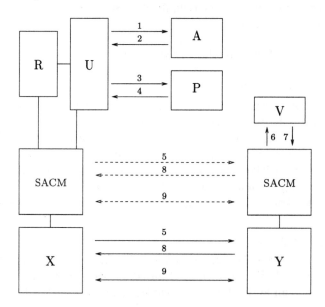

Figure 6.7.   SESAME protocol using X.509

1. SES-AS-REQ

The user sponsor U sends an authenticator $AuthPK_{R-A}$ to the authentication server A. The protocol, that is described in Section 2.5.3.3, is used in this step.

The user R uses strong authentication to authenticate to the system. This means that the authentication server A knows whether or not the log-in has been successful.

$$U, r_U, RL_{TGT_R}, Cert_R, AuthPK_{R-A}$$

2. **SES-AS-REP**

The authentication server A checks the certificate $Cert_R$, extracts the user's public key, and verifies the authenticator $AuthPK_{R-A}$. A returns a key package to U encrypted with the user's public key ($KeyPK_{A-R-P}$). In this setting, the authentication server uses the identification number of $Cert_R$ as the PPID (Section 6.5.3.1) and puts it inside the ticket granting ticket TGT_R. The response also contains an authenticator $AuthPK_{A-R}$, of which the data field contains $KeyPK_{R-P}$, to authenticate the authentication server A to the user sponsor U (mutual authentication). With this the user is protected against possible rogue authentication servers impersonating the real servers.

$$TGT_R, KeyPK_{A-R-P}, AuthPK_{A-R}$$

3. **SES-PAS-REQ**

The user sponsor decrypts the incoming key package $KeyPK_{R-P}$ with the private key of the user R. In the same way as the authentication server A, the authenticator $AuthPK_{A-R}$ is verified. The user sponsor U then forwards a request for a PAC to the privilege attribute server P. In this example, it includes a flag to indicate that the PAC should be delegatable, inside the requested privileges $ReqPriv_R$.

$$RL_{PAC_R}, r_U^{(1)}, TGT_R, AuthSK_{U-P}, ReqPriv_R$$

4. **SES-PAS-REP**

The privilege attribute server decrypts TGT_R to obtain the session key k_{UP}. With this it verifies the authenticator $AuthSK_{U-P}$. As it sees that there already is a PPID in TGT_R, it copies this value into the returned PAC PAC_R. To make delegation possible, it also creates a PV/CV pair (Section 6.5.3.2) with $PV_R = h(CV_R)$. The check value is then transmitted to the client encrypted with the session key.

Since the application client X generates the basic session key k_{XV}, to be used between X and the application server Y, and then uses public-key cryptography to transmit it to Y, there is no need to send back a new session key package and/or ticket as would be the case in the Kerberos scenario.

$$PAC_R, ENC(k_{UP})(r_U^{(1)}, CV_R)$$

5. SES-INIT-CTXT

The application client X generates the new basic session key k_{XV}. The public key PK_V of the target application server's PAC validation facility V can then either be pulled from a directory or is cached in the client computer.

This step of the protocol is based upon the ECMA-206 Association Context Management [80] protocol.

The key package contains an authenticator $AuthPK_{R-V}$ to let the target PVF V verify the PPID identified inside PAC_R, and an authenticator $AuthPK_{X-V}$ (containing $KeyPK_{X-V}$ in the data field) to authenticate the application client to the application server. The check value CV_R is also encrypted with the self-created session key k_{XV}.

The SESAME token is sealed with IK_{XY} (see below) to provide data authentication. The token contains all the information which V needs to derive IK_{XY}.

Let M be the SESAME token :

PAC	PAC_R
check value	$ENC(k_{XV})(CV_R)$
Key package	$KeyPK_{X-V}$
Authenticator 1	$AuthPK_{R-V}$
Authenticator 2	$AuthPK_{X-V}$
Miscellaneous	$Cert_X, Cert_R, r_X, t_X$
Random off-sets	rs_1, rs_2
Target application server	Y

Resulting in the message :

$$SEAL(IK_{XY})(SEAL(k_{XV})(M), X, t_X, n_X)$$

The integrity and confidentiality dialogue keys IK_{XY} and CK_{XY} are used later on to protect the messages between the application client X and the application server Y; they are computed by applying one-way functions to the basic key k_{XV} and the random offsets (rs_1, rs_2) supplied by the application client X (principle of key-offsetting explained in Section 6.4.2.3).

$$IK_{XY} = h_1(k_{XV}, rs_1)$$
$$CK_{XY} = h_2(k_{XV}, rs_2)$$

6. SACMToPVF

The application server Y then passes the information received from X on to the PAC validation facility V for processing (through its SACM module). This transfer of information takes place within one computer, and SESAME assumes that the host's access control mechanisms provide sufficient protection for these messages.

$$SEAL(k_{XV})(M)$$

7. PVFToSACM

The PAC validation facility V decrypts the key package $KeyPK_{X-V}$ with its private key and obtains the basic key k_{XV}. The PAC validation facility then performs the following checks :

- It validates the authenticator $AuthPK_{X-V}$. If this check is successful V has authenticated X and has a confirmation by X on the key package $KeyPK_{X-V}$.

- It validates the authenticator $AuthPK_{R-V}$ with the public key contained in the certificate $Cert_R$.

- It verifies the seal on the entire message with k_{XV}.

- It checks that the target Y identified inside this message matches the identity of the server on whose behalf the PAC validation facility is currently acting.

- It verifies the digital signature on PAC_R with the privilege attribute server P's public key.

- It checks that the $PPID_R$ value inside the PAC matches the identification number of the certificate $Cert_R$ that was used to validate the authenticator $AuthPK_{R-V}$.

- It decrypts the check value package $ENC(k_{XV})(CV_R)$ with the session key k_{XV} to obtain CV_R.

- It applies whatever access control checks are necessary (e.g., DTQ_R), based on the attributes inside the PAC, the identity of the client X and the identity of the server Y.

The PAC validation facility then supplies Y with the integrity and confidentiality dialogue keys and the check value. Again, it is assumed that access control mechanisms provide sufficient protection for this message.

$$IK_{XY}, CK_{XY}, CV_R$$

8. SES-INIT-CTXT-COMPLETE

The server Y now validates the seal with key IK_{XY} on the message received in step 5 of the protocol. Y then authenticates itself to X by sealing a message under the shared dialogue integrity key IK_{XY}.

$$SEAL(IK_{XY})(t_X, n_Y)$$

9. SES-DATA

As of this moment, X and Y are able to exchange data that can be protected against changing and/or snooping. SESAME does not use the Kerberos defined KRB-PRIV and KRB-SAFE, but instead defines its own message format.

$X \rightarrow Y$	$SEAL(IK_{XY})(t_X^{(i)}, n_X^{(i)}, m)$	data auth.
$X \rightarrow Y$	$SEAL(IK_{XY})(t_X^{(i)}, n_X^{(i)}, ENC(CK_{XY})(m))$	int. & confidentiality
$X \leftarrow Y$	$SEAL(IK_{XY})(t_Y^{(i)}, n_Y^{(i)}, m)$	data auth.
$X \leftarrow Y$	$SEAL(IK_{XY})(t_Y^{(i)}, n_Y^{(i)}, ENC(CK_{XY})(m))$	int. & confidentiality

In some cases, the application server Y might need to access another application server Z on behalf of the user. The protocol that is used to achieve this is illustrated in the following steps (see also Figure 6.8).

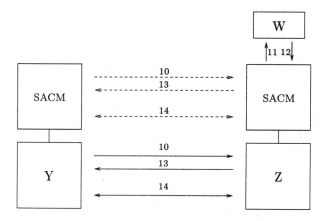

Figure 6.8.   SESAME protocol with delegation

10 SES-INIT-CTXT

Only the case where the new target application's PAC validation facility W's public key PK_W is known to the application server Y is considered here.

Let M' be the SESAME token :

PAC	PAC_R
check value	$ENC(k_{YW})(CV_R)$
Key package	$KeyPK_{Y-W}$
Authenticator	$AuthPK_{Y-W}$
Miscellaneous	$Cert_Y, r_Y, t_Y$
Random off-sets	rs_3, rs_4
Target	Z

Resulting in the message :

$$SEAL(IK_{YZ})(SEAL(k_{YW})(M'), Y, t'_Y, n'_Y)$$

The integrity and confidentiality dialogue keys IK_{YZ} and CK_{YZ} are computed by applying one-way functions to the basic key k_{YW} and the random offsets (rs_3, rs_4) supplied by Y.

$$IK_{YZ} = h_1(k_{YW}, rs_3)$$
$$CK_{YZ} = h_2(k_{YW}, rs_4)$$

11 SACMToPVF

The application server Z then passes the information it has received from application server Y on to his PAC validation facility W for processing.

$$SEAL(k_{YW})(M')$$

12 PVFToSACM

The PAC validation facility decrypts the key package $KeyPK_{Y-W}$ with its private key in order to obtain the basic session key k_{YW}. It performs the following checks :

- It verifies the authenticator $AuthPK_{Y-W}$ to authenticate Y and to get confirmation on the key package $KeyPK_{Y-W}$.

- It verifies the seal on the entire message with k_{YW}.

- It checks that the target Z identified inside this message matches the identity of the application server on whose behalf the PAC validation facility is currently acting.

- It verifies the digital signature on PAC_R with the privilege attribute server P's public key.

- It decrypts the check value package $ENC(k_{YW})(CV_R)$ and checks if $PV_X = h(CV_R)$.

- It applies whatever access control checks are necessary, based on the attributes inside the PAC (e.g., DTQ_R), the identity of the application server Y, and the identity of application server Z.

The PAC validation facility then supplies Z with the integrity and confidentiality dialogue keys and the check value.

$$IK_{YZ}, CK_{YZ}, CV_X$$

13 SES-INIT-CTXT-COMPLETE

The server Z authenticates itself to Y by sealing a message under the shared dialogue integrity key IK_{YZ}.

$$SEAL(IK_{YZ})(t_Y, n_Z)$$

14 SES-DATA

The servers Y and Z may then exchange data with the same messages as those used in step 9.

6.7   ANALYSIS OF SESAME

There is still plenty of work to do on SESAME in the future if SESAME is to continue to be successful in helping people protect their valuable computer resources. Looking back at the whole implementation process, and taking into account the latest developments in security technology, the following problems and possible solutions can be identified (some of these objections were met by the designers of the SESAME architecture but have not been implemented into the current SESAME V4):

1. Due to cryptographic regulations in force the SESAME project had to replace the DES algorithm in the SESAME distribution at [216] by a simple XOR operation. Therefore anyone who installs the SESAME software should replace this by an actual DES implementation (many are available on the Internet). Although this is a fairly easy task, it has been made easier by including the DES in the version for Linux that can be downloaded from [216].

2. Table 6.5 gives an overview of the actual cryptographic algorithms used in SESAME V4. In view of recent developments [29, 77, 193], it is recommended to increase the bit-length for RSA to 1024 bits, to replace the DES by another symmetric key algorithm with a key length of more than 80 bits and a larger block length (e.g., SQUARE [66] or RC-5 [208]), and to replace MD5 with a 160-bit hash function such as RIPEMD-160 [78] or SHA-1 [94]. The SESAME code was written in a modular way so that these changes need a minimal effort.

3. The private key of the user, used to generate their digital signatures, is only protected in the current release of SESAME by the underlying OS's (UNIX) access controls. To solve this, Smart Cards should be used or a protection scheme with a passphrase (as in the PGP system) needs to be implemented.

4. The message structure in step SES-DATA needs to be reorganized. To improve the security, the message to provide data confidentiality and data authentication should be replaced by the following (reversing the sealing and encrypting sequence):

Table 6.5.   Cryptographic primitives used by SESAME

$SEAL(K_{AB})(m)$	DES CBC-MAC
$ENC(K_{AB})(m)$	DES in CBC mode together with MD5
$SIGN(K_A^{-1})(m)$	RSA (512 bits) together with MD5
$ENC(K_A)(m)$	RSA (512 bits)
$h(m)$	MD5

$$ENC(CK_{XY})(m, t_X^{(i)}, n_X^{(i)}, SEAL(IK_{XY})(m))$$

This is known to be good practice, e.g., by Menezes, van Oorschot and Vanstone in [181].

5. As suggested in Section 6.6.1, the symmetric-key encrypted message in its current form does not provide data authentication and confidentiality protection in a secure way. Suppose a block cipher is used in the CBC mode and the message $ENC(k_{AB})(m, h(m), m', h(m, h(m), m'))$ is sent. Then the message $ENC(k_{AB})(m, h(m))$, obtained by cutting off the last blocks, is also a valid message. To obtain data authentication the sealed message should be used.

6. When the SESAME consortium decided to use attribute certificates to implement role based access control with delegation, this was of course fueled by the ECMA initiative in that area [81]. At that time it was also the only known solution. In recent years there have been other solutions suggested such as the SDSI certificates [88] (Section 1.7.2) and the addition of proprietary extensions to the certificates based on the X.509 standard [131]. Therefore it should be investigated whether any of these new ideas can be incorporated into SESAME.

7. Although the decision not to award any cryptographic keys to the user sponsor might have been justifiable at the start of the SESAME project, the same thing can no longer be said in 1998. The *Trojan Horse* attack in which an attacker subverts the security of the system by replacing the user sponsor with a tampered version is very realistic and provides a real threat. As modern client work stations can be operated by a more secure OS, such as Windows NT or Linux, it would be a big improvement to rewrite the protocols to use these user sponsor's credentials. E.g., if the user has a Smart Card and the user sponsor is assigned a public/private keypair, the Station-To-Station protocol (Section 2.5.5.4) could be used to this end.

8. The communication between the PAC validation facility and the application server is assumed to be secure. This is not always the case in reality, especially if the PAC validation facility is serving several application servers

at the same time. Since both of them have a public/private key-pair, the protocol only needs a minor update to incorporate data authentication and confidentiality services on this link. This would enhance the overall security of the system considerably.

9. The SESAME architecture [81] was designed in a way to make it possible to implement any possible security policy. However if this is not needed and e.g., the password based log-in does not need to be supported, the authentication server can be omitted. The main purpose of the authentication server is to provide a user with a strong secret to prove its identity in return for a weaker secret (the password). If all users have their own public-key pairs there is no need for this anymore and the architecture can be simplified by removing the authentication server. The resulting change in the protocols should only be minor.

10. Finally, an even bigger change would be to remove the Kerberos compatibility completely and design the protocols from scratch. This could lead to a more generic protocol such as those described in ISO/IEC 9798-3 [128] or ISO/IEC 11770-3 [130].

7 SECURING APPLICATIONS WITH THE GSS-API

7.1 INTRODUCTION

Applications that want to take full advantage of the benefits of the Kerberos or SESAME architecture, need to be *Kerberized* or *sesamized*. This Chapter describes in some detail how applications can be *sesamized* [6, 7, 9].

The chapter begins with a description of the Generic Security Service Application Program Interface (GSS-API) and in particular how to use the GSS-API to secure applications. Fortunately, Kerberos and SESAME both adopt the GSS-API, thus minimizing the programming effort needed. The next section then describes how the SESAME GSS-API was used to secure two user level applications, `telnet` and the `rtools`. Both of these applications are notoriously insecure. The last section describes the *sesamization* of a non-user level application, in particular how SESAME security was added to the remote procedure call (RPC).

7.2 GSS-API

The GSS-API [167, 169] is a software specification for providing security services to networked applications in a generic fashion. The specification defines security services and primitives at a level independent of both underlying mechanism and programming language environment (it assumes the existence of complementary specifications for language and implementation specifics).

There are two distinct components to a GSS-API implementation: an *interface* to a set of security services, and *mechanisms* that provide the services. The interface is provided to a caller through a GSS-API library that can be linked to the application code. The interface hides from the application the specific details of the mechanism. A mechanism is usually a security architecture, for example Kerberos or SESAME, and typically exists on secured hosts.

There are two main benefits derived from separating the interface and mechanism: the programmer only requires limited knowledge of how the security services are implemented, and it aids in source level portability of applications (in general requiring applications only to be rebuilt with a new implementation of the library). The GSS-API specification addresses four specific goals [169]:

- *Mechanism independence*: The GSS-API defines an interface to security services at a generic level that is independent of particular underlying mechanisms.

- *Protocol environment independence*: The GSS-API is independent of the communication protocol suite.

- *Protocol association independence*: The GSS-API's security context construct is independent of protocol association constructs.

- *Suitability to a range of implementation placements*: GSS-API clients should not be constrained to reside within any trusted computer base perimeter defined on a system where the GSS-API is implemented.

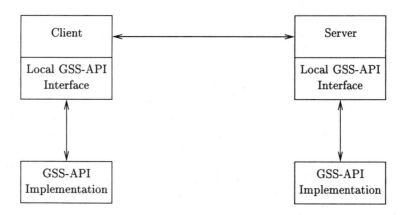

Figure 7.1.   Conceptual model of the GSS-API

Figure 7.1 shows the conceptual model of the GSS-API. The arrows indicate network communication. An application itself provides the communications, calling on the GSS-API in order to provide data authentication and data confidentiality to these communications. A GSS-API caller accepts *tokens* (such as a ticket) provided to it by its local GSS-API implementation and transfers these tokens to a peer on a remote system. That peer passes the received tokens to its local GSS-API implementation for processing.

Before entities can take part in the GSS-API security process they must possess appropriate credentials. The structure of these credentials is mechanism specific, and at the GSS-API level are treated as opaque quantities. It is the responsibility of the underlying mechanism to ensure only those entities entitled can gain access to credentials. The GSS-API process assumes that entities have access to credentials before beginning.

For client processes often the credentials available are those of the user accessing the client process, and who wish to perform some function on a server. These type of 'user' credentials are typically obtained through a login process e.g., in SESAME they are obtained using the 'ses_login' or 'strong_login' programs. The credentials may be tickets, cryptographic keys, PACs or a combination depending on the underlying mechanism.

In most cases the server process has credentials created for it when the server is installed in the system. These 'server' credentials are installed in an area accessible to the server process and are protected by some underlying mechanism to ensure only the server process can access the credentials. The server credentials are typically as simple as a cryptographic key that can be used by the server to prove its identity. Note that in some cases it is more appropriate for a server to use credentials that are 'user' credentials, and these are obtained in a similar fashion to the client 'user' credentials.

The GSS-API is session oriented and it separates the operations of initializing a session (called a security context) and achieving peer entity authentication, from providing per message data authentication and data confidentiality for messages subsequently transferred within the context.

To establish a context, the entities involved in the process pass credential tokens to each other to prove their identity, and then session data is established at each entity to be used in subsequent data transfers. This session data is opaque to the GSS-API level and is accessed through a context handle. When establishing a security context, the GSS-API also allows the client to delegate its credentials to the server. This allows the server (which usually does not have credentials that would allow context establishment) to initiate its own security context on behalf of the initializing client.

7.2.1   Interface Descriptions

The GSS-API is a product of the IETF Common Authentication Technology Working Group (CAT-WG) [121], with the original intention to provide portability of applications between the Kerberos (Chapter 5) architecture and the Distributed Authentication Security Service (DASS) (Section 8.6). Its role has been somewhat expanded, and is now emerging as a standard in the Internet Community for securing networked applications.

The GSS-API [165, 238] has been incorporated into many security technologies, some examples are OMG-CORBA [194], Kerberos [168], DCE [212], SPX [225], KryptoKnight [184], SPKM [1], and SOCKS [178]. The version 1

Table 7.1.   GSS-API version 2 function calls

Call	Description
Credential Management Calls	
GSS_Acquire_cred	acquire credentials for use
GSS_Release_cred	release credentials after use
GSS_Inquire_cred	display information about credentials
GSS_Add_cred	construct credentials incrementally
GSS_Inquire_cred_by_mech	display per-mechanism credential information
Context-Level Calls	
GSS_Init_sec_context	initiate outbound security context
GSS_Accept_sec_context	accept inbound security context
GSS_Delete_sec_context	flush context when no longer needed
GSS_Process_context_token	process received control token on context
GSS_Context_time	indicate validity time remaining on context
GSS_Inquire_context	display information about context
GSS_Wrap_size_limit	determine GSS_Wrap token size limit
GSS_Export_sec_context	transfer context to other process
GSS_Import_sec_context	import transferred context
Per-message calls	
GSS_GetMIC	apply integrity check, separate from message
GSS_VerifyMIC	validate integrity check token and message
GSS_Wrap	optionally encrypt and encapsulate
GSS_Unwrap	decapsulate, and optionally decrypt
Support Calls	
GSS_Display_status	translate status code to printable form
GSS_Indicate_mechs	indicate mech_types supported on system
GSS_Compare_name	compare two names for equality
GSS_Display_name	translate name to printable form
GSS_Import_name	convert printable name to normalized form
GSS_Release_name	free storage of normalized-form name
GSS_Release_buffer	free storage of printable name
GSS_Release_OID	free storage of OID object
GSS_Release_OID_set	free storage of OID set object
GSS_Create_empty_OID_set	create empty OID set
GSS_Add_OID_set_member	add member to OID set
GSS_Test_OID_set_member	test if OID is member of OID set
GSS_OID_to_str	display OID as string
GSS_Str_to_OID	construct OID from string
GSS_Inquire_names_for_mech	name types supported by mechanism
GSS_Inquire_mechs_for_name	mechanisms supporting name type
GSS_Canonicalize_name	translate name to per-mechanism form
GSS_Export_name	externalize per-mechanism name
GSS_Duplicate_name	duplicate name object

specification originally had around 20 calls. Version 2 [169] is a result of industry feedback and has over 30 calls. It adds a number of new features such as the sharing of contexts across processes. Version 2 has superseded Version 1.

The GSS-API calls can be divided into four groups. Table 7.1 gives the version 2 calls. A full description of each call can be found in the version 2 specification [169].

7.2.2   A GSS-API Example

To illustrate the use of the GSS-API for securing applications, a simple client-server application is secured. Experience with the GSS-API [7, 9] has shown that it requires a reasonably small number of code changes to convert an insecure client-server application into a GSS-API secured one.

Client

> Connect to server
> **do**
>> generate client-message
>> send client-message
>> receive server-message
>> process server-message
> **until** NOMOREDATA
> generate terminate-message
> send terminate-message

Server

> **while** TRUE
>> wait for client connection
>> **do**
>>> receive client-message
>>> process client-message
>>> **if** terminate-message
>>> **then** NOCONNECTION
>>> **else** generate server-message
>>>> send server-message
>>> **endif**
>> **until** NOCONNECTION
> **endwhile**

Figure 7.2.   Pseudocode for an insecure client/server application

The pseudocode in Figure 7.2 is for a simple insecure client-server application. There are no security services provided to the application, so masquerading as client or server, and copying and modifying data during transfer would not be difficult.

To secure the application, GSS-API calls should be added to the appropriate positions in the code to establish a secure context between client and server, and then to provide data protection for the data sent between client and server within this context. The procedure is illustrated in Figures 7.3 and 7.4.

Client

```
connect to server
get server's name
GSS_Import_name()
 do
   GSS_Init_sec_context()
   send client-token
   receive server-token
    If MUTUAL_REQUESTED
    then
       GSS_Init_sec_context()
    endif
 until SECURITY-CONTEXT-ESTABLISHED
 do
   generate client-message
   GSS_Wrap()
   send client-message
   receive server-message
   GSS_Unwrap()
   process server-message
 until NOMOREDATA
generate terminate-message
GSS_Wrap()
send terminate-message
receive context-token
GSS_Process_context_token()
```

Figure 7.3.   Pseudocode for a GSS-API secured client

The client calls GSS_Init_sec_context() to establish a secure context to the server, and requests mutual authentication to be performed in the course of context establishment. GSS_Init_sec_context() returns an output token to be passed to the server, and indicates that mutual authentication has been requested.

The server acquires the appropriate credentials to enable connection acceptance with a call to GSS_Acquire_cred(). It receives the client's connection and passes the received token to GSS_Accept_sec_context(). If the token is acceptable, it provides an output token to be passed back to the client.

If mutual authentication was requested the client passes the received token to a successive call to GSS_Init_sec_context() which processes data included in the token in order to achieve mutual authentication. If mutual authentication is successful a security context is established.

Server

```
get server's name
GSS_Import_name()
GSS_Acquire_cred()
 while TRUE
  wait for client connection
  do
    receive client-token
    GSS_Accept_sec_context()
    send server-token
  until SECURITY-CONTEXT-ESTABLISHED
  do
    receive client-message
    GSS_Unwrap()
    process client-message
    if terminate-message
    then NOCONNECTION
        GSS_Delete_sec_context()
        send-context-token
        GSS_Release_cred()
    else
        generate server-message
        GSS_Wrap()
        send server-message
    endif
  until NOCONNECTION
endwhile
```

Figure 7.4.   Pseudocode for a GSS-API secured server

The client generates a data message and then passes this to GSS_Wrap(). GSS_Wrap() performs data authentication, and (optionally) confidentiality processing on the message. The client sends the output message to the server.

The server passes the received message to GSS_Unwrap() which inverts the encapsulation performed by GSS_Wrap(), decrypts the message if the original confidentiality feature was applied, and validates the data authentication.

When the client and server have completed their operations, the server calls GSS_Delete_sec_context() to flush context-level information. Optionally the server-side application may provide a buffer to GSS_Delete_sec_context(), to receive a context-token to be transferred to the client in order to request that client-side context level information be deleted.

If a context-token is transferred, the client passes the context-token back to the function GSS_Process_context_token() which deletes the client's context information.

It should be clear from this example that the securing of existing applications is reasonably straight forward and can be done without knowledge of underlying mechanisms or modification to communication protocols.

7.2.3 The Different GSS-API Versions

Table 7.3 shows the GSS-API calls supported by version 1 [167], version 2 [169] and the SESAME version of the GSS-API [13, 14]. The SESAME GSS-API includes all the version 1 calls together with additional calls that support access control and digital signatures. These additional calls, which are not currently part of the version 2 specification, are shown in Table 7.2.

The new SESAME V4 calls are as follows:

- GSS_Get_attributes(): get attributes associated with credentials or security context. For SESAME this returns the user's access identity, role and group membership, the audit identity, controls and restrictions.

- GSS_Modify_cred(): request a set of privileges and controls, optionally replacing existing credentials or creating a new set. The effect of this interface is cumulative on a set of credentials.

- GSS_Set_default_cred(): permits a user to indicate which credential is to be interpreted as the default.

- GSS_Release_priv_attribute_set(): discard a set of privilege attributes.

- GSS_Release_targ_control_set(): discard a set of target controls.

- GSS_Sign() and GSS_Verify(): these are per message calls that apply and validate a digital signature to the message. In this way it is possible to build a non-repudiation of origin service.

Table 7.2.   Extra SESAME GSS-API calls

Access Control Calls
GSS_Get_attributes
GSS_Modify_cred
GSS_Set_default_cred
GSS_Release_priv_attribute_set
GSS_Release_tag_control_set
Digital Signature Calls
GSS_Sign
GSS_Verify

Table 7.3.   Comparison of GSS-API implementations

GSS-API Call	Version 1	Version 2	SESAME V4
Credential Management Calls			
GSS_Acquire_cred	X	X	X
GSS_Release_cred	X	X	X
GSS_Inquire_cred	X	X	X
GSS_Add_cred		X	
GSS_Inquire_cred_by_mech		X	
Context-Level Call			
GSS_Init_sec_context	X	X	X
GSS_Accept_sec_context	X	X	X
GSS_Delete_sec_context	X	X	X
GSS_Process_context_token	X	X	X
GSS_Context_time	X	X	X
GSS_Inquire_context		X	
GSS_Wrap_size_limit		X	
GSS_Export_sec_context		X	
GSS_Import_sec_context		X	
Per-message Calls			
GSS_GetMIC	X	X	X
GSS_VerifyMIC	X	X	X
GSS_Wrap	X	X	X
GSS_Unwrap	X	X	X
Support Calls			
GSS_Display_status	X	X	X
GSS_Indicate_mechs	X	X	X
GSS_Compare_name	X	X	X
GSS_Display_name	X	X	X
GSS_Import_name	X	X	X
GSS_Release_name	X	X	X
GSS_Release_buffer	X	X	X
GSS_Release_OID		X	
GSS_Release_OID_set	X	X	X
GSS_Create_empty_OID_set		X	
GSS_Add_OID_set_member		X	
GSS_Test_OID_set_member		X	
GSS_OID_to_str		X	
GSS_Str_to_OID		X	
GSS_Inquire_names_for_mech		X	
GSS_Inquire_mechs_for_name		X	
GSS_Canonicalize_name		X	
GSS_Export_name		X	
GSS_Duplicate_name		X	

7.2.4   Limitations of the GSS-API

The GSS-API has a number of limitations:

1. Mechanism Negotiation

   The GSS-API specification indicates that the GSS-API may be implemented as an interface to a set of mechanisms. The specification however does not describe how to chose a mechanism. This may be necessary where applications are secured with a GSS-API implementation that supports a number of mechanisms. Two parties may want to first determine whether they share a common mechanism, and which one to use, before normal context establishment is performed. A simple and protected GSS-API negotiation mechanism is defined in [14] by Baize and Pinkas.

2. Message Based Specification

   The GSS-API is designed to protect discrete messages using GSS-API routines within the established security context. Each of the routines, for example GSS_Wrap() and GSS_Unwrap() is designed for discrete message packets, and they are not suited for protocols where a data stream is sent from one peer to another (for example the telnet protocol). To overcome this in the SESAME telnet, the GSS_Wrap_Char() and GSS_Unwrap_Char() routines were added that provide efficient processing for a single character.

3. Security Context Establishment

   The message protection calls can be used only after a security context has been established. Without an established context the calls fail. In many situations this session establishment is suitable and the GSS-API works satisfactory. In other situations, such as email, session establishment may not be suitable. An extension to the GSS-API to allow protection of an independent data unit is described by Adams in [3].

4. Access Control and Delegation Extensions

   The GSS-API specification currently does not support security attributes other than a single identity and does not allow fine control of delegation. Parker and Pinkas specify the exchange of a variety of security attributes, and the construction of authorization functions using these attributes including delegated ones, and fine control over delegation in [198].

7.3   TELNET

telnet is a client-server based program that allows users to work on remote computers. The main goal of telnet is to make an environment-independent representation of the transmitted data. It was meant to be used both for terminal to mainframe connections, for terminal to terminal connections, and for process to process communications. Nowadays, it is mainly used to get a remote shell across the network.

7.3.1 Security Issues

`telnet` is still one of the most popular applications. In most cases it is used without any security considerations at all and therefore remains one of the most vulnerable programs.

It can be exposed to the following attacks (see Chapter 4 for more information):

- TCP hijacking: since the session is not encrypted.

- Sniffing: passwords are sent in the clear on the network.

- TTY hijacking: the user is linked to the server through a tty.

- Finally the whole `telnet` session can be eavesdropped to reveal any possibly confidential information typed in by the user or sent by the server.

This means that the following options needed to be added to `telnet`, to make it secure.

1. A stronger authentication mechanism needs to be implemented. The current `telnet` implementations are based on passwords, or on the caller's IP address.

2. To ensure data confidentiality, users should be given the possibility to encrypt their `telnet` session, both from the client to server and server to client.

These security services can be provided using the SESAME GSS-API (with some minor changes). The result is named `s-telnet` (SESAME `telnet`). In the following sections the changes to the basic `telnet` are explained in some detail.

7.3.2 Authentication Framework

The `telnet` AUTHENTICATION option and SESAME's GSS-API are used to add strong authentication to `telnet`.

Starting with its October 1995 release, the BSD UNIX `telnet` source code also has a built-in facility to negotiate this authentication [33]. This facility is a framework for any security system to perform the authentication, but it does not actually implement any authentication mechanism.

For mutual authentication with SESAME, the client-server exchanges were implemented as depicted in Figure 7.5 The implementation is straight-forward and follows closely the general mechanism, explained in Section 7.2. The client remains in `GSS_Init_sec_context()` until it receives the token with which the server authenticates (mutual authentication).

7.3.3 Encryption Framework

`telnet` has in the past included facilities to add encryption. Two Internet-Drafts exist, but both have expired. The described protocols were never promoted to the level of an RFC. The first Internet-Draft [31] described the ENCRYPT

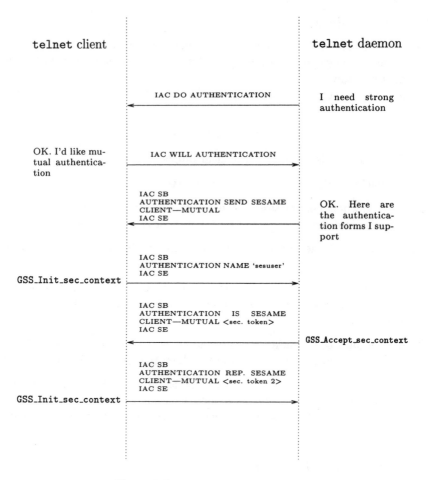

Figure 7.5.   s-telnet authentication

option, which could start and/or stop encryption of the data stream from client to server or vice-versa, independent from the authentication stage. It dates from 1992. One year later, the second Internet-Draft [32] described the AUTH_ENCRYPT option, which would replace both the AUTHENTICATION and ENCRYPT options. By putting these two commands together, the data stream is ensured to be encrypted as soon as entity authentication has been successful. This would eliminate the window of vulnerability to an active attack, in between the successful authentication step and the negotiation of the ENCRYPT option. Some kind of support of the ENCRYPT option has been added to the 1991 release of telnet, but this code was only meant for experimental purposes and is not available outside the U.S. and Canada.

This does not constitute a big problem for the SESAME implementation of s-telnet. The encryption option negotiation is not a requirement for s-telnet. s-telnet was dedicated to SESAME authentication and encryption, so the client can rely on the server's capabilities to encrypt/decrypt with the proper session key once a security context has been initiated. s-telnetd listens on a specific port and is not required to be compatible with a telnet client which does not offer SESAME authentication. On the contrary, s-telnet is *required* to have strong SESAME authentication, not just *offer* it as an option.

As explained in the AUTH_ENCRYPT Internet-Draft, encryption should start as soon as successful authentication has taken place. Therefore, referring to Figure 7.5, the encryption starts immediately after the 6th message that concludes the authentication stage.

7.3.4   Implementation using the SESAME GSS-API

Encryption with the GSS-API in the case of telnet is not so straight forward because of the way telnet processes its data stream.

To protect the data confidentiality, the GSS-API provided by SESAME offers two calls: GSS_Wrap() and GSS_Unwrap(). These functions encrypt the input buffer with the session key created during the establishment of a secure context and then put the result, encapsulated in a SESAME structure containing miscellaneous information, in an output buffer.

As pointed out in Section 7.2, the best place in the existing source code to include the GSS-API calls for encrypting and decrypting data is:

- Call GSS_Wrap() before sending any data to the network.

- Call GSS_Unwrap() after retrieving any data from the network.

However, some additional care needs to be taken. telnet puts data from the network in a buffer (circular buffers are used in the client). These buffers can be flushed anytime: if the data makes part of an option negotiation, it can either be immediately processed (putting the client or server in another 'state'), or, if it is (part of) a suboption, it is pushed in the suboption buffer until an IAC SE is received. Data meant for the (pseudo)terminal can also be treated immediately. So except for suboption negotiation, telnet is never waiting for a complete token to be received.

If n bytes (using GSS_Wrap()) need to be encrypted from a buffer before sending it, it is necessary to send a token of length $N > n$. At the other side of the communication, it is only possible to unwrap this token when all N bytes are received. This creates two problems:

1. The receiving side has to wait until N bytes are received. As it does not know N beforehand, this length has to be sent before sending the token released by GSS_Wrap. Another possibility (for example used in the telnet suboptions) would be the use of an escape character.

2. The encryption implies a network traffic overhead. This might not seem important but it is. In most cases, for client to server traffic n is much

smaller than N. Even worse in the usual case (character-by-character mode) characters are sent over the network one by one (when the client host is slow and the user is typing extremely fast it can happen that more than one character is sent at once). While this is a bad characteristic of telnet (one character typed is one full IP packet on the network), using the SESAME GSS-API would make it even worse: a bunch of miscellaneous information is added to the one encrypted character.

Another issue is the fact that telnet can be run in two modes: a character-by-character mode, and a line-by-line mode.

The line-by-line mode was used in old terminals (e.g. IBM 2741) and is less interactive than the character-by-character mode. Still for use in some programs, the line-by-line concept had some advantages (fast local echo). Therefore, a more modern line-by-line mode was implemented for some systems, called the LINEMODE and described in [30].

Many interactive programs (e.g., pine or tin) can only be used in the character-by-character mode, so this mode should also be supported. The problem with doing so is that SESAME's GSS-API does not provide a reliable way to securely encrypt one character at a time. Since GSS_Wrap() is based on the DES in CBC mode, there would be some synchronization problems as well as some performance issues.

To solve all previously mentioned problems, it was decided to add two new GSS-API calls: GSS_Wrap_char() and GSS_Unwrap_char(). These are implemented using the DES in CFB mode. The encryption of one character relies on the precedent characters. The implementation also results in an output token of exactly the same length as the input token, so that simple calls to these GSS-API routines can be made without needing to add another buffer to telnet, and there is no increase in network traffic due to encryption.

One limitation though of replacing the conventional wrapping routines with these new DES CFB routines, is that these routines do not produce output that is ASN.1 compliant as required by the GSS-API standard [165, 169].

Table 7.4.   Performance results for SESAME telnet

Security Service	T1	T2
Single Authentication	430 ms	215 ms
Mutual Authentication	445 ms	240 ms
GSS_Wrap character	24.0 μs	17.8 μs
GSS_Unwrap character	7.20 μs	5.60 μs

7.3.5 Performance

This section outlines the performance of *sesamized* `telnet`, the results being for a single computer (both client and server running on the same machine) a Pentium 120 MHz, 16 MB RAM (T1), and a Pentium 200MHz MMX, 64 MB RAM (T2) both running Redhat Linux.

`telnet` traditionally used username and password for authentication and provided no data protection. The *sesamized* `telnet` provides the option of SESAME single or mutual entity authentication and full data protection.

Table 7.4 shows the results for *sesamized* `telnet`. Note that there was no observable difference in interactive performance between `telnet` and *sesamized* `telnet`.

7.4 RTOOLS

The BSD `rtools` are a suite of remote host-to-host communication programs that were introduced with BSD4.2, and are found on most BSD-derived systems. They have also been included and/or ported to most other UNIX-based systems due to their popularity and usefulness. One of the major features of the tools is the ability to access resources (files, programs) on the remote host without explicitly logging in to the remote host. This is most useful in `rcp` and `rsh` commands, which may be invoked from shell scripts to automate some process for the user. At the same time this feature is also their biggest weakness, and the reason that they have been disabled in security conscious environments. The default authentication is very weak, and easily overcome.

There have been other attempts at securing the `rtools`. The `rtools` supplied with BSD4.4-Lite (and derived systems such as FreeBSD and OpenBSD), have been secured using Kerberos V4. The implementation was not achieved using the GSS-API, but with the native Kerberos API. SSLrsh is a version of the standard *rshd* and client (`rsh`, `rcp` and `rdist`) that have been secured using SSL. SSH is a complete `rsh`, `rcp` and `rdist` replacement, using public-key authentication and data is protected with session keys that are regenerated every hour. Broom and Ashley [36] argue that the main reason for the inadequacy of these tools is the fact that programs such as SSH are not part of a comprehensive security architecture.

In this section the *sesamizing* of three of the rtool programs `rlogin` (remote login), `rsh` (remote shell) and `rcp` (remote copy) is described.

7.4.1 rlogin

This program is typically used when logging in to another Unix system to use interactive facilities (shell, editors, curses based programs). Redirection of input and output does not work well with `rlogin` (`rsh` was intended for that use), since the client puts the terminal in 'raw' mode. If there is no entry for the originating host in the */etc/hosts.equiv* database, or in the user's personal ˜*/.rhosts* database, then the user is prompted for a password during login. Typical usage is: *rlogin remote-host [-l username]*, where *remote-host* is the destination computer and the option *-l username* specifies the username to login to on the remote host (if different from the local username).

7.4.2 rsh

This program is used for running non-interactive commands on remote hosts without having to login manually to the host(s) concerned. This is used, for example to run a program on the remote host and display the output on the user's terminal. The difference between rsh and rlogin is that rsh allows no interactivity, and also allows redirection of both the input (STDIN) and the output (STDOUT) of the remote process to other processes on either the client host or the remote host. Output from a program on one remote host can even be used as the input to a program on another remote host, using two separate invocations of rsh with a shell pipeline (using the Unix shell pipe mechanism). rsh depends on a */etc/hosts.equiv* and ˜*/.rhosts* file with valid entries. Typical usage is:

- *rsh remote-host ls*, which runs the command *ls* on the destination computer *remote-host*;

- *rsh remote-host ls | more*, which is the same as the previous example, but it pipes the output from the remote command to a local invocation of *more* (a text scrolling utility).

7.4.3 rcp

rcp executes in the same fashion as the standard Unix copy program cp, but is capable of handling slightly different parameters. These parameters indicate to rcp that a source file may be located or is to be transferred to a particular HOSTNAME under a particular USERID. rcp depends on a working */etc/hosts.equiv* and ˜*/.rhosts* file. The syntax for rcp is :

- *rcp -r -p [[userid@hostname:]filename] [[userid@hostname:]filename]*

  rcp can offer different modes:

1. Local to local:

   Here the user did not provide a HOSTNAME or USERID for either source or target. rcp simply substitutes the arguments into a standard Unix copy cp command and executes it, for example:

   - *rcp /tmp/test /tmp/test.new*

   This copies the file *test* in the *tmp* directory on the local computer, to a new file called *test.new* in the same directory on the local computer.

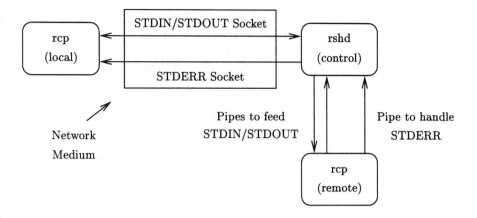

Figure 7.6.   rcp local to remote and remote to local

2. Local to Remote and Remote to Local:

    The user has supplied a HOSTNAME and a USERID for either the source or
    the target (but not both). rcp detects which of the two modes was selected.
    Depending on which mode was selected, a function is executed via use of
    rcmd() (a function that rtools uses to talk to the *rshd* daemon) on the
    remote host. Figure 7.6 gives a general overview of the configuration of the
    two computers and the use of rcmd() to help achieve these modes:

    - rcp calls rcmd() which executes a command on the remote host (via
      rshd);
    - *rshd* on the remote host detects a request for service;
    - *rshd* does its authentication and if successful then forms two sockets,
      one to handle STDIN and STDOUT, and another for STDERR;
    - *rshd* then executes the requested command on the remote computer.

    Typical syntax for this mode is:

    - *rcp userid@hostname:filename filename (remote to local)*

    In this case the source procedure (the functions that sends the file) is exe-
    cuted on the remote host, and the target procedure (function that receives
    the file) is executed on the destination (local) computer.

    - *rcp filename userid@hostname:filename (local to remote)*

    In this case the target procedure is executed on the remote host, and the
    source procedure is executed on the local computer.

3. Remote to Remote:

When this mode has been selected by the user (that is both source and target have a HOSTNAME and USERID) then rcp simply executes rcp (using rsh) on the source host but with the parameters configured to execute as a LOCAL to REMOTE mode.

7.4.4   Existing Security of rshd and rlogind

This section outlines the existing operation of the *rshd* and *rlogind* daemons (the daemons used by the rsh, rcp and rlogin programs).

rshd is the daemon used by both rsh and rcp. When a service request is received the following protocol is initiated:

1. The server checks the client's source port. If the port is not in the range 512-1023, the server aborts the connection.

2. The server reads in a number, if it is non-zero it is interpreted as the port number of a secondary port to be used for the STDERR. A second connection is then created to the specified port on the client's computer. The source port of this second connection is also in the range 512-1023.

3. Two usernames are retrieved on the initial socket. These usernames are interpreted as the user identity on the client's computer, followed by the user identity to use on the server's computer.

4. *rshd* then validates the user by using the files */etc/hosts.equiv* and the ˜*/.rhosts*.

rlogind is the daemon used by rlogin. When a service request is received the following protocol is initiated:

1. The server checks the client's source port. If the port is not in the range 512-1023, the server aborts the connection.

2. Once the source port has been checked, *rlogind* proceeds with the authentication process outlined for *rshd*. It then allocates a pseudo terminal, and manipulates file descriptors so that the slave half of the pseudo terminal becomes the STDIN, STDOUT and STDERR for a login process. If automatic authentication fails, the user is prompted to log in as if on a standard terminal line.

As the above descriptions show, the existing authentication methods are quite weak, and potentially easily circumvented by various spoofing techniques. Where users have direct access to a workstation on the network, there are various ways in which computer identifications can be spoofed. Added to this, some users might naively assume their workstation is secure, and possibly create entries in the remote˜*/.rhosts* file to allow automatic access from their personal workstation.

The basic attacks consist of:

- Spoofing (forging) the identity of the computer. It is possible to setup a computer with the same network address as a 'trusted' computer, and use that to obtain access to some secured host that allows rtools connections from the trusted host. Although usually the time interval in which the network address is available to the attacker is short, it is long enough to enable the attacker to rsh into the remote computer, and plant a suitable ~/.rhosts file to allow later access.

- Spoofing (forging) the identity of a user on the client host. When only a user on a host is trusted, it means that the attacker must convince the remote host that the attacker is indeed the user with permission to access.

7.4.5   Writing a Common Library

Since there was such a large amount of code that would be common to both servers, and also common to all clients, it made sense to develop a library of functions that could be used by all client and server applications. This reduced the amount of code changes and also provided a simple interface to the GSS-API routines.

The two servers that needed to be secured, *rlogind* and *rshd*, had the following common requirements:

- Perform SESAME authentication;

- And if successful then get the name of the remote user;

- Verify that the user is the same as the user on the destination computer and if they are allowed to login to that account (through a ~/.rhosts file);

- Wrap the data transfers in both directions.

A common library for both servers and clients was written that would enable the servers to authenticate the clients (with mutual authentication if needed) and secure the data streams, with a minimum of changes to the original code.

7.4.6   Authentication

7.4.6.1   Server Authenticating a Client.   The interface provided to the server programs was simplified to allow a single line change in the server code to do the full client and server authentication, with all of the work being done in the library. After the SESAME authentication had been performed, the normal server processing was resumed, with the exception that the paranoia (client source port below 1024) checking was deleted. The paranoia code is no longer needed as SESAME guarantees that a PAC that is accepted by GSS_Accept_sec_context() is the verified user, and it doesn't matter if the client computer has been compromised, the SESAME system itself is secure, so a SESAME identity cannot be faked in any way.

For each server, the calls to accept the SESAME connection were identical, and consisted of calling `rauth_init()`, and then calling `rauth_accept_client()`.

7.4.6.2   Client Authenticating to Server.   After making the initial TCP connection to the server, the client calls `rauth_init()`. It then accesses the function `rauth_client_login()`, to obtain a PAC and transfer it to the application server and receive the server's PAC for mutual authentication. After this authentication takes place, normal client processing is resumed.

7.4.7   Wrapping of the Data

Securing the streams was less straight forward than the authentication. Normally the rtools put the network stream in non-blocking mode, and expect the network as a stream, reading a variable number of bytes from 1 up to a maximum buffer size, and writing anywhere from 1 to maximum buffer size back down the stream. The problem here was to convert the `GSS_Wrap()` and `GSS_Unwrap()` procedures which worked on blocks of data (each block must be read in completely before it can be decoded), into a stream.

Buffering was needed for the block to stream conversion, as the size of the blocks sent by a transmitting end of the application could be anywhere from 1 to the maximum buffer size. An encrypted block could have been limited to one byte for sending, which would have made buffering unnecessary, but it would have added far too much overhead. The application data would also have comprised approximately 0.5% of the total data transferred. For user input applications such as `rlogin`, encrypting single bytes is unavoidable, as each keypress must be encrypted then sent to the server (which usually echoes the character back, doubling the bandwidth wasted). For large transfers, such as screen output or copying files to/from the remote, it is avoidable.

In the securing of `telnet`, two new routines were added GSS_Wrap_char() and GSS_Unwrap_char(). These were included for efficient encryption and decryption of single characters. Because the `rtools` use a single library for encryption and decryption, it was decided not to use these routines (they are potentially only useful for rlogin). Hence the timing for encrypting and decrypting single characters in `rlogin` is slower than `telnet`. The difference however is not noticeable to the user.

7.4.7.1   Writing Encrypted Data.   For writing data out securely, it would have been quite simple to just divide the output into manageable blocks. As it turns out, `GSS_Wrap()` can accept any arbitrary sized block, so the encrypted write becomes a simple process of encrypting the passed data as one block, then writing the resultant block down the network with a header containing enough information ('magic ID', data length) so that the reading process can reassemble the block.

The routine `secure_write()` emulates the semantics of the normal write system call, so that minimal changes to the I/O code of the application/server needed to be made. Also, it allows different types of encryption (or no encryption at all) to be plugged in, with no further changes to the application code. On successful write of the data, it returns the amount that is written out (which may be less than was requested), or -1 on error.

7.4.7.2 Reading Encrypted Data.   Reading the data presented a slightly different problem, as the application expected the same semantics as read on a non-blocking channel (that is that the read attempt would read as many characters as were available on the stream, then return). With the encrypted stream, the entire block had to be read (in blocking mode) in one piece. The block was then decoded and stored into a buffer, and the requested amount of data was returned if it was less than the encoded block size, or else the entire contents of the decoded block were returned.

The routine `secure_read()` emulates the semantics of the read system call, for the same reasons as `secure_write()` emulates the write system call. On successful completion, it returns the amount of data read (which may be less than requested) to the caller, or -1 on error, 0 if no data available.

It was also necessary to add in a call that would tell how much data was left in the buffer of the cipher object. This was needed as the application would not always read in the entire amount of data that was contained in a block of data, and the excess needed to be buffered. The existing I/O transfer loops (transferring data from the network to the user or sub-program), waited for data via the `select()` system call, tried to read as much as possible from the network, output that to the user/program, then waited for more data via `select()` again.

A small loop was inserted into the section that read from the network which would read data from the cipher object, write it to the user/program then check if any data was left in the cipher buffer, and then loop back to the read again.

The routine for checking for data (`secure_pending()`) returns the number of bytes remaining in the buffer of the cipher object, or 0 if no data was in the buffer.

There was one further situation that had to be dealt with, and that is when the application was reading data from the stream, then writing it out to a non-blocking pipe (for example the screen, or a pseudo-TTY) it might not have been able to accept all of the data. In this case, the application would attempt to read in as much as possible from the network, then store the result in a buffer which was then fed to the user/program as it could accept it. In this case, a simple loop as above was not possible, but by using `secure_pending()`, and if the cipher buffer had data and by selecting only the output pipe, a successful work around was created. `rlogin` used blocking I/O extensively for communication to/from the child shell on the remote end, and for communication with the user on the client end.

7.4.7.3 Non-blocking I/O.   In the application, the option to put the network stream into non-blocking mode was turned off. If it was left on, reading of a block of encrypted data would mean polling or waiting for the end of the encryption block, or to keep retrying to send all of the encryption block before returning. Since polling is bad for CPU usage, turning it off seemed the best way, and does not appear to have affected the operation of the programs. This is also the approach taken by the BSD4.4 rtools, which had been secured with Kerberos.

7.4.7.4 Out-of-Band Data.   One problem that did prove quite interesting to solve was when *rlogind* sent out-of-band data to the client. Out-of-band data is used as urgent data, which the network attempts to deliver as fast as possible to the receiver, possibly ahead of data that is sent normally. During normal operation, if a read request for normal data is attempted, and there is out-of-band data waiting to be read, the read fails until the out-of-band data is read from the network.

On the surface, this does not appear to be much of a problem, since the data is transferred in blocks. Unfortunately, TCP does not keep message boundaries, so each of these blocks may need to built out of many small reads, each of which may possibly be interrupted by out-of-band data. Therefore, the token reading routines needed to be modified to expect interruption by out-of-band data and to be able to resume an interrupted token read at any time. This complicated the code for reading a token, and also complicated the `secure_read()` function slightly, as it needed to be able to restart the token read if the previous one failed with out-of-band data.

Unfortunately, this extra complexity had to be catered for, even though the existing method worked fine on the loopback connection, and possibly even fine over a LAN where the network transfers are high speed, and the data would not be spread out over a number of TCP packets. Over a slower link, there is more latency in the network, and out-of-band data may arrive in the middle of one of the encrypted blocks, causing the read to fail, and requiring a restart on the block read.

7.4.8 Delegation of Privileges

SESAME delegation was required for securing of `rcp` in remote to remote mode. In the first phase of `rcp` remote to remote, a security context was established from the local computer to the source host. The delegation option in `GSS_Init_sec_context()` and `GSS_Accept_sec_context()` was used to delegate the credentials to the source host. These credentials could then be used by the source host in establishing context with the target host.

7.4.9 Performance

This section outlines the performance of the *sesamized* `rtools`, the results being for a single computer (no network latency) using Pentium 120 MHz, 16 MB RAM (T1), and Pentium 200MHz MMX, 64 MB RAM (T2) both running Redhat Linux.

The `rtools` traditionally had very weak entity authentication and no data protection. The *sesamized* `rtools` provide the option of SESAME single or mutual authentication and full data protection.

Table 7.5 shows the results for *sesamized* `rtools`. Note that there was no observable difference in the performance of `rlogin` and only a small observable difference in performance of `rsh` and `rcp`.

Table 7.5.   Performance results for SESAME `rtools`

Program	Security Service	T1	T2
rlogin	Single Authentication	390 ms	190 ms
	Mutual Authentication	410 ms	210 ms
	`GSS_Wrap` character	42.0 μs	32.1 μs
	`GSS_Unwrap` character	13.0 μs	10.1 μs
rsh	Regular 'rsh cat file'	7.98 s	5.11 s
	SESAME 'rsh cat file'	14.9 s	6.41 s
rcp	Regular 'rcp file'	3.43 s	3.29 s
	SESAME 'rcp file'	10.4 s	5.41 s

7.5   RPC

The Remote Procedure Call (RPC) allows a client to execute procedures on remote networked servers. It has two main uses:

1. It can be used as a programming tool for building networked applications. It allows the programmer to concentrate on the application and use RPC for the transport.

2. It is the foundation of a number of system utilities such as the Network File System (NFS) and the Network Information System (NIS).

The Open Network Computing (ONC) version of RPC from Sun Microsystems is arguably the most popular (probably because Sun Microsystems released the source code to the public), and it is this version that was secured with SESAME.

A simple RPC application consists of a single client that communicates with a single server (the machine that actually executes the procedure). The client application requests execution of the procedure using RPC calls that pass arguments to the the server procedure, and retrieve the results. To the client it appears that the procedure was executed locally, and execution is synchronous, the same as for local procedures.

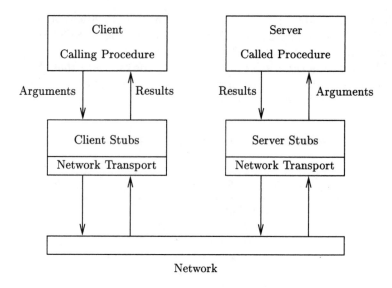

Figure 7.7.   The remote procedure call

RPC uses a request and reply communication model (Figure 7.7). The client procedure sends request messages to the server procedure which returns reply messages. The client and server processes communicate by means of two stubs, one for the client and one for the server. A stub is a communications interface that implements the RPC protocol and specifies how messages are constructed and exchanged. The stubs contain functions that map simple local procedure calls into a series of network RPC function calls. The client calls procedures found in its stub that use the RPC library to find a remote process and then make requests of it. This remote process, in turn, listens to the network through the server stub. The server executes service routines when requested.

ONC RPC provides a machine independent data representation known as the External Data Representation (XDR). Client and server stubs are responsible for translating data in and out of this form. The XDR library contains filters for translating built-in C types as well as more complex types like strings and variable-length vectors.

7.5.1 Review of Other Research

For some time ONC RPC has provided an authentication service. The service is available with different strengths (call flavors): none (no authentication), Unix (simple user identification based on Unix UID and GID), DES (DES encryption of client and server keys), and Kerberos (the full Kerberos authentication system). Unfortunately, although client and server can be authenticated at a strong level using the DES or Kerberos flavors of authentication (Unix is very weak), ONC RPC does not provide any protection to the data being transferred.

Lately there have been attempts to provide additional security services to ONC RPC to make it at least as secure as industry standards require. OpenVision Technologies [133] has produced an ONC RPC secured with a Kerberos version of the GSS-API. This is believed to be the first version of a GSS-API ONC RPC. OpenVision used the Kerberos V5 implementation of the GSS-API, which provides Kerberos authentication services and additional data protection.

Sun Microsystems itself has followed on after the research of OpenVision Technologies. They have produced their own GSS-API ONC RPC [86] and have produced an Internet RFC based on their experience [85]. Again they have used a Kerberos V5 implementation of the GSS-API and provide the same security services as OpenVision's original version.

7.5.2 Overview of the Implementation

The mechanism independence of the GSS-API enabled the work of OpenVision and Sun Microsystems to be the basis of the SESAME version of GSS-API ONC RPC. This was not through use of their code but by re-securing ONC RPC following the guidelines set out in RFC2203 [85]. The mechanism independence of the GSS-API was proved, because the SESAME ONC RPC was built exactly to the guidelines specified in the RFC. Basing the security on SESAME has provided additional security services to ONC RPC, the most important of which are use of public-key technology and RBAC.

Similarly to the RFC a new authentication flavor AUTH_RPCSEC_GSS was added that provides SESAME security services: secure single or mutual authentication that occurs on the first access of the client to the server, data protection services for the arguments and results transferred, and also SESAME RBAC.

ONC RPC is very modular. The client calls clnt_create() which returns a client structure. If the client wishes authentication with the server it calls one of the four authentication flavor routines: auth_none(), auth_unix(), auth_des() or the new routine auth_rpcsec_gss(). The authentication details are stored in the client structure. When the client processing has finished the authentication details and client handle are destroyed using the auth_destroy() and clnt_destroy() calls.

7.5.3 Authentication

Authentication occurs only once. The authentication is performed and the authentication structure is created by the auth_rpcsec_gss_create() routine. The authentication credentials of the client and server are created by the SESAME implementation and are accessible through the GSS_Init_sec_context() call. As a result of the call two items are created and returned: a token which must be sent to the server, and the client context handle which is used to identify the secure context the client uses to talk to the server. The token is sent to the server and the client waits for a reply.

The server takes the call and notes the call is a RPCSEC_GSS_INIT, which tells the server that authentication and context establishment is required. The server calls GSS_Accept_sec_context() and passes the token received from the client into it. If successful, a call to the function auth_rpcsec_gss_reply() is made. In this reply message, the server adds its context handle and if mutual authentication was requested, the server's token.

The server's context handle had to be sent back to the requesting client as the server has no state. There was also the option to store the server context handle local to the server and use a hash function to retrieve the context. The hash key would then be sent by the client to the server. Instead the server's context handle was sent each time. Note there are no security implications to this decision as the context handle is a pointer to a data structure in the server. An attacker cannot benefit from the pointer.

The client gets the reply. If mutual authentication was requested, the client loops through the GSS_Init_sec_context() loop passing in the received server token and if successfully authenticated, a successful reply is returned to the client code and a client authentication structure is updated accordingly. A secure context has now been created between the client and server.

It should be noted that there is an underlying incompatibility between the stateless nature of RPC and the 'once only' authentication of SESAME RPC. For the system to operate correctly it is assumed that the RPC server stays up for at least the first few RPC requests (to complete the context establishment). If the RPC server at any later time crashes, context establishment has to be performed again.

7.5.4 Secure Parameter Passing

AUTH_RPCSEC_GSS provides data authentication, data confidentiality or both on all data transferred along the secure context channel. This is achieved by the GSS_Wrap() and GSS_Unwrap() routines of the GSS-API. There are two places data is currently protected during transfer: the arguments passed from the client to the server and the results passed from the server to the client.

The arguments to be passed to the server are added to the outgoing stream in two possible places, depending on which protocol the client is using to communicate with the server (TCP or UDP). Both of these modules XDR encode the arguments using the XDR routine passed via the call. The calls were replaced at these two places with a new ClientWrap_Args() routine. This determines if the authentication flavor is AUTH_RPCSEC_GSS and if the phase is RPCSEC_DATA. If so the arguments were XDR'ed into a stream of bytes. This stream is then passed through GSS_Wrap() and the result is a protected stream. This protected stream is then placed directly onto the outgoing network XDR stream. If the authentication flavor is not AUTH_RPCSEC_GSS the call to GSS_Wrap() is skipped, and the original XDR routine call is made.

At the server end again there are the TCP and UDP modules. Both modules have a get_args() routine. The XDR call inside this routine is replaced with a ServerUnwrap_Args() routine. This routine detects whether the flavor

is AUTH_RPCSEC_GSS and if the phase is RPCSEC_DATA. If so the server passes the
stream through GSS_Unwrap() to get a XDR stream with the arguments. This
stream is then XDR decoded using the XDR routine supplied. The arguments
are passed to the server to start the server call.

The results are placed into a reply message structure. The XDR routine
is replaced with a ServerWrap_Args() function. This routine simply XDRs the
message and the resultant stream is wrapped with GSS_Wrap() and placed on
the transport XDR stream.

On the client end the un-XDR routine for the reply message is replaced with
a ClientUnwrap_Args() routine. This routine un-XDRs the stream and gives
back the reply message to the client.

7.5.5   Closing The Security Context

When all communications with the server have finished, the client calls the
function Auth_Destroy() which normally would clear and free memory for the
standard three authentication flavors. With AUTH_RPCSEC_GSS() flavor not only
does this have to be done, but it also has to close down the context channel on
the client's end and the server end as well.

This is achieved by the client calling GSS_Destroy_sec_context(), and setting the phase to RPCSEC_GSS_DESTROY and calling the server. The server calls
the function GSS_auth_rpcsec_destroy after noting the phase. A new function was added, called auth_rpcsec_destroy(). This function is similar to the
auth_destroy(). The only difference is that this new routine passes the client
CLIENT handle which is needed to make a call to the server, where as the earlier
routine used the AUTHENTICATION structure.

7.5.6   SESAME RBAC Service

SESAME's authorization service is based on a PAC being sent from the client
to the server when access is attempted. The PAC contains the privileges of the
user. There are two different methods for providing authorization using this
PAC:

- SESAME authorization: the SESAME system can be configured to control
  access to the server, by examining the PAC and disallowing access if the
  PAC's privileges are insufficient.

- Server based authorization: the SESAME system can be configured to allow
  full access to the server, and let the server use the PAC to determine if the
  request should be satisfied.

Of course a combination of the two methods is also possible. For the server
to use the PAC privileges, the server must call a GSS-API routine that extracts
the privileges from the PAC. The routine is called GSS_Get_attributes(). If this
GSS-API routine is called when a Kerberos mechanism is being used, the call
simply returns the identity of the client (because Kerberos does not transport

privileges). In the SESAME system a call to GSS_Get_attributes() returns the user's identity, roles, groups (supersets of roles) and other information about the user.

The important design decision was to keep ONC RPC GSS-API generic, so that it can be used with any mechanism. Hence the SESAME specific code was placed in the actual server service routines rather than in the RPC code.

7.5.7   Outstanding Issues

The following issues need to be investigated:

- GSS-API security routines can provide protection against replay attacks. But RPC is capable of receiving out of order messages, that is a message that needs to be replayed due to a time-out on either the server's end or the client's end. Therefore the replay and out of sequence flags have to be turned off (not selected) for the GSS-API GSS_Init_sec_context() call.

  The solution to out of sequence or replay attacks suggested by RFC2203 [85] was the use of a sequence window. The sequence window value is set to the sequence window length supported by the server for this context. This window would specify the maximum number of client requests that may be outstanding for this context at a time, and these may be out of order. The client may use this number to determine the number of threads that can simultaneously send requests on this context.

- The GSS_Wrap and GSS_Unwrap routines protect the arguments and results of RPC calls from being tampered with. The AUTHENTICATION structure, and the request and reply messages structures are still being transmitted in the clear across the network, and the verifier fields have not been set up or checked.

7.5.8   Performance

Table 7.6.   Performance results for SESAME ONC RPC

Flavor	Security Service	T1	T2
Unix	Single Authentication	0.44 ms	0.32 ms
	Procedure Call	0.60 ms	0.35 ms
SESAME	Single Authentication	395 ms	210 ms
	Mutual Authentication	420 ms	230 ms
	Call	0.66 ms	0.42 ms
	Call (Data Auth.)	3.4 ms	2.4 ms
	Call (Data Auth.+Conf.)	3.6 ms	2.5 ms

This section outlines the performance of *sesamized* RPC, the results being for a single computer (no network latency) using Pentium 120 MHz, 16 MB RAM (T1), and Pentium 200MHz MMX, 64 MB RAM (T2) both running Redhat Linux.

The *sesamized* RPC provides the options of SESAME single or mutual authentication, none, data authentication, data authentication and confidentiality protection, and support for SESAME RBAC. Table 7.6 shows the results for the *sesamized* RPC.

There is a noticeable performance degradation with SESAME RPC over Unix flavor RPC. A RPC call is almost an order of magnitude slower (i.e., 0.35ms to 2.4ms). This would be particularly significant if an application required a large number of RPC calls. Therefore, some work is required to improve the efficiency of the SESAME RPC implementation.

III Other Security Solutions

8 SECURITY ARCHITECTURES

8.1 INTRODUCTION

Chapters 5 and 6 reviewed the Kerberos and SESAME security architectures. In this chapter other important security architectures are reviewed. They are classified as architectures because similarly to Kerberos and SESAME they provide an infrastructure to secure a networked environment. The infrastructure may include components such as on-line security servers, off-line security servers, security APIs, etc. The architectures included in this chapter are Yaksha, KryptoKnight, DCE, DSSA and DASS/SPX.

8.2 YAKSHA

The goal of Yaksha was to start from the Kerberos architecture, and make changes to remove some limitations and add additional security services. Yaksha had five specific design goals:

1. Compromise of the KDC should not allow the attacker to impersonate a client to the server or vice versa.

2. To remove Kerberos' vulnerability to dictionary attacks.

3. Make minimal changes to the Kerberos protocol.

4. To work with Smart Cards.

Table 8.1. Notation used to describe the simplified Yaksha protocols

c	Name of the client
tgs	Name of the ticket granting service
s	Name of the server
T_{exp}	Requested expiry time on the ticket
T	A timestamp
N	A nonce
K_c	Client's password
K_{tgs}	Long term secret key known only to the KDC and TGS
K_s	Server's long term secret key
k_{c-tgs}	Session key shared between the TGS and the client
k_{c-s}	Session key for use between the client and the server
$ENC(K)(M)$	Symmetric encryption of message M under key K
TGT_{c-tgs}	Ticket granting ticket for the client
TKT_{c-s}	Server ticket
PK_i	Public key of party i
PK_i^{-1}	Private key of party i
$ENC(PK)(M)$	Message M encrypted with public key PK
$SIGN(PK^{-1})(M)$	Message M signed with private key PK^{-1}
$CA_i(PK)$	A certificate for the public key PK issued by party i
$PK_{c,temp}$	A temporary public key for client c
PK_{cc}^{-1}	User's part of its private key PK_c^{-1} (user's smart card)
PK_{cY}^{-1}	Yaksha's part of the user's private key PK_c^{-1}
PK_{ss}^{-1}	Server's part of its private key PK_s^{-1} (user's smart card)
PK_{sY}^{-1}	Yaksha's part of the server's private key PK_s^{-1}
PK_{YTGS}^{-1}	Long term private key known only to Yaksha and TGS

5. Provide digital signatures and key escrow services.

Yaksha is a recent development of Bell Atlantic [101, 102, 103] with its beginnings around 1994. The motto of Yaksha given on the Bell Atlantic web site is "Yaksha: Towards Reusable Security Infrastructures". To meet this design goal, the Yaksha system starts with Kerberos and replaces the symmetric key authentication with a public-key solution based on an RSA variant [34, 104]. The name Yaksha is from Hindu mythology, Yaksha being a creature that guards the gates of Heaven.

8.2.1 Yaksha Protocol

In the following text the Yaksha protocols are described as defined by Ganesan [102]. They are based on a simplified version of the Kerberos V5 protocol as defined by Neuman and Ts'o [191] and explained in Section 5.5. The notation used in the protocols is outlined in Table 8.1.

Figure 8.1 shows the Yaksha protocol. The Kerberos authentication server has been renamed to Yaksha, and there are six messages in the Yaksha protocol, the same as Kerberos. The most important difference in the protocol is that Yaksha uses a public-key based solution for authentication rather than a symmetric key solution. Also the system authenticates all of the components, that is client, Yaksha, ticket granting server and (application) server, whereas in Kerberos the authentication server and ticket granting server are not authenticated.

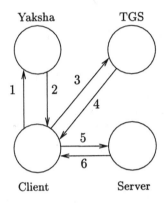

Figure 8.1.   Yaksha protocol

A description of the six steps in the protocol are as follows (see [102] for a more detailed description). For each step in the protocol the difference with Kerberos is described.

1. Client $\rightarrow$ Yaksha : $c, tgs, T_{exp}, SIGN(PK_{cc}^{-1})(CA_c(PK_{c,temp}), N)$

   The first three components are identical to Kerberos. The last part is a certificate generated by the client for its temporary public key together with a nonce. This part is signed by the client with its part of its regular private key. When the Yaksha server receives the message the client can be immediately authenticated by checking the validity of the temporary certificate.

2. Yaksha $\rightarrow$ Client : $ENC(PK_{c,temp})(k_{c-tgs}, T_{exp}, N),$
   $$SIGN(PK_{YTGS}^{-1})(TGT_{c-tgs}),$$
   $$SIGN(PK_{cY}^{-1})(CA_c(PK_{c,temp})$$

   The first two components are identical to Kerberos, except for the fact that they are signed. The third component is the temporary certificate signed by both the client and the Yaksha server. This is important later because it stops the Yaksha server and client from generating false TGTs.

3. Client $\rightarrow$ TGS : $s, T_{exp}, N,$
$$SIGN(PK_{c,temp}^{-1})(SIGN(PK_{YTGS}^{-1})(TGT_{c-tgs})),$$
$$ENC(k_{c-tgs})(T, ...)$$
$$SIGN(PK_{cY}^{-1})(CA_c(PK_{c,temp})$$

The only modifications to the Kerberos message are to attach the dual signed temporary certificate to the message, and to take the TGT from Yaksha and sign it with the client's private temporary key. The TGS can authenticate the user immediately.

4. TGS $\rightarrow$ Client : $ENC(k_{c-tgs})(k_{c,s}, T_{exp}, N, s),$
$$SIGN(PK_{sY}^{-1})(TKT_{c-s}),$$
$$SIGN(PK_{tgs}^{-1})(SIGN(PK_{YTGS}^{-1})(TGT_{c-tgs}))$$

The first component is identical to Kerberos. The second component has the client's server ticket this time signed by Yaksha with its part of the server's private key. The last component is to ensure that a false TGS cannot masquerade to the server.

5. Client $\rightarrow$ Server : $ENC(k_{c-s})(T, ...),$
$$SIGN(PK_{c,temp}^{-1})(SIGN(PK_{sY}^{-1})(TKT_{c-s})),$$
$$SIGN(PK_{cY}^{-1})(CA_c(PK_{c,temp}))$$

The first component is identical to Kerberos. The second component (the client's server ticket) has only been modified such that it is signed both by the ticket granting server and client. The final component is added so that the server can validate the client's ticket.

6. Server $\rightarrow$ Client : $SIGN(PK_{ss}^{-1})(SIGN(PK_{sY}^{-1})(TKT_{c-s}))$

Similarly to Kerberos mutual authentication is not mandated. The server proves its knowledge of its long term secret key to authenticate itself to the client.

The author confirms that the protocol is not as efficient as it could be, but the aim was to keep it as close as possible to Kerberos. At this stage Yaksha only works within a single Kerberos realm, however the author notes the protocol could be extended for inter-realm functions.

8.2.2   Digital Signatures and Key Escrow

One of Yaksha's aims is to add digital signatures and key escrow to Kerberos. The digital signatures are provided by two additional messages [102] not part of Kerberos. These messages allow documents to be signed by generating a document hash and encrypting it with the appropriate RSA keys. The benefit of the scheme is that the same infrastructure can be used for both authentication and non-repudiation of origin.

Key escrow is possible with Yaksha since the Yaksha server generates the session keys. The session keys can be provided to an authority, the benefit of using Yaksha is that although the authority can decrypt the session messages, it can never impersonate the user. The user never has to reveal its private RSA key. A more detailed review of using Yaksha key escrow is presented in [103].

8.2.3 Further Information

Bell Atlantic provides a web site for Yaksha Information [101]. It contains a number of papers and presentations relating to Yaksha.

8.3 KRYPTOKNIGHT

The goal of the KryptoKnight project was to design authentication and key distribution protocols for a low-level networking environment or for small low power devices. The design had to take into account the limitations of these scenarios: small packet sizes, low bandwidth, high transmission costs, limited processing, limited storage, real time needs and export restrictions [132].

KryptoKnight thus has four specific goals:

1. Minimize bandwidth usage and computational overhead.

2. The technology must be exportable.

3. Flexibility is required in the protocols.

4. The design must be scalable.

KryptoKnight has incorporated many of the ideas from Kerberos and is similar in many ways. For example it uses an on-line KDC, it supports multiple realms, provides authentication, key distribution, data protection and single sign-on.

The goals of KryptoKnight however are different to those of Kerberos and it differs in a number of ways [144]:

- Uses hash functions rather than DES for authentication and encryption of tickets (for export reasons since hash functions are not normally subject to export restrictions). It has the added advantage of being computationally less expensive than DES encryption.

- Provides a range of protocols for authentication and key distribution (Kerberos provides only a single protocol).

- Gives an excellent analysis of the protocols under the assumption that the CBC encryption mode of block ciphers is secure.

- Supports the version 4 style inter-realm protocols, insisting that each realm that needs to communicate share a cryptographic key.

- Instead of relying on Kerberos's synchronized clocks, uses nonces instead.

- All protocols minimize the number of messages, length of messages and the amount of encryption.

- Does not provide many of the new features of Kerberos V5 such as delegation, authorization data areas, and postdated and renewable tickets.

KryptoKnight has been under development at the IBM Research Division since about 1992. There are a number of papers describing different components of its development [25, 26, 27, 115, 184]. It is the foundation for the IBM Network Security Program (NetSP), and there are a number of products available (some examples are the security infrastructure, client/server applications and firewalls). KryptoKnight offers the application developer the GSS-API so once the security infrastructure has been purchased, application developers are free to secure their applications.

8.3.1 Protocols

KryptoKnight provides a range of protocols:

- 2-party

- 3-party

- Inter-Domain

- User

In the following sections describing the KryptoKnight protocols, we use the notation from Table 8.2.

Table 8.2.   Notation used in the KryptoKnight protocols

A, B	Network entities performing mutual authentication
N_A, N_B	Nonces
K_A	Long term secret key shared between A and the KDC
K_{AB}	Long term secret key shared between A and B
k_A	Session key for A
k_{AB}	Session key for A and B
$MAC(K)(M)$	Message authentication code of message M computed with key K
$ENC(K)(M)$	Encryption of message M under a secret key K

8.3.2   2-Party Protocols

8.3.2.1   2-Party Mutual Authentication Protocol.   The foundation for the design of the KryptoKnight protocol suite is the 2-party mutual authentication protocol (KryptoKnight refers to it as the 2PAP protocol). The protocol is shown in Figure 8.2 and it is assumed that A and B share cryptographic keys before the protocol begins and want to mutually authenticate each other.

1. $A \rightarrow B : N_A$

2. $B \rightarrow A : N_B, MAC(K_{BA})(N_A, N_B, B)$

3. $A \rightarrow B : MAC(K_{AB})(N_A, N_B)$

The number of message flows (three) is minimal for a nonce-based protocol. The combined size of all messages is also minimal. The use of nonces means that no state information is required (compared with synchronized clocks or counters). The use of a one-way hash function (used for constructing the MACs) is also beneficial for export.

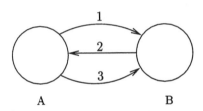

Figure 8.2.   KryptoKnight 2-party mutual authentication protocol

8.3.2.2   2-Party Key Distribution Protocol.   The 2-party authentication protocol leads onto a 2-party key distribution protocol (KryptoKnight refers to it as the 2PKDP protocol). In this scenario, A wants a new session key from the KDC. This is shown in Figure 8.3.

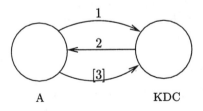

Figure 8.3.   KryptoKnight 2-party key distribution protocol

1. $A \rightarrow KDC : N_A$

2. $KDC \rightarrow A : N_{KDC}, MAC(K_A)(N_A, N_{KDC}, KDC) \oplus k_A$

3. $A \rightarrow KDC : MAC(k_A)(N_A, N_{KDC})$ (Optional)

In this protocol A is authenticated to the KDC, and the KDC provides a session key to A. Before the protocol begins it is assumed that A and the KDC share a cryptographic key. The third message is optional giving confirmation to the KDC that A received the new session key, and would require the KDC to keep state between flows 2 and 3.

8.3.2.3   2-Party Authenticated Key Distribution Protocol.   The 2-party key distribution protocol has the problem that the second message has no integrity protection (how does A know that KDC generated the message). KryptoKnight provides an alternative 2-party authenticated key distribution protocol (called 2PAKDP). This protocol provides both key distribution and authentication of messages. This is shown in Figure 8.4

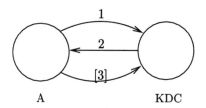

Figure 8.4.   KryptoKnight 2-party authenticated key distribution protocol

1. $A \rightarrow KDC : N_A$

2. $KDC \rightarrow A : MAC(K_A)(N_A, N_{KDC}, KDC),$
    $\qquad\qquad\qquad ENC(K_A)(MAC(K_A)(N_A, N_{KDC}, KDC)) \oplus k_A$

3. $A \rightarrow KDC : MAC(k_A)(N_A, N_{KDC})$ (Optional)

In the second message, an encryption is used on the second component, so that A has to decrypt the component to find the new key. This verifies the new key originated at KDC. Again the last message confirms to KDC that A received the new session key.

8.3.3   3-Party Protocols

The 3-party protocols are used when two network entities A and B want to authenticate each other followed by a secure communications session. A and B initially have no shared secret and one of them must contact the KDC with whom they each share a secret. Note the similarities with Kerberos in the following protocols.

8.3.3.1   A-B-K Pull. In this model it is assumed that A is unable, unauthorized or unwilling to contact KDC, and allows B to contact KDC. The protocol is a construction of the 2PAKDP and 2PAP protocols. This is shown in Figure 8.5.

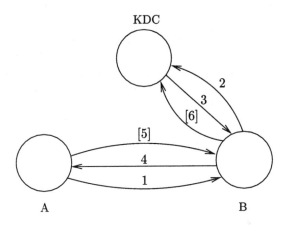

Figure 8.5.   KryptoKnight ABK 3-party key distribution protocol

1. $A \rightarrow B : N_A$

2. $B \rightarrow KDC : N_A, N_B, A$

3. $KDC \rightarrow B : MAC(K_A)(N_A, k_{AB}, B),$
$ENC(K_A)(MAC(K_A)(N_A, k_{AB}, B)) \oplus k_{AB},$
$MAC(K_B)(N_B, k_{AB}, A),$
$ENC(K_B)(MAC(K_B)(N_B, k_{AB}, A)) \oplus k_{AB}$

4. $B \rightarrow A : MAC(K_A)(N_A, k_{AB}, B),$
$ENC(K_A)(MAC(K_A)(N_A, k_{AB}, B)) \oplus k_{AB},$
$N_B, MAC(k_{AB})(N_A, N_B, B)$

5. $A \rightarrow B : MAC(k_{AB})(N_A, N_B), MAC(K_A)(N_A, k_{AB})$
(Last Component Optional)

6. $B \rightarrow KDC : MAC(K_A)(N_A, k_{AB}), MAC(K_B)(N_B, k_{AB})$ (Optional)

The A-B-K Pull protocol begins with A contacting B challenging it to authenticate based on a nonce N_A. B contacts KDC passing along A's identifier and nonce N_A and its own nonce N_B. KDC replies by sending two tickets each containing the new session key k_{AB}. Having received the tickets, B extracts k_{AB} and checks its integrity and freshness. B forwards to A the appropriate ticket and adds its own nonce along with authentication information. A extracts and verifies k_{AB}, verifies the authentication expression from B, and replies with its own authentication information. Optionally A can add a confirmation token that completes mutual authentication between A and KDC. B authenticates A. B can optionally forward A's token as well as its own token to KDC in the last flow.

8.3.3.2   K-A-B Push.   In this model it is assumed that B is unable, unauthorized or unwilling to contact KDC, and allows A to contact it. The main difference between the A-B-K Pull protocol and the K-A-B Push protocol is that the protocol provides authentication of the forward flows to KDC (KDC has authenticated A and B before issuing the session key). The most important consequence is that the direct handshake between A and B is no longer needed. This is shown in Figure 8.6.

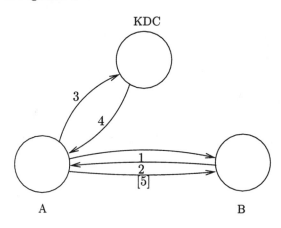

Figure 8.6.   KryptoKnight KAB 3-party key distribution protocol

1. $A \rightarrow B : N_A$

2. $B \rightarrow A : N_B, MAC(K_B)(N_A, N_B, B)$

3. $A \rightarrow KDC : N_A, N_B, B, MAC(K_A)(N_A, MAC(K_B)(N_A, N_B, B), A)$

4. $KDC \rightarrow A : MAC(K_A)(N_A, k_{AB}, B),$
   $\qquad\qquad ENC(K_A)(MAC(K_A)(N_A, k_{AB}, B)) \oplus k_{AB},$
   $\qquad\qquad MAC(K_B)(N_B, k_{AB}, A),$
   $\qquad\qquad ENC(K_B)(MAC(K_B)(N_B, k_{AB}, A)) \oplus k_{AB}$

5. $A \rightarrow B : MAC(k_{AB})(N_A, N_B), MAC(K_B)(N_B, k_{AB}, A),$
   $\qquad\qquad ENC(K_B)(MAC(K_B)(N_B, k_{AB}, A)) \oplus k_{AB}$
   $\qquad\qquad$ (First Component Optional)

8.3.3.3   Other 3-Party Protocols.   There are other 3-party protocols [132] that are not described here. These include protocols that use time-stamps and are even closer to the Kerberos protocol.

8.3.4   Inter-Domain Protocols

KryptoKnight calls the Kerberos realms *domains*. In the case of Kerberos the load for the inter-realm protocol is placed on the client. KryptoKnight on the other hand to be more flexible allows the 3-party protocols to be extended for inter-domain communication, thus not restricting the inter-domain communication to a single protocol. A detailed review of the inter-domain protocols is given in [132].

8.3.5   User Protocols

In addition to the 2-party, 3-party, and inter-domain protocols, KryptoKnight offers protocols for human users. These include a single sign-on protocol, a single sign-on protocol for mobile users, and a password changing protocol. A detailed review of the user protocols is given in [132].

8.3.6   Further Information

The IBM Zurich Research Laboratory provides a web-site for KryptoKnight information [159]. It contains a number of papers and other information relating to KryptoKnight. IBM also has numerous documents related to NetSP products, and these can be found by using the search engine available from the main IBM Home Page [119].

8.4   DCE SECURITY

The goal of the Distributed Computing Environment (DCE) was to provide a comprehensive solution for building a distributed computing system. This solution contained a number of services, one of those being the security service. This section deals with the security service only.

DCE security had 5 main goals:

1. Allow a user a single sign-on to the network.

2. Provide authentication of network entities.

3. Provide data protection to data during transit.

4. Provide an authorization service (including delegation).

5. Provide security APIs for secure application development.

DCE's security is based on Kerberos V5 with additions for an authorization service. Its services are in fact very similar to those of SESAME but it does not provide public-key based services and the authorization scheme is based on user identification and group membership rather than roles.

DCE [114, 118, 145, 212] was developed by the Open Software Foundation (OSF), a non-profit consortium promoting the development of open computing. Development of DCE began in the late 1980s, and there has been renewed interest. The aim of DCE was to provide a vendor-neutral open development environment, with suitable security. Lately OSF has joined forces with the X/Open group to form a new organization called the Open Group. The Open Group looks after the ongoing development of DCE.

8.4.1 Security Services

DCE security comprises three security services:

- An authentication service providing mutual authentication of clients and servers (based on Kerberos V5).

- An authorization service that supplies information about user privileges to servers (similar to SESAME).

- A registry service containing information for the authentication service and authorization service. The registry is similar to the central databases of Kerberos and SESAME.

DCE provides a secure RPC library that can be used by application developers to allow applications to access the authentication and authorization services. For non-RPC applications an implementation of the GSS-API is also available.

8.4.1.1 Authentication Service. The authentication service is based on Kerberos V5 and is not described here as it has been detailed in Section 5.5. The DCE authentication service has two main differences to the Kerberos V5 implementation [195]:

- The DCE security servers are able to interpret both DCE and Kerberos principal names (for backward compatibility).

- Communication with the DCE security servers uses the DCE RPC and also supports the standard Kerberos communication protocols (for backward compatibility).

8.4.1.2 Authorization Service. DCE has adopted the same approach as SESAME to provide an authorization service. It also uses Privilege Attribute Certificates (PACs) from a dedicated server called the Privilege Server (PS). The security attributes in the DCE PAC contain the principal's identity and group-related information. The DCE PAC is shown in Table 8.3.

The *authentication flag* identifies whether the certificate was authenticated by the DCE authentication service (a client is able to present unauthenticated PACs). The *Cell UUID* is the cell in which the principal is registered. DCE uses the term *cell* to describe a Kerberos *realm* and the term Universal Unique Identifier (UUID) to uniquely identify every resource in the system. The principal UUID identifies the principal whose privileges are stored in the PAC. The rest of the PAC contains the *groups* that the principal is a member of.

Table 8.3.   DCE privilege attribute certificate (PAC)

Authentication Flag
Cell UUID
Principal UUID
Primary Group UUID
Secondary Group UUIDs
Foreign Group UUIDs

DCE uses the Kerberos V5 authorization field to store the PAC. When a client requests a Ticket Granting Ticket (TGT) from the Authentication Server (AS), the TGT has an empty authorization field. The PS fills this field with the PAC when a valid request is received.

DCE uses Access Control Lists (ACLs) extensively. Unlike traditional ACLs that are normally only used to control access to files, the ACLs of DCE are used to access all services.

Unlike SESAME, DCE does not provide a server-side component for verifying the PAC and performing access control decisions. DCE provides only an API for building the component.

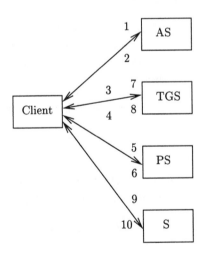

Figure 8.7.   DCE protocol

8.4.1.3   The Complete Service.   The complete DCE security service is as follows (the numbers relate to those used on Figure 8.7). Note the similarity to

Kerberos and SESAME in the protocol. Typically all of the security services are implemented as part of the one server called *secd*:

1. A user logs into the AS.

2. The AS returns a TGT for the Ticket Granting Service (TGS).

3. The user presents the TGT to the TGS.

4. The TGS returns a ticket for the PS called the Privilege TGT (PTGT). To keep DCE compatible with Kerberos, the TGS views the PS as any other application server.

5. The client presents the PTGT to the PS.

6. The PS returns the PTGT to the client with the user's PAC information filled in. This is the completion of the login process.

7. When a client wants to access a server, the client supplies the TGS with the PTGT and requests a ticket to the application server (S).

8. The TGS returns with a ticket to the application server called the Privilege Service Ticket (PST).

9. The client presents the PST containing the PAC information to the server.

10. The server receives the PST checks its ACL which contains a list of UIDs and GIDs that are allowed access to see if access should be granted.

A session key is established similarly to Kerberos and this is used by DCE's RPC mechanism for secure client/server communication.

DCE is designed to be scalable to a very large environment. It provides full inter-cell protocols to allow clients in one cell to access servers in foreign cells. DCE uses a hierarchy of cells, and the client walks the tree to the final destination, with the PS and ACLs in each cell left to ensure the security policy is enforced.

8.4.2   DCE Security APIs

DCE provides a very large set of APIs. The advantage of this is that it is flexible enough to provide a wide range of security services. The disadvantage of this is that the programmer can easily get lost among the security services. The DCE Security API consists of five separate APIs [118]. The positioning of these APIs is shown in Figure 8.8.

- *Authenticated RPC API*: Allows client and servers to mutually authenticate and establish secure communications.

- *sec_login API*: Allows servers to set up their DCE identity and security attributes.

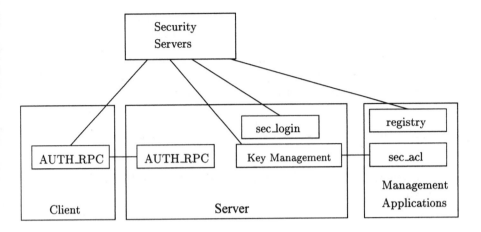

Figure 8.8.   Positioning of the DCE security APIs

- *Key Management API*: Allows servers to manage their secret keys.

- *Registry API*: Offers access to information stored in the security registry.

- *sec_acl API*: Allows management applications to control remote ACLs.

8.4.3   DCE 1.1 Security Enhancements

DCE 1.1 provides a number of security enhancements over the original release DCE 1.0. The major enhancements are [118]:

- Delegation: A client can delegate its privileges to a server so that it can act on behalf of the client. The final server can reliably determine the identities of the originating client as well as that of the intermediate server(s).

- GSS-API: The GSS-API was added. This allows non-RPC applications access to DCE security services.

- ACL Library: Simplifies the task of writing an ACL manager.

- Audit API: Allows an application to record security relevant activity.

8.4.4   DCE 1.2 Security Enhancements

The DCE 1.2 security extensions include:

- Full compatibility with MIT's Kerberos V5 (previous versions had no interoperability commitment).

- Public-key support for user login (so that the security servers need not store the long term secrets of users). As a transition aide, a new 'keystore' server was provided. This server stores private keys for users or sites without access to hardware-based cryptographic tokens or secure filesystems.

- Allows user-to-user authentication, that allows both client and server components of an application to act on behalf of users (normally servers have long term secret keys associated with them but in this case can use the user's credentials).

- Global group that allows principals from a foreign cell to be added to a group in the local cell.

- Improvement in the efficiency of the Security Server so that it is no longer a bottleneck for very large installations.

8.4.5   Further Information

The Open Group maintains a web site of DCE information [68]. It contains details on obtaining DCE, research papers and other DCE information sources.

8.5   DSSA

The goal of the Distributed System Security Architecture (DSSA), was to provide a comprehensive security solution for very large distributed heterogeneous environments. Hence the goals were greater than most other architectures and included:

1. Authentication of users and network entities.

2. Key distribution.

3. Data protection of data in transit.

4. Use of Smart Cards.

5. Secure software loading.

6. Mandatory and discretionary access control.

7. Delegation of identity based privileges.

8. Digital signatures.

9. Scalable to a very large environment.

Unlike most other security architectures, DSSA was designed to have no on-line authorities.

DSSA was a development of the Digital Equipment Corporation (DEC) and had its beginnings around 1985. It was an architecture that was intended for implementation across the entire DEC product line including all operating systems, applications and hardware components [106]. The aim was that the architecture was grand enough to be suitable for all DEC products and would discourage any ad hoc or duplicate efforts within DEC.

The implementation of DSSA was never completed (possibly due to the enormity of the task), and a subset of security services similar to that provided by Kerberos was implemented in an authentication architecture called DASS. There are a number of papers that give details about DSSA [28, 106, 108, 135, 164]. The implemented DASS security architecture is discussed in the next section.

8.5.1   Protocols

DSSA was designed for a very large distributed system. It was also designed so that there was no need for on-line authorities in any of the protocols.

To implement such a scheme, DSSA instead relied on the following technologies:

- Public-key based technologies.

- A unique global naming system.

- Certificate authority hierarchy.

- A publicly accessibly directory for certificates.

Every entity in the DSSA system had the following:

- A unique global name.

- An RSA key pair with the secret key held by the entity, and the public key stored in a publicly available certificate signed by an appropriate certificate authority.

8.5.1.1   Security Services.
Similarly to other security architectures a core security service provided by DSSA was mutual authentication of client and server, followed by key exchange, and data protection. The difference with DSSA though is that no on-line authority is used in the process.

The following is an example of a DSSA protocol for single authentication and key exchange (the numbers refer to those on Figure 8.9):

1. The client sends a message to a server claiming its global identity.

2. The server issues a random challenge to the client.

3. The client signs the challenge and returns it to the server.

4. The server uses the publicly available certificate to check the signature. If the client was authenticated then the server generates a session key, and encrypts it with the client's public key, and forwards it to the client. The client can decrypt the session key and a session is thus established.

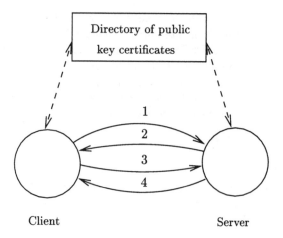

Figure 8.9.   DSSA mutual authentication and session establishment protocol

Any two entities in the DSSA system can authenticate and establish a secure session without the need for on-line authorities. Similarly to KryptoKnight, DSSA uses a challenge response protocol to ensure freshness rather than relying on synchronized clocks.

8.5.1.2   Access Control.   DSSA access control is based on the global identifier. The system works as follows (see Figure 8.10):

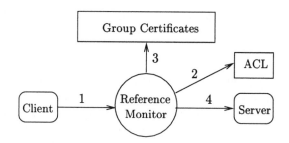

Figure 8.10.   DSSA access control

1. The client applies to a server's reference monitor for access to the server. DSSA assumes a secure reference monitor exists on each computer providing services, and must be accessed by the client (it is similar to the SESAME PVF).

2. The reference monitor accesses the server's access control list (ACL) to see if the client's global identifier exists in the list.

3. Alternatively the client may be a member of a group, with the group name being stored in the ACL. To check if this is the case, the reference monitor must access the public group certificates.

4. If either case is valid, then the reference monitor allows access to the server.

Note the differences in the access control services between SESAME and DSSA. In SESAME a Privilege Attribute Certificate (PAC) is retrieved by the client from an on-line privilege attribute server, and is passed from client to server when access is attempted (this is termed an *on-line push* model). In DSSA the reference monitor acting on behalf of the server may have to retrieve the client's privileges from an off-line created certificate (this is termed an *off-line pull* model.)

There are also some similarities in the access control schemes of DSSA and SESAME. DSSA and SESAME both use a specialized access control module to determine if access should be granted. In DSSA it is called the reference monitor and in SESAME the PVF. The idea behind both schemes is that a small verifiable piece of code does the access control rather than the application servers. Another similarity is the use of groups in DSSA and roles in SESAME to reduce maintenance in a very large environment.

DSSA was also designed to support both discretionary access control and mandatory access control. In the second case security classifications are used to control access.

A final note about access control is that DSSA supports delegation. If an entity wants another entity to act on its behalf, it creates a delegation certificate giving the new entity the right to use its global identity. This can occur along a chain of delegations [108].

8.5.1.3   Secure Software Loading.   DSSA tries to protect fraudulent or altered services from running in a DSSA system. DSSA does this by creating for all software components a message authentication code (MAC) and any time a software component is loaded its MAC can be checked against an expected value stored in a publicly available certificate. If the operating system is being loaded then its MAC is checked by the computer hardware, if an application program is being loaded it can be checked by the operating system.

8.5.1.4   Revocation.   There are several things that may need to be revoked in a DSSA system:

- Privileges in ACLs.

- Group membership.

- Certificates of authentication.

- Certificates of delegation.

Immediate revocation is a problem because it requires either that a system does not cache any data, or a mechanism that notifies all system entities when something has changed. The first requirement is unacceptable for performance and the second requirement is impractical. DSSA relies on two mechanisms for revocation:

- Certificates expire.

- The security policy of the organization decides whether an application should use cached information or information should be retrieved from the original source.

8.5.2   Further Information

DSSA development ceased around 1990 and was superseded with a sub-development focusing on authentication only. This sub-development is called DASS or SPX and is reviewed in some detail in the next section.

8.6   DASS/SPX

Following the work of DSSA, DEC focussed on producing an authentication service. This authentication service was called the Distributed Authentication Security Service (DASS) and similarly to DSSA was based on public-key technology. The service was prototyped in a system called SPX [225]. The DASS/SPX system had similar goals to Kerberos and these included:

1. Authentication of users and network entities.

2. Key Distribution.

3. Data Protection of data in transit.

4. Single Sign-On.

5. Delegation of identity based privileges.

6. Scalable to a very large environment.

The earliest publications of DASS/SPX were in the early 1990s [107, 225] with two RFCs released in 1993 for SPX Telnet [4] and for DASS [143]. Versions of DASS/SPX were trialled by customers and a Beta version including a GSS-API implementation and documentation were made available to the public [218]. The name DASS is used to describe the architecture and SPX (pronounced Sphinx) is used to describe the implementation.

8.6.1   Protocols

The DASS/SPX network authentication service is based on X.509 Public Key Certificates and on hierarchically organized Certification Authorities. It consisted of the following components:

Table 8.4.   GSS-API calls implemented by DASS/SPX

```
GSS_Acquire_cred()
GSS_Init_sec_context()
GSS_Accept_sec_context()
GSS_Display_name()
GSS_Display_status()
GSS_Import_name()
GSS_Release_buffer()
GSS_Release_name()
```

- An implementation of a subset of the GSS-API providing an authentication service to applications. The GSS-API calls implemented by DASS/SPX are shown in Table 8.4.

- A server application called the Certificate Distribution Center (CDC) that was used to distribute public key certificates. It was envisaged that this would eventually be replaced with an infrastructure such as X.500 directory service.

- A server application called the Login Enrollment Facility (LEAF) that is used mainly to provide users with their encrypted private keys for initialization. It was envisaged that this would be replaced when Smart Cards became more readily available.

- Support applications for generating public keys, creating certificates, enrolling users and managing passwords.

8.6.2 Authentication and Key Distribution

The DASS/SPX authentication exchange is illustrated in Figure 8.11. The steps are as follows (see [225]):

1. A user requests the CDC for a certificate for a server.

2. The CDC issues the certificate to the user.

3. The user verifies the certificate using the public keys of its trusted CAs.

4. The user then generates an authentication DES key for this session, and uses the server's public key to make an authentication token consisting of:

   - Name of the server.
   - Ticket containing delegation public key and validity interval signed with the user's long term private key.

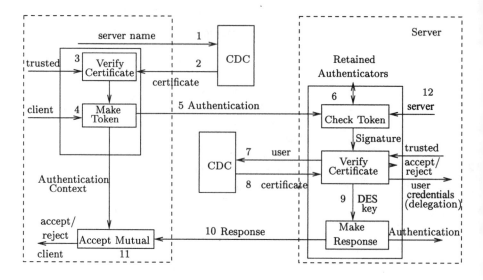

Figure 8.11.   DASS/SPX authentication and key distribution

- The encrypted DES key with the server's public key.
- The signature on the encrypted DES key using the delegation private key, or if delegation is being performed, the delegation private key encrypted under the DES key.
- An authenticator, which is a timestamp and cryptographic checkvalue computed using the DES key over a buffer containing the timestamp, directory flag, and channel binding.

5. The authentication token is transferred by the application to the server.

6. The server unwraps the received authentication token by using its private key to decrypt and recover the DES authenticating key, and then verifies the validity of the authenticator. If delegation is not being performed, the server checks the signature on the encrypted DES key using the public key in the ticket. If delegation is being performed, the server decrypts the delegation private key with the DES key, and checks it against the public key in the ticket. At this point the verifier knows it has a good authenticator, but not the identity of the principal who made it.

7. The server uses the claimed identity, to request a certificate from the CDC.

8. The CDC returns the certificate to the server.

9. The server uses its trusted CAs to verify the user's identity. When delegation is requested, there is an additional step of installing the user's credentials.

10. If mutual authentication is required, the server returns the authenticator to the user (only the server should be able to extract the DES key).

11. The user checks the authenticator and accepts or rejects mutual authentication.

DASS/SPX protects against replay attacks on authentication exchanges by using timestamps. It was decided that challenge-response exchanges were not suitable.

8.6.3 User Credential Initialization

The LEAF facility is used to provide the user with encrypted copies of their long-term private keys. In order to retrieve an encrypted private key, a user must present evidence of knowing the password. LEAF maintains a copy of the encrypted private key with a one-way hash of the user's password.

The steps for users to retrieve their private key are as follows (see [225]):

1. The user after entering their name is prompted for a password, initiating a login request to the LEAF.

2. The username, a one-way hash of the password, a timestamp, and a random nonce to be used as a DES key when the LEAF returns the user's encrypted private key is sent to the LEAF. To prevent the hash of the password and the nonce from being viewed, they are encrypted with the public key for the LEAF service.

3. LEAF reads the user's encrypted private key and the hashed password from the CDC. These are both encrypted with a DES key, and this DES key encrypted with the LEAF's public key. The LEAF then delegates the DES key using its private key, and decrypts the user information with the DES key.

4. If everything checks out, the CDC returns the user's private key encrypted with the nonce used as the DES key. Otherwise an invalid password error is returned. The benefit of using the LEAF is that password guessing attacks require contacting the LEAF each time.

5. The user creates a new short-term RSA delegation key, and creates its login ticket containing a validity interval, user uid, newly generated short-term public key, all signed with the long term private key.

6. The user gets their trusted CA certificates from the CDC.

7. Each certificate is verified using the user's public key, derived from its private key.

User credentials are saved locally in a file on the workstation, protected from unauthorized access by the file system.

8.6.4 DASS/SPX Versus Kerberos

DASS/SPX and Kerberos provide comparable services, the main ones being entity authentication, key distribution and data protection. The designers of DASS/SPX even concede [225] that the design was influenced by Kerberos, and similarly to Kerberos, DASS/SPX stores its secret keys in the local workstation.

There are however major differences between Kerberos and DASS/SPX. DASS/SPX uses a hybrid of public-key and secret key technology, whereas Kerberos only uses secret key. The benefit of using public-key technology is that no on-line servers are required, and it makes scaling easier.

8.6.5 Further Information

Although DASS/SPX attracted much attention in the network security community, development ceased in 1992 with 2.4 being the final version.

9 SECURE INTERNET TECHNOLOGIES

9.1 INTRODUCTION

This chapter continues the theme of the previous chapter in discussing a number of recent network security proposals. The previous chapter focussed on the security architectures and comprehensive technologies for providing network security infrastructure. This chapter discusses technologies that focus on particular applications, or components of the network. In some cases the solutions are complete (in that they provide both application and security services), in others they provide a component that can be added to an application. Specifically, this chapter discusses PEM, PGP, S/MIME, SSL, SSH, IPSEC and CDSA.

9.2 PRIVACY ENHANCED MAIL (PEM)

Privacy Enhanced Mail is the oldest secure e-mail protocol still in use. The first version dates from 1985 and the definitive version originated in February 1993. PEM is one of the standards to secure Internet electronic mail. It is specified in RFCs 1421-1424 [15, 138, 146, 166]. A major short-coming of PEM is that it only supports mail bodies according to RFC822 [65], thus only ASCII text. Another reason why PEM has not been very successful on the Internet has been the lack of freely available and easy to use implementations.

PEM offers the four cryptographic services and the scenario outlined in section 1.4.3. It uses both symmetric key technology and public-key technology.

The number of supported algorithms is very limited. To obtain data confidentiality, the DES in CBC mode is used. To exchange the Data Encryption Key (DEK) and to sign the messages, RSA is applied together with the MD5 hashing algorithm (for the digital signature). Unfortunately, the name they chose for the signature is the MIC (Message Integrity Check) and this term has been defined otherwise in Chapter 1 of this book.

The key management is strictly hierarchical and is specified in detail in RFC1422 [146]. The key management protocol is based on X.509 certificates and uses the X.500 directory services. To solve the problem of defining the CAs, PEM has defined the two top levels of CAs: the Policy Certification Authorities (PCA) and the ultimate arbiter, the Internet Policy Registration Authority (IPRA) (see Figure 9.1). Each PCA must list its official policy with the IPRA. PEM is very strict with certificates and Certificate Revocation Lists (CRLs). The result is a high confidence level in the correctness of a certificate.

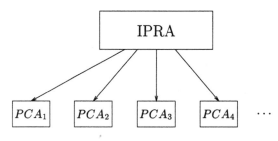

Figure 9.1.   CA hierarchy according to PEM

9.2.1 Structure of a PEM message

Messages sent using PEM are first converted to a canonical form so that they all follow the same conventions with respect to white space, carriage returns and line feeds. This transformation is done to eliminate the effects of all the message transfer agents that modify the messages from the sender to the receiver. Without conversion, these changes would affect the results of functions such as hash comparisons.

A PEM message consists of a header and the encrypted data (body), separated by a blank line (see Figure 9.2). The header consists of the following fields:

1. The first field within the header is the `Proc-Type`. It contains the version number (4 in the example) and the services that are offered by this PEM message.

   - `MIC-CLEAR`: text is sent in the clear. A non-PEM compliant mail reader is also able to read this message.
   - `MIC-ONLY`: the message has been signed and then encoded to represent the messages independent of the mail platform.

```
-----BEGIN PRIVACY-ENHANCED MESSAGE-----
Proc-Type: 4,ENCRYPTED
Content-Domain: RFC822
DEK-Info: DES-CBC,BFF968AA74691AC1
Originator-Certificate:
MIIB1TCCAScCAWUwDQYJKoZIhvcNAQECBQAwUTELMAkGA1UEBhMCVVMxIDAeBgNV
BAoTF1JTQSBEYXRhIFN1Y3VyaXR5LCBJbmMuMQ8wDQYDVQQLEwZCZXRhIDExDzAN
5XUXGx7qusDgHQGs7Jk9W8CW1fuSWUgN4w==
Key-Info: RSA, I3rRIGXUGWAF8js5wCzRTkdh034PTHdRZY9Tuvm03M+NM7fx6
qc5udixps2LngO+wGrtiUm/ovtKdinz6ZQ/aQ==
Issuer-Certificate:
MIIB3DCCAUgCAQowDQYJKoZIhvcNAQECBQAwTzELMAkGA1UEBhMCVVMxIDAeBgNV
BAoTF1JTQSBEYXRhIFN1Y3VyaXR5LCBJbmMuMQ8wDQYDVQQLEwZCZXRhIDExDTAL
EREZd9++32ofGBIXaialnOgVUnOOzSYgugiQO77nJLDUjOhQehCizEs5wUJ35a5h
MIC-Info: RSA-MD5,RSA, UdFJR8u/TIGhfH65ieewe21OW4tooa3vZCvVNGBZi
rf/7nrgzWDABz8w9NsXSexv AjRFbHoNPzBuxwmOAFeAOHJszL4yBvhG
Recipient-ID-Asymmetric:
MFExCzAJBgNVBAYTA1VTMAwHgYDVQQKExdSUOEgRGFOYSBTZWN1cm1OeSwgSW5j
LjEPMAOGA1UECxMGQmVOYSAxMQ8wDQYDVQQLEwZOT1RBU1k==
Key-Info: RSA, O6BS1ww9CTyHPtS3bMLD+LOhejdvX6Qv1HK2ds2sQPEaXhX8E
hvVphHYTjwekdWv 7x0Z3Jx2vTAhOYHMcqqCjA==qeW1j/YJ2Uf5ng9yznPbtDOm
YloSwIuV9FRYx+gzY+8iXd/NQrXHfi6/MhPfPF3d

jIqCJAxvld2xgqQimUzoS1a4r7kQQ5c/Iua4LqKeq3ciFzEv/MbZhA==
-----END PRIVACY-ENHANCED MESSAGE-----
```

Figure 9.2.   Example PEM message

- ENCRYPTED: the message has been signed, encoded and then encrypted with the DEK.
- CRL: the message contains a certificate revocation list (Section 1.7.1).

2. The second field describes the Content-Domain and this is usually RFC822 compliant text.

3. In case of an encrypted message there is a first DEK-Info field. It specifies the symmetric algorithm used and also what initial value (IV) was used in the CBC mode.

4. With the Originator-Certificate field the public key or the certificate of the sender of the message can be obtained.

5. The Key-Info field is optional but is used most of the time when encryption is applied to the whole message. It contains the algorithm used to transfer the DEK and the DEK enciphered with the public key of the sender. The reason for this is that when the message is filed, the sender would be unable to decipher the message since the DEK is normally only enciphered with the public key of the recipient of the message. This would mean that only the recipient could read the filed message.

6. Next is the Issuer-Certificate field that contains the certificate of the issuer of the sender's certificate. It is clear that when the issuer's CA is low

in the CA hierarchy, all of the other issuers' certificates can also be found here. This enables the recipient of the mail message to verify the whole certificate chain.

7. The `MIC-Info` field consists of three sub-fields. The first one gives the hash algorithm used, the second one the digital signature algorithm and the third one the actual value of the signature. When the message is ENCRYPTED, the MIC is also enciphered with the DEK so that no one other than the intended receiver can verify the MIC and thus nobody can check whether a certain message has been sent. These sub-fields are described in detail in RFC1423 [15].

8. One of the last fields in the header of the message is the `Recipient-ID -Asymmetric`. Similarly to the `Originator-Certificate`, it contains the address of the issuer of the recipient's certificate and its validity period.

9. The final `Key-Info` field, containing the DEK enciphered with the public key of the recipient, completes the information needed by the intended recipient to reconstruct the whole message.

9.3 PRETTY GOOD PRIVACY (PGP)

PGP was initially the result of one man's work: Phil Zimmerman. It is a complete e-mail security package that provides cryptographic services and compression. Even better, the complete package (including the source code) can be obtained without charge from numerous points on the Internet. Due to the lack of cost and the quality of the available implementations, PGP has become very popular on the Internet and has become a *de facto* standard.

The algorithms used by PGP are:

- RSA and MD5 for the digital signature;

- IDEA for bulk encryption;

- RSA for key management (as in PEM).

The international version (2.6.3i) supports RSA keys of up to 2048 bits long. IDEA is a block cipher invented by Lai, Massey and Murphy [160] that uses a 128-bit key (rendering exhaustive key search unlikely). It is patented, but PGP has obtained a license to use it for free in any non-commercial applications.

The key management scheme implemented by PGP is novel. Contrary to the strictly hierarchical system of X.509, it is based on a *web of confidence* (trust of peers). Each PGP user locally has two files containing their *key-rings*. The public key-ring is a list of all the public keys of the people the user usually corresponds with. Each participant in the PGP scheme asks their friends to digitally sign their public key, thus generating a type of 'certificate'. These are not real certificates since they are not issued by a Trusted Third Party (TTP), but this is sufficient in closed and/or restricted communities. There are also

PGP servers on the Internet where you can obtain public keys and these offer greater confidence. Other possibilities for broadcasting the public key include putting it in the finger information or home-page of the user. A clear advantage of this kind of system is speed. Obtaining a secure X.509 certificate (Verisign class 2) can be a very lengthy and costly procedure and until one has received it, it is impossible to start securing the e-mail. With PGP, it is sufficient to simply install the program, and generate a key pair. Revoking a key is however very difficult, sometimes even impossible. The value of the non-repudiation service offered is legally very doubtful because of the absence of an official TTP (i.e., a TTP that is bound by law or through a contractual agreement with its customers).

9.3.1   PGP Message

A PGP message is generated in the following way. The sender first hashes the message and, using their private key, digitally signs the hash result. When the receiver eventually gets the message, this signature can be verified to ensure the authenticity of the message. The signature and the original message are now concatenated into one single message. The resulting message is compressed using the Liv-Zempel algorithm (as in the ZIP format). This message is split into 64-bit blocks and they are encrypted using IDEA in cipher-feedback (CFB) mode with the DEK (PGP calls this the session key). The DEK is also encrypted with the public key of the recipient using the RSA algorithm. The concatenation of the encrypted blocks and the encrypted DEK, is then encoded using the Base-64 algorithm. The output of this is ASCII, which means that it can be incorporated into an RFC822 message body. At the receiver's end, all of these transformations can be inverted and the recipient is able to read the message.

9.3.2   PGP 5.0

In 1997 a new release of PGP emerged, Version 5. It naturally supports the PGP/MIME [87] protocol which combines the MIME messaging capabilities [99] with the PGP security enhancements.

The new features are:

■ More user-friendly, integration into several MS-Windows based e-mail clients (Eudora, Outlook).

■ Choice of algorithms:

1. DSS or RSA for signing.
2. SHA-1 for hashing.
3. Diffie-Hellman or RSA for public-key encryption.
4. IDEA, triple DES or CAST [2] for bulk encryption.

■ Key server integration: although sticking to the web of trust, PGP now offers a directory solution for storing and retrieving the public keys on-line.

9.4   SECURE/MULTIPURPOSE INTERNET MAIL EXTENSIONS (S/MIME)

Early in 1995, several major e-mail vendors (Microsoft, Lotus, Qualcomm) collaborated with RSA Data Security to design a secure, interoperable messaging standard. The result of their work is S/MIME [79]. It integrates MIME with the PKCS#7 standard [139].

9.4.1   Public Key Cryptographic Standards (PKCS)

The PKCS standard is an initiative of RSA Data Security. It was written in 1991 when the need for a standard, specifying how public-key cryptography should be applied, became obvious. Other big corporations (Microsoft, Digital) have also adopted and incorporated PKCS into their product line.

PKCS#7 [139] is a list of specifications of how to apply public-key cryptography to offer all the security services (data confidentiality, data origin authentication, data integrity and non-repudiation). Messages that have been encrypted using PKCS#7 can be viewed and verified independent of the platform used. PKCS#7 contains both algorithm specific and algorithm independent encryption standards. This means that some algorithms are supported explicitly while others need to obey certain syntax rules to obtain interoperability. DES, RSA and Diffie-Hellman are supported completely. Furthermore, PKCS#7 also defines algorithm independent standards for digital signatures, digital envelopes and certificates.

The syntax allows recursion, so that, for example, one envelope can be nested inside another, or one party can sign some previously enveloped data. PKCS#7 allows arbitrary attributes, such as the signing time, to be authenticated along with the content of the message. A degenerate case of the syntax provides a means for disseminating certificates and certificate revocation lists (CRLs).

PKCS#7 supports two kinds of certificate schemes: one based on X.509 (Section 1.7.1) and one defined in PKCS#6. There are six types of PKCS#7 messages:

1. Data

2. EnvelopedData: encrypted data

3. SignedData: data + digital signature

4. SignedandEnvelopedData

5. DigestedData: data + hash

6. EncryptedData: encrypted data without the DEK.

9.4.2   Version 2

S/MIME recommends two symmetric encryption algorithms: RC2 [209] and triple-DES. The key-size of RC2 can be adjusted to 40 bits, which was the maximum strength allowed for export outside of the U.S. (until 1997). As recent experiments (see Section 1.4.1.1) and literature study have shown [29], 40 bit keys do not result in a secure system with the current state of computing. Such a system can be broken in a matter of hours on a medium sized university network, or in minutes if one implements a hardware solution using technology like FPGA (Field-Programmable Gate Arrays) technology.

The key management is based on X.509 certificates. Since S/MIME is new, it supports the Version 3 certificates (PEM does not). The RSA public-key cryptosystem is used to generate digital signatures and exchange keys.

In RFC2311 [79], the new content-type *application/x-pkcs7-mime* is defined, to specify that a MIME body part has been cryptographically enhanced according to PKCS#7. S/MIME uses the MIME security multi-parts. PKCS#7 describes a series of encodings to transfer messages over 7-bit electronic mail systems but MIME solves this with its content transfer encodings. With regular PKCS#7 there are no restrictions on the format of the data that is encrypted or signed, but in S/MIME this data needs to be a MIME entity on its own. This allows the result of removing the signature and/or encryption to be passed on directly to the MIME engine. Table 9.1 contains an overview of the new MIME types and when a mail agent should use them.

9.4.3 Version 3

Halfway through 1997 after a long debate in the IETF group it was clear that there were some major objections to S/MIME becoming an Internet standard:

1. The name S/MIME was rumored to be a trademark owned by RSA Data Security. If S/MIME wanted to become an RFC, the RSA company would have to forego on this trademark.

2. S/MIME requires support for the RC-2 cipher. RC-2 is a block cipher that has been designed by RSA Data Security but its details had *never* been published. An alleged description has been leaked to the Internet and implementations following these guidelines are compatible with software products by RSA.

3. The description of S/MIME specifies that a 40-bit implementation of RC-2 needs to be supported, so that U.S. companies can sell their software overseas. As mentioned before, this does not offer a sufficiently high level of security.

In June 1997 the second objective was resolved, when RSA Data Security published RC-2 [209]. Because RC-2 dates back to the 80's it is very slow so it should be replaced by a modern algorithm such as RC-5 or SQUARE.

RSA Data Security also put out a bulletin that the name S/MIME was not a trademark but that only the S/MIME-Enabled logo was trademarked. Products that are allowed to use this seal are guaranteed to be interoperable.

In November 1997 a new version of S/MIME (version 3) was released [204]. Although it is closely based on the previous version, there are some minor

Table 9.1.   Mime types in S/MIME

MIME types	When to use
application/pkcs7-mime	- To send enveloped data. - To send signed data to S/MIME only capable recipients and when multipart/signed messages are expected to not arrive intact. - To send a message containing certificates.
multipart/signed	Default for sending a signed message; required when sending a signed message to a mix of recipients where S/MIME capabilities are not known for all recipients.
application/mime	To send multipart/signed messages to recipients who may or may not be S/MIME-capable and the message is expected to not arrive intact.
application/pkcs10	To send a certification request to a certification authority.

additions to the cryptographic infrastructure. For example 2-key triple-DES for bulk encryption, Diffie-Hellman for key management, and DSS for digital signatures are now also supported. Increasing the number of algorithms was inspired by the IETF's comments above.

A big improvement are the new security extensions defined in [116] that are targeted to work with both versions of S/MIME although some of them require the use of version 3. These security extensions include:

1. Signed receipts.

   Non-repudiation of delivery (Section 1.2.3) is provided by returning a signed receipt to the sender of the message. It is implemented in such a way that it also guarantees that the recipient was able to verify the signature on the original message. This means that a signed receipt can only be requested when the original message is signed. The signed receipt may optionally be encrypted to provide data confidentiality.

2. Security labels.

   Security labels are tags that can be put into a message that allows a security gateway to decide whether or not a particular person should see a particular message. They do not enforce policy, only state it. The message is still fully readable. This is used by some organizations to help prevent people who shouldn't see a message (such as a mailing list message) from seeing it.

3. Secure mailing lists.

   Sending S/MIME agents must create recipient-specific data for each recipient of the message. This can become quite cumbersome when sending mail to a mailing list (containing a large number of members). Therefore Mail List Agents (MLA) are used to perform the recipient-specific encryption for every recipient.

   The MLA acts as a message expansion point. The sender of the message directs the message to the MLA. The MLA then redistributes the message to all the members of the mailing list. The MLA thus provides cryptographic and expansion services for the mailing list.

9.5   SECURE SOCKETS LAYER (SSL)

SSL provides client/server authentication, data authentication and data confidentiality. It is specified in an Internet Draft [100] and was originally an initiative of Netscape Communications. It has become very popular as there are also some free implementations (SSLeay and SSLRef). The latest release of SSL is version 3.0.

The IETF working group on transport layer security has adopted SSL 3.0 in its first release of TLS (1.0) [74] with some minor changes. The TLS standard is expected to become the most widely implemented security standard in the near future.

SSL offers the cryptographic services in a layer, situated underneath the application layer and on top of the transport layer (see Figure 3.2). This allows for security to be added to specific applications without needing to rewrite a lot of code.

The set of cryptographic algorithms that is supported by SSL is very elaborate. The interested reader is referred to [100] for more details.

9.5.1   Structure

The structure of the SSL protocol is outlined in Figure 9.3. It consists of two levels: one containing the Record Layer Protocol and the other four other protocols.

9.5.2   Record Layer

The Record Layer provides three core services: fragmentation, compression and encryption. Each message passes through these three functions before it is sent

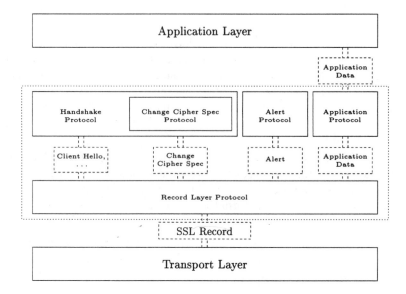

Figure 9.3.   SSL structure

down to the transport layer. The variables `Session State` and `Connection State` contain the names of the algorithms to use and the values of (or the pointers to) the cryptographic keys. These have been negotiated before in the handshake protocol.

It is important to distinguish between a session and a connection. A *connection* is set up every time there is a physical connection. It is not necessary to go through the handshake protocol for every new connection. Therefore, if previously arranged keys and algorithms are used, the *session* is resumed. This implies that there can be more than one connection in a single session.

9.5.3 Higher Level

9.5.3.1 Handshake Protocol. With this protocol the client and server negotiate the version of the protocol (2.0 or 3.0) to be used, the cryptographic algorithms and the setup of the keys. It is also possible to include entity authentication in this step (one-way or mutual).

The sequence of messages exchanged is illustrated in Figure 9.4.

1. The `Hello Request` is sent by the server to request a `Client Hello` from the client. This implies that the client has instigated the connection by requesting the appropriate URL (not shown on Figure 9.4). If the client receives this message during the handshake process, it simply ignores it.

2. The `Client Hello` contains:

    ■ Protocol version.

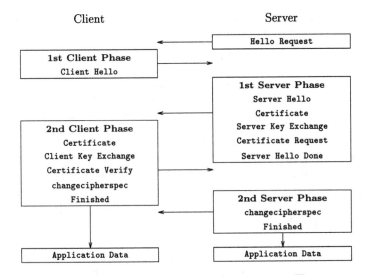

Figure 9.4.   SSL 3.0 handshake protocol

- A random number, used later on in the generation of the session keys.

- A session ID, to check whether a new session needs to be set up.

- A list of cryptographic options: key exchange algorithm, hash algorithm, etc.

- A list of the compression methods that are supported by the client.

After sending this message, the client waits for a `Server Hello`. If it receives any other type of message, this results in a fatal error and the handshake needs to be restarted.

3. During the **1st Server Phase**, the server sends the following messages:

- The `Server Hello` acknowledges which version of the SSL protocol is supported (less than or equal to the version of the client). The server also generates a random number and returns the session ID from the `Client Hello` if it agrees to pick up the old session. A choice is also made from the set of cryptographic options and compression methods that were proposed by the client.

- If the server authenticates to the client, the `Certificate` of its public key is included.

- With the `Server Key Exchange`, the key exchange algorithm is specified. It can either be Diffie-Hellman (Section 2.5.4.1), RSA (Section 2.5.5.3) or Fortezza (the Smart Card implementing the KEA (Key Exchange Algorithm) recently published as [192]).

- If the server wants the client to authenticate (mutual authentication), it sends a **Certificate Request**.

- The messages are concluded with the **Server Hello Done**.

4. The client responds accordingly (**2nd Client Phase**):

- If the server requested for it, it sends its **Certificate**.

- With the **Certificate Verify**, the client proves to the server that it is in possession of the private key that corresponds to the public key in its **Certificate** by digitally signing a specific message (Section 2.5.3.3).

- The **Client Key Exchange** contains the necessary information so that both parties are able to calculate all the session keys. The rules to generate them are specified in the Internet Draft.

5. Both parties now send in turn the **Finished** message, preceded by the **changecipherspec** (detailed in the next section). These are the first messages that use the newly agreed upon keying material. They contain two HMAC-like MACs (the first one with MD5, and the second with SHA-1) on all the previous messages in the handshake protocol.

As explained in Section 2.5.1 the procedure by which the server authenticates also provides key confirmation of the session key to the client.

9.5.3.2   Change Cipher Spec Protocol. This protocol is actually a subroutine of the handshake protocol. Its primary target is to specify to the other party that there has been a change in the cryptographic options. A signal consisting of a byte with value 0x01 is transmitted. Afterwards both parties use the values that have been agreed upon in the previous handshake protocol.

9.5.3.3   Alert Protocol. This protocol deals with the errors. The messages contain two parts. In the first one, the actual error is described, and in the second the *level* of the error is specified.

Two levels have been defined:

- *Warning*: this indicates a possible problem. An example of this is the close_notify that specifies that the sender does not send any more messages in the current session.

- *Fatal*: this interrupts the current session, and also means that the current session cannot be resumed in the future. An example of this is the bad_record_mac indicating that the MAC of a message or the message itself has been tampered with.

9.5.3.4   Application Protocol. The application protocol is responsible for passing the messages from the application layer to the record layer protocol.

9.5.4   SSL 3.0 versus SSL 2.0

Although SSL 2.0 has not been discussed explicitly in this chapter, the main differences with version 3.0 are still outlined as there are still many implementations that only support version 2.0. The version 2.0 of SSL has multiple security problems. Claessens, Vandenwauver, Preneel and Vandewalle showed in [63] how they can be (ab)used to build an actual attack. All of the problems have been solved in version 3.0.

- The MAC construction in SSL 2.0 is a very simple one and has a certificational weakness. It also supports only MD5 as the hash function and this also has some weaknesses as outlined by Dobbertin in [77].

- The integrity of the handshake messages is not guaranteed. This means that an active attacker can intercept and change these messages so that the client and server agree on a low level of security.

- In SSL 2.0 the shared secret consists of 128 bits, of which 88 bits are sent in the clear. An attacker is thus able to obtain the `Master Secret` and all its derived keys in one step. Also all the MAC keys are limited to 40 bits. Usually, the export regulations only ensure that the level of data confidentiality does not exceed 40 bits and they do not care about the level of data authentication.

- The client authentication token is not dependent on any recent information when a session is resumed.

9.6   SECURE SHELL PROTOCOL (SSH)

The goal of SSH is to provide a set of tools that allow secure communications over insecure networks. In particular SSH was designed:

1. To provide replacements for the BSD rtools (rlogin, rsh and rcp);

2. To provide secure X11 sessions;

3. To provide arbitrary TCP/IP port forwarding over encrypted channels.

In particular SSH was to provide entity and data authentication, data confidentiality, and data compression for the applications mentioned above. The authors have also noted that they have avoided on-line authorities in any of the SSH protocols, due to the risk to the whole system if an on-line authority is compromised.

The SSH development began at Helsinki University of Technology, Finland in the early 1990's. It is now being maintained by two companies: SSH Communications Security and Data Fellows. It is becoming increasingly popular and is widely used in the Internet community. There are both commercial versions and free versions available giving support for Windows, Unix, VMS, OS/2, Macintosh and Amiga. The currently available version of SSH is 1.0, and the version 2 protocols are being standardized by the IETF's Secure Shell Working Group [219] with a number of Internet Drafts available [240, 241, 242, 243]. SSH is produced in Finland and hence is not constrained by United States export regulations. However U.S. citizens need to download a special version because of the patent on RSA in the U.S.

9.6.1 Protocols

This section outlines the SSH version 2 protocols that are currently being standardized [219]. The SSH protocol provides secure versions of the BSD rtools, secure X11 sessions and secure TCP/IP port forwarding. To provide these services it relies on three major components:

1. A *transport layer protocol* that provides server authentication followed by a key exchange for data confidentiality and data authentication. It also provides data compression. It is expected that the transport layer protocol runs on top of a reliable data stream such as TCP/IP.

2. A *user authentication protocol* that authenticates users to the server. It runs on top of the transport layer protocol.

3. A *connection protocol* that provides interactive login sessions, remote execution of commands, and forwarded TCP/IP and X11 connections. All of these connections are multiplexed into a single encrypted tunnel.

A secure transport layer connection is established first, followed by user authentication and then a connection protocol for one of the applications.

All SSH protocols are designed to have the following properties:

1. All cryptographic algorithms are well known and well analyzed;

2. All algorithms use key sizes that are secure against even the strongest cryptoanalytic attack;

3. All algorithms are negotiated.

9.6.1.1 Transport Layer Protocol.

The transport layer protocol provides server authentication followed by session establishment for data confidentiality, data authentication and data compression. The authentication is host based and the protocol provides no user authentication. The client initiates the connection and the algorithms for authentication, key exchange, message encryption, message integrity, and compression are all negotiated.

For example the following symmetric key ciphers are defined: triple DES, blowfish in CBC mode, RC-4 stream cipher, IDEA in CBC mode, CAST-128 in CBC mode and no encryption. Similarly for the other algorithms; the key exchange is primarily Diffie-Hellman, and keys are re-exchanged at regular intervals.

It is assumed that every server has a private key and this is used during server authentication. The client stores the server's public key, or can retrieve a suitably certified public key certificate for the server. Note that the server authentication is not mandatory, it is possible to have key exchange without it (although this is not recommended).

A full description of the connection protocol can be found in [243].

9.6.1.2   User Authentication Protocol.   Once a secure transport layer session has been established (the server is authenticated and a secure channel created) the client user can be authenticated. This is possible using 3 methods:

1. Public-key authentication of the user;

2. Password authentication of the user;

3. Public-key authentication of the user's host.

The client initiates the connection, the server determines the algorithms that can be used for authentication and returns a list to the client. The client then selects the most convenient algorithm from the list.

A full description of the user authentication protocol can be found in [240].

9.6.1.3   Connection Protocol.   After user authentication the connection protocol is used to provide interactive login sessions, remote execution of commands, forwarded TCP/IP and X11 connections. As a result there can be multiple connections, each multiplexed into a single encrypted tunnel.

A full description of the transport layer protocol can be found in [241].

9.7   INTERNET PROTOCOL SECURITY (IPSEC)

IPSEC provides improved security to the Internet Protocol (see Figure 3.2). IPv4 is the current version of the Internet Protocol and provides no security features at all. IPv6 is destined to be its replacement in the near future and must include IPSEC. However most of the current implementations of IPSEC have been written for IPv4 as it might take a long time before IPv6 will be deployed on a large scale.

The goals of IPSEC are:

1. To provide data authentication to IP packets (to reduce IP spoofing and to also provide the possibility of non-repudiation).

2. To provide data confidentiality and data authentication to the payload of IP packets.

Development of IPv6 has been underway since the early 1990s. There are a number of Internet RFCs [10, 11, 12, 70, 141, 182] that describe in detail the IPv6 security. It is important to note that RFCs 1525-1727 will probably be replaced by the current Internet Drafts [147, 148, 149] in September 98. IPv6 is predicted to be phased into the Internet starting around the year 2000.

9.7.1   Security Services

IPv6 includes two mechanisms for providing security:

1. IP authentication header (AH).

2. IP encapsulating security payload (ESP).

Both of these headers are new to IPv6.

9.7.1.1   IP Authentication Header. The IP authentication header is a mechanism to provide strong data authentication to IP datagrams. It could also provide non-repudiation depending on the algorithm used.

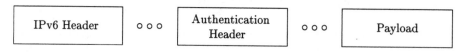

Figure 9.5.   IP authentication header

Figure 9.5 shows the authentication header as an extra header after the IPv6 header. Systems that are not concerned with security can ignore the header. The authentication header contains authentication data that is calculated over the whole IP packet except for those fields which change in transit. To identify the packet, each authentication header has a Security Parameter Index (SPI) that was agreed on by the two communicating parties. There is usually a different SPI for each direction. The size of the authentication data varies depending on the algorithm used.

The specification for the algorithms for the authentication data, and the issue of key management are considered outside the scope of the authentication header specification [10]. One algorithm that must be implemented is keyed MD5, and it is described separately in RFC1828 [182]. To conform to the authentication header specification, an implementation must at least support this algorithm.

9.7.1.2   IP Encapsulating Security Payload. The authentication header described in the previous section does not provide confidentiality protection for the IP payload. This has been moved to a separate header, so that in areas with cryptographic restrictions, at least the authentication header can be used.

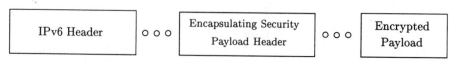

Figure 9.6.   IP ESP header

Figure 9.6 shows the ESP header as an extra header after the IPv6 header, and the payload is now encrypted. The ESP header must be used together with the authentication header as shown by Bellovin in [20]. The purpose of the ESP header is to allow encryption of the IP payload.

There are two modes for the ESP. *Tunnel-mode* ESP where the original IP datagram including headers and payload is encrypted and placed in a datagram with unencrypted IP headers. In *Transport mode* ESP, the ESP header is inserted into the IP datagram and the payload is encrypted.

To identify the packet to the receiver, an SPI is agreed upon by the two communicating parties. Similar to the authentication header, the algorithm and the key management scheme are considered outside the scope of the specification [11]. One algorithm that must be implemented is DES-CBC and it is described in RFC1829 [141]. To conform to the ESP header specification, an implementation must at least support this algorithm. For some implementations the DES is not considered to be secure enough (Section 1.4.1.1) and therefore several other algorithms have been suggested. All of them except for the 3DES [142] are however still in the Internet Draft stage.

9.7.2 Security Failure

The IPv6 specification also notes that if either the authentication data or ESP data is invalid, then the IP datagram must be discarded and the failure recorded in an audit log. The recorded data should contain an SPI value, date/time received, and sending and destination IP addresses.

9.7.3 Key Management

Although the IPv6 specification does not dictate any particular key management scheme for IPv6 it does give some examples that may be usable in the Internet environment [12]:

1. Manually distributed.

2. Needham and Schroeder key distribution.

3. Diffie and Hellman key distribution.

Recently considerable effort has been dedicated to the definition of the actual key management protocols. The current IPSEC protocols for key management can be cataloged using two types:

1. Protocols that define the procedures and packet formats to establish, negotiate, modify and delete secure communications. There have been two proposals: the Simple Key-management for Internet Protocols (SKIP), and the Internet Security Association and Key Management Protocol (ISAKMP) [174].

The main difference between these two is their location in the TCP-IP network model. SKIP is situated at the IP layer and provides a session-less key management. ISAKMP is implemented in the application layer and provides a framework but does not actually define the key-exchange algorithm.

In September 96, IPSEC announced that ISAKMP would be the key management protocol for IPSEC v4 and v6. SKIP has since not been supported in the IETF but still appears in Sun products.

2. Protocols that specify key exchange mechanisms. The OAKLEY Key Determination Protocol (Oakley) [196] and the Internet Key-Exchange (IKE) [113] are two examples of these protocols.

9.8 COMMON DATA SECURITY ARCHITECTURE (CDSA)

CDSA [37] is a specification for a set of layered security services designed to address communications and data security problems in Intranet and Internet environments.

The specification was initiated by the Intel Architecture Labs (IAL), and now has received support from a range of commercial organizations and standardizing bodies. The specification is now managed by the Open Group. The IAL broadly defined the CDSA to have two objectives: to encourage interoperability through security standards, and offer components of security to the industry at large. Specifically it was designed with peer-to-peer distributed systems, and client-server applications in mind in an environment with personal computers (PCs).

A reference implementation of CDSA (Version 1.2) was made available by Intel for the Windows platform [122]. The Open Group adopted CDSA 2.0 as a security standard. When CDSA is referred to in this section, the Open Group standard is targeted.

9.8.1 Threats

The CDSA's goal is to defend against two types of attacks:

- An attack by software running on the platform. This could be a virus, trojan horse, or software used to discover secrets stored on the system;

- An attacker has an opportunity to replace system software and observe all communications of a system.

9.8.2 Model

CDSA is a set of layered services and associated Application Programming Interfaces (APIs). The lowest layers begin with fundamental components such as cryptographic tools. The layers build up to complex services such as secure transaction protocols and key management mechanisms.

The standard lists five design principles for CDSA:

- A layered service provider model: CDSA is built up from a set of layers, each providing services to the layer above it;

- Open model: CDSA is fully disclosed for peer review, standardization, and adoption by the industry;

- Modularity and extensibility: components of each layer can be chosen as separate modules and new modules can be inserted in each layer;

- Value in managing the details: CDSA attempts to hide security related details from the application layer (for simplicity);

- Embrace emerging technologies: support of portable digital tokens (such as Smart Cards) and digital certificates.

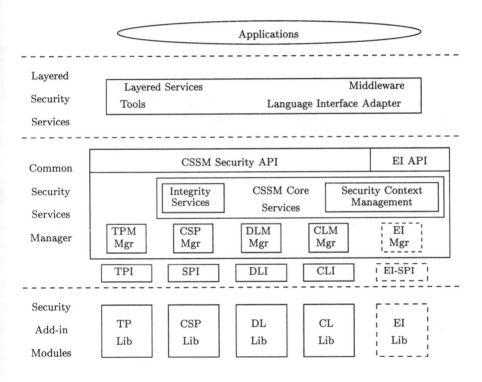

Figure 9.7.   The CDSA model

CDSA is built of three basic layers as shown in Figure 9.7:

- Layered Security Services;

- The Common Security Services Manager (CSSM);

- Security Add-In Modules.

9.8.3   Layer 1 : Layered Security Services

Layered security services are between the application layer and CSSM layer (Figure 9.7). The standard defines that software at this level may:

- Define high-level security abstractions (such as secure electronic mail);

- Provide transparent security services (such as secure file systems or private communications);

- Make CSSM security services accessible to applications developed in languages other than the C language;

- Provide tools to manage the security infrastructure.

Applications have the choice of using the CSSM APIs directly or using the layered services.

9.8.4   Layer 2 : Common Security Services Manager

The aim of the CSSM is to integrate and manage all security services. It defines a set of APIs to support development of applications, and also a Security Programming Interface (SPI) for interfacing with the add-in security modules.

The standard defines a set of core services that are common to all security services:

- Dynamic attachment of all add-in security modules;

- Enforced verification and identification procedures when dynamically extending services;

- General integrity services.

Module managers are responsible for matching API calls to one or more SPI calls, that result in an add-in module performing the required operation.

The CSSM API is partitioned into sets (see Figure 9.7):

- Core services;

- Security context management services;

- Integrity services;

- Basic module managers (MM).

There is a MM for each functional subset and this includes:

- Cryptographic Services Manager (CSP Mgr): defines a common API for accessing all of the cryptographic add-in modules. All cryptography functions are implemented by the CSPs.

- Trust Policy Services Manager(TPM Mgr): the API allows applications to request security services that require 'policy review and approval' as the first step in performing an operation. Approval can be based on the identity, integrity and authorization.

- Certificate Library Services Manager(CLM Mgr): the API allows applications to manipulate memory-resident certificates and certificate revocation lists. Operations include creating, signing, verifying and extracting field values from certificates.

- Data Storage Library Services Manager (DLM Mgr): the API must allow applications to search and select stored data objects, and also information about the stored data.

CSSM allows elective MMs (EI Mgr)). They define additional APIs for new category services. An example of an elective category given in the specification is Key Recovery.

CSSM also provides a set of integrity services, that can be used by the CSSM, module managers, add-in modules, and applications to verify the integrity of themselves and other components in the CSSM environment.

9.8.5 Layer 3: Security Add-In Modules

CSSM supports interfacing to sets of add-in modules. The four basic categories are:

- Cryptographic Service Providers (CSPs);

- Trust Policy Modules (TPs);

- Certificate Library Modules (CLs);

- Data Storage Library Modules (DLs).

Each add-in module is installed with CSSM. The installation records in the CSSM registry the module's identifying name, a description of the services it provides, and the information required to dynamically load the module.

9.8.5.1 Cryptographic Service Providers (CSP). The CSPs are modules that perform cryptographic functions and they may also implement one or more of the following functions:

- Bulk encryption;

- Digital signature algorithm;

- Cryptographic hash algorithm;

- Unique identification number;

- Random number generator;

- Secure key storage;

- Custom facilities unique to the CSP.

  CSPs must also provide:

- Key generation or key import;

- Secure storage for cryptographic keys and other variables.

A CSP can also manage other services such as key escrow, key archiving and key recovery.

9.8.5.2 Trust Policy Modules (TP). TP modules implement policies defined by authorities and institutions. Three basic action categories exist for all certificate-based trust domains:

- Actions on certificates;

- Actions on certificate revocation lists;

- Domain specific actions (such as issuing a check or writing to a file).

When a TP function has determined the trustworthiness of an action, the TP invokes library functions to carry out the actions.

9.8.5.3 Certificate Library Modules (CL). CL modules implement manipulation of memory-resident certificates and CRLs. The API defines generic operations that should be supported by every CL module. Each module implements the operations specific to its certificate data format (e.g. X.509 or SDSI).

9.8.5.4 Data Storage Library Modules (DL). The DL module provides stable storage for security-related data objects. These objects can be certificates, CRLs, cryptographic keys, policy objects or application specific objects. Stable storage can be provided by a range of mechanisms:

- Commercial database;

- File system;

- Hardware based;

- Remote directory services;

- Memory storage.

9.8.5.5   Multi-Service Library Module.   Vendors are also able to build add-in modules that provide services for CSSM APIs from multiple CSSM functional categories. A multi-service module is an add-in module that implements CSSM functions from two or more functional categories.

9.8.6   Interoperability

Interoperability is essential among CDSA systems and components within the systems.

The standard lists the following interoperability goals:

- Applications written to the CSSM API operate using add-in service modules from multiple vendors.

- Applications run on different CSSM implementations.

- Applications can use a particular add-in service module through different CSSM implementations and obtain the same results.

- Applications can use different implementations of the same add-in services and obtain the same results.

10 COMPARISON OF THE SECURITY SOLUTIONS

10.1 INTRODUCTION

This chapter attempts to compare the security solutions that have been reviewed in the previous chapters. Comparison of security solutions can be difficult because the designers had different motives, and aimed at solving particular requirements. The solutions are therefore compared in a number of different ways [8]:

1. Categorizing the type of solution;

2. Positioning in the networking model;

3. Security services provided;

4. Cryptographic primitives used;

5. Applications and availability;

6. Standardization.

For each of these alternatives an attempt is made to show the differences between the security solutions.

Table 10.1.   Categories

Solutions	Application	Layer	Infrastructure	Protocol
Kerberos			X	(X)
SESAME			X	(X)
Yaksha			X	(X)
KryptoKnight			X	(X)
DCE			X	(X)
DSSA			X	(X)
DASS/SPX			X	(X)
PEM	X			(X)
PGP	X			(X)
S/MIME	X			(X)
SSL		X		(X)
IPSEC		X		(X)
SSH	X			(X)

10.2   CATEGORIZING THE TYPE OF SOLUTION

There seems to be four main methods for solving the network security problem:

1. Secure particular applications. For example build secure versions of TELNET, FTP, email, corporate applications and so on.

2. Secure particular layers of the networking hierarchy. For example physical layer, IP layer, transport layer and so on.

3. Provide an infrastructure for securing applications. This means providing components for security such as on-line security servers and security APIs.

4. Define security protocols that can be implemented by all.

Of course a combination of the approaches is also possible. Table 10.1 shows the four categories and where each of the solutions fits into the categories. An X indicates the solution is aimed at this category, the (X) indicates that the category is a side affect of the first category.

10.3   POSITIONING IN THE NETWORKING MODEL

In Chapter 3 the OSI (Figure 3.1) and TCP/IP (Figure 3.2) networking models were presented. Recently there has been a change in the TCP/IP model as the sockets layer has been added as a layer between the transport layer and application layer.

Putting the security solutions at different layers in the model has two main affects: how the applications interact with the security services and what security services are available to the applications.

Applications that use security services at the application layer have to be modified to use these services. For example applications must be modified to make calls to the Kerberos or SESAME security libraries. This means that the application code not only performs the function of the application, but must also be aware of the security services it would like to use.

Providing security services below the application layer means that applications (at least in theory) do not have to be as security aware (in some cases not at all). For example, in the case of SSL, applications that are built using the normal socket library, can be SSL secured by simply rebuilding them with a new SSL socket library. This means it is possible to turn an insecure application into a more secure one without changing a line of application code.

Table 10.2.   TCP/IP layers

Solutions	Physical	Networking	Transport	Application
Kerberos				X
SESAME				X
Yaksha				X
KryptoKnight				X
DCE				X
DSSA				X
DASS/SPX				X
PEM				X
PGP				X
S/MIME				X
SSL			X	
IPSEC		X		
SSH				X

Table 10.2 shows the positioning of each of the security solutions in the TCP/IP model. It should be noted that almost all security solutions are at the application layer, although SSL and IPSEC are at the transport (or the sockets layer) and networking layer respectively.

The difference in the security services that can be provided at the different layers is described in the next section. In general the higher the security solution is in the hierarchy, the greater the possibility to provide additional services.

Table 10.3.   Acronyms for Table 10.4

Acronym	Meaning
SS	Single sign-on for users
EA	Entity authentication
DC	Data confidentiality
DI	Data integrity
KD	Key distribution
NR	Non-repudiation
AU	Auditing
AC	Access control
KE	Specifically designed for key escrow

Table 10.4.   Security services

Solutions	SS	EA	DC	DI	KD	NR	AU	AC	KE
Kerberos	X	X	X	X	X				
SESAME	X	X	X	X	X	X	X	X	
Yaksha	X	X	X	X	X				X
KryptoKnight	X	X	X	X	X				
DCE	X	X	X	X	X		X	X	
DSSA		X	X	X	X				
DASS/SPX	X	X	X	X	X				
PEM		X	X	X	X	X			
PGP		X	X	X	X	X			
S/MIME		X	X	X	X	X			
SSL		X	X	X	X				
IPSEC		X	X	X	X				
SSH		X	X	X	X				

10.4 SECURITY SERVICES PROVIDED

Table 10.4 shows the security services provided by each of the applications. Note the definition of the acronyms in Table 10.3.

The first security service that is only offered by most of the security architectures (Kerberos, SESAME, Yaksha, KryptoKnight, DCE and DASS/SPX) is a single sign-on for users. That is, users of the secured network log on once to the network, are provided with credentials, and then use these to access resources across the network. The advantages of a single sign-on solution have been recognized for some time with Kerberos being the most well known example.

In all technologies, entities can be authenticated, and data is protected while in transit with options for both confidentiality and integrity protection. All solutions provide facilities for key distribution, e.g., session key establishment.

In SESAME, PEM, PGP and S/MIME non-repudiation is technically realized by using digital signatures. It is not clear whether non-repudiation (in the legal sense) can be provided by protocols that are situated underneath the application layer, such as SSL. This is mainly due to the fact that these protocols are concerned with securing the dataflow. The cryptographic protection is removed when the data is received, and the original unsecured information is passed to the application. Another problem is that in principle lower layers are transparent for the user. So the user is not necessarily aware of the fact that some kind of digital signing is being performed.

An extensible set of audit tools is provided by SESAME, and DCE (from version 1.1) provides an auditing API. The other solutions provide only limited auditing facilities.

One of the main features of SESAME and DCE is access control, and in particular role based access control for SESAME. None of the other solutions provide an access control service.

Yaksha is the only solution particularly designed to support key escrow, although it is technically possible for key escrow to be implemented in any of the solutions.

10.5 TYPES OF CRYPTOGRAPHIC PRIMITIVES USED

Table 10.6 shows the cryptographic primitives used by each of the solutions. Note the acronyms used are shown in Table 10.5. All of the solutions (except KryptoKnight) make use of symmetric key cryptography (and in most cases this involves use of DES). KryptoKnight is the only solution that uses one-way functions instead of DES and this is for export reasons. Almost all of the solutions make use of public key technology. It is mainly the older solutions (Kerberos, KryptoKnight, and DCE) that don't make use of it (although DCE from version 1.2 uses public-key technology for user authentication). Compression algorithms are used by the three email applications and SSH.

10.6 APPLICATIONS AND AVAILABILITY

This section describes the availability of the applications and security solutions. The availability is broken down into two possibilities: available in the public domain and available from a commercial organization. The applications are those available either in the public domain or commercially.

Kerberos, SESAME, DCE and SSL have probably been best supported at this stage in terms of the applications. Note that Yaksha and DSSA have never been released in either the public domain or commercially.

Table 10.5.   Acronyms used in Table 10.6

Acronym	Meaning
SK	Symmetric Key Cryptography
PK	Public Key Cryptography
CO	Data Compression
OW	One-Way Function
MAC	Message Authentication Code
DS	Digital Signature

Table 10.6.   Cryptographic primitives used

Solutions	SK	PK	CO	OW	MAC	DS
Kerberos	X			(X)	X	
SESAME	X	X		X	X	X
Yaksha	X	X		X	X	X
KryptoKnight				X	X	
DCE	X			(X)	X	
DSSA	X	X				X
DASS/SPX	X	X				
PEM	X	X	X	(X)	X	X
PGP	X	X	X	(X)		X
S/MIME	X	X	X	(X)	X	X
SSL	X	X	(X)	(X)	X	X
IPSEC	X	X		X	X	(X)
SSH	X	X	X	(X)	X	X

10.7 STANDARDIZATION

Standardization is a necessary feature for the success of any security solution for a number of reasons:

- Customers are wary of products that are proprietary and lock the customer to one particular supplier.

- Manufacturers who produce their products to known standards, or who publish their standards in the public domain, have greater opportunity of interoperability with other manufacturers.

Table 10.7. Availability and applications

Solutions	Commercial	Public	Applications
Kerberos	X	X	telnet, rTools, RPC, NFS ...
SESAME	X	X	telnet, rTools, RPC, NFS ...
Yaksha			
KryptoKnight	X		
DCE	X		telnet, rTools, RPC, NFS ...
DSSA			
DASS/SPX		X	telnet
PEM	X		email
PGP	X	X	email
S/MIME	X		email
SSL	X	X	telnet, ftp, www browser/server
IPSEC	X	X	
SSH	X	X	rTools

Table 10.8. Standards used

Solution	Standards
Kerberos	RFC1510, GSS-API
SESAME	X.509, GSS-API, ECMA-219, ECMA-235
Yaksha	
KryptoKnight	GSS-API
DCE	Open Group,GSS-API
DSSA	
DASS/SPX	RFC1507, X.509, GSS-API
PEM	RFC1421, RFC1422, RFC1423
PGP	Internet Draft
S/MIME	Internet Draft
SSL	Internet Draft
IPSEC	RFC1825 to RFC1829
SSH	Internet Draft

- Manufacturers who produce APIs based on a particular standard (for example the GSS-API) allow programmers to reuse their existing experience in the standard. This makes the product more attractive to potential customers.

Table 10.8 shows the standards used in the design of the security solution. It is interesting to note that almost every solution is standardized in some way in the public domain.

ACL	Access Control List
AH	Authentication Header
API	Application Program Interface
AS	Authentication Server
AKEP	Authenticated Key Exchange Protocol
ARP	Address Resolution Protocol
ATM	Automatic Teller Machine
BSD	Berkeley Software Distribution
CA	Certification Authority
CBC	Cipher Block Chaining
CCITT	Now known as ITU-T
CDC	Certificate Distribution Center
CDSA	Common Data Security Architecture
CERT	Computer Emergency Response Team
CFB	Cipher Feedback
CGI	Common Gateway Interface
CL	Certificate Library
CORBA	Common Object Request Broker Architecture
CRL	Certificate Revocation List
CSF	Cryptographic Support Facility
CSP	Cryptographic Service Provider
CSSM	Common Security Services Manager
DARPA	Defence Advanced Research Project Administration
DASS	Distributed Authentication Security Service
DCE	Distributed Computing Environment
DEK	Data Encryption Key

DES	Data Encryption Standard
DL	Data Storage Library
DMZ	Demilitarized Zone
DNS	Domain Name System
DoD	Department of Defense
DSA	Digital Signature Algorithm
DSS	Digital Signature Standard
DSSA	Distributed System Security Architecture
DTQ	Delegate Target Qualifier
ECB	Electronic Code Book
ECC	Elliptic Curve Cryptography
ECMA	European Computer Manufacturers Association
ESP	Encapsulating Security Payload
EU	European Union
FAR	False Acception Rate
FIPS	Federal Information Processing Standard
FRR	False Rejection Rate
FPGA	Field-Programmable Gate Arrays
FSP	File Service Protocol
FTP	File Transfer Protocol
GID	Group Identifier
GSS-API	Generic Security Services API
IAB	Internet Architecture Board
IAL	Intel Architecture Laboratories
ICMP	Internet Control Message Protocol
IEC	International Electrotechnical Commission
IETF	Internet Engineering Task Force
IKE	Internet Key Exchange
IP	Internet Protocol
IPRA	Internet Policy Registration Authority
IPSEC	IP Security
IRTF	Internet Research Task Force
ISAKMP	Internet Security Association and Key Management Protocol
ISP	Internet Service Provider
ISO	International Standards Organization
ITU-T	International Telegraph Union - Telecommunications
KDS	Key Distribution Server
KEA	Key Exchange Algorithm
LAN	Local Area Network
LEAF	Law Enforcement Access Field

	Login Enrollment Facility
MAC	Message Authentication Code
MDC	Manipulation Detection Code
MIC	Message Integrity Check
MLA	Mail List Agents
MM	Module Managers
NBS	National Bureau of Standards
NFS	Network File System
NIS	Network Information System
NNTP	Network News Transfer Protocol
OFB	Output Feedback
OMG	Object Management Group
ONC	Open Network Computing
OOB	Out of Band
OSF	Open Software Foundation
OSI	Open System Interconnection
OSPF	Open Shortest Path First
PAC	Privilege Attribute Certificate
PCA	Policy Certification Authority
PCBC	Propagating Cipher Block Chaining
PEM	Privacy Enhanced Mail
PGP	Pretty Good Privacy
PKCS	Public-Key Cryptographic Standards
PKM	Public Key Management
PIN	Personal Identification Number
POP	Post Office Protocol
PPID	Primary Principal Identifier
PS	Privilege Server
PST	Privilege Service Ticket
PTGT	Privilege Ticket Granting Ticket
PV/CV	Protection Value / Control Value
PVF	PAC Validation Facility
RBAC	Role Based Access Control
RFC	Request For Comment
RPC	Remote Procedure Call
RIP	Routing Information Protocol
RSA	Rivest Shamir Adleman
SACM	Secure Association Context Manager
SDSI	Simple Distributed Security Infrastructure
SHA	Secure Hash Algorithm

SKIP	Simple Key Management for Internet Protocols
S/MIME	Secure / Multipurpose Internet Mail Extensions
SMTP	Simple Mail Transfer Protocol
SNMP	Simple Network Management Protocol
SPI	Security Parameter Index
	Security Programming Interface
SPKI	Simple Public Key Infrastructure
SSH	Secure Shell Protocol
SSL	Secure Sockets Layer
STDERR	Standard Error
STDIN	Standard Input
STDOUT	Standard Outout
TCP	Transmission Control Protocol
TGS	Ticket Granting Server
TGT	Ticket Granting Ticket
TFTP	Trivial File Transfer Protocol
TLS	Transport Layer Security
TP	Trust Policy
TTP	Trusted Third Parties
XDR	External Data Representation
UDP	User Datagram Protocol
UID	User Identifier
US	User Sponsor
U.S.	United States of America
UUCP	Unix to Unix Copy
UUID	Universal Unique Identifier
WAN	Wide Area Network
WWW	World Wide Web

Appendix B
CD-ROM

The CD-ROM that accompanies this book has been included so that SESAME V4 can be evaluated. It contains the following files and guides:

- Unix: SESAME V4 c-sources, patch and documentation. Before installing please read carefully the LICENCE agreement included in Appendix C.

- Redhat Linux V5:

  - Linux specific patch for the SESAME V4 sources. This includes a build file and installation and configuration guide.

  - Sesamized applications: `telnet`, `rtools`, RPC. An installation and configuration guide is provided for the applications.

The easiest way to get started is to open the `index.html` file with your favorite web browser. An up to date distribution of SESAME V4 is available at **https://www.cosic.esat.kuleuven.ac.be/sesame**.

Appendix C
SESAME V4 Licence Agreement

The "SESAME partners" : Bull SA, International Computers Ltd, Siemens Nixdorf Informationssysteme AG and Software and Systems Engineering Ltd have developed the SESAME Technology, which is a software for securing distributed applications. The SESAME Technology software is mainly distributed in source code form, with all modules written in the C programming language. The SESAME Technology belongs to Bull SA, International Computers Ltd, Siemens-Nixdorf Informationssysteme AG and Software and Systems Engineering Limited, and is being made available for use on the following basis.

The SESAME partners grant you a licence as follows to the SESAME Technology software:

1. LICENCE

The SESAME partners grant you a free non-exclusive, non-transferable licence for the SESAME Technology software accompanying this Agreement (the "SESAME Technology") and its associated documentation, subject to all of the following terms and conditions. In accepting a copy of the SESAME Technology you agree to the following terms and conditions of this Agreement.

This licence permits you to use, copy, and modify the SESAME Technology solely for experimental purposes within your organisation.

2. LIMITATIONS ON LICENCE.

a. You may only use, copy, and modify the SESAME Technology as expressly provided for in this Agreement. You must reproduce and include this Agreement, and SESAME copyright notices on any copy and its associated documentation.

b. No part of the SESAME Technology may be incorporated into any program or other product that is sold, or for which any revenue is received without written permission of one of the SESAME partners. A licence on commercial terms will be required in this case.

c. No part of the SESAME Technology may be installed or configured for a customer as a service for which any revenue is received without written permission of one of the SESAME partners. A licence on commercial terms will be required in this case.

d. If you wish to use the SESAME Technology within your organisation for non-experimental purposes, including without limitation as part of your normal operations, you must obtain the written permission of one of the SESAME Partners, which will normally be granted on favourable terms.

e Use or export of the SESAME Technology may require specific licences from the national authorities. It is the responsibility of any person or organisation contemplating use or export to obtain such a licence before exporting or using.

f. All rights not expressly granted herein are reserved to the SESAME partners.

3. NO SESAME PARTNERS OBLIGATION:

You are solely responsible for maintaining the SESAME Technology and the security of the operating environment in which the SESAME Technology may be used. You are solely responsible for all of your costs and expenses incurred in connection with the distribution and the use of the SESAME Technology, and the SESAME partners shall have no liability, obligation or responsibility therefore. The SESAME partners shall have no obligation to provide maintenance, support, upgrades, or new releases to you.

4. NO WARRANTIES OF PERFORMANCE.

THE SESAME TECHNOLOGY AND ITS ASSOCIATED DOCUMENTATION ARE LICENSED "AS IS". THE SESAME PARTNERS HEREBY DISCLAIM ALL REPRESENTATIONS AND WARRANTIES, EXPRESS, IMPLIED OR STATUTORY, AS TO THE PERFORMANCE OR FITNESS FOR ANY PARTICULAR PURPOSE OR FREEDOM FROM INFRINGEMENT OF INTELLECTUAL PROPERTY RIGHTS OF THE SESAME TECHNOLOGY AND ITS ASSOCIATED DOCUMENTATION AND ANY INFORMATION SUPPLIED AT ANY TIME IN RELATION THERETO. THE ENTIRE RISK AS TO THE RESULTS AND PERFORMANCE OF THE SESAME TECHNOLOGY IS ASSUMED BY YOU. SHOULD THE SESAME TECHNOLOGY PROVE DEFECTIVE, YOU ASSUME THE ENTIRE COST OF ALL NECESSARY SERVICING, REPAIR, OR CORRECTION.

5. LIMITATION OF LIABILITY.

NEITHER THE SESAME PARTNERS NOR ANY OTHER PERSON WHO HAS BEEN INVOLVED IN THE CREATION, PRODUCTION OR DELIVERY OF THE SESAME TECHNOLOGY SHALL BE LIABLE TO YOU OR TO ANY OTHER PERSON, IN CONTRACT OR OTHERWISE, FOR ANY DIRECT, INDIRECT, SPECIAL, INCIDENTAL, CONSEQUENTIAL, OR PUNITIVE DAMAGES, EVEN IF THE SESAME PARTNERS HAVE BEEN ADVISED OF THE POSSIBILITY OF SUCH DAMAGES, OR FOR ANY LOSS OF USE, PROFIT, BUSINESS OR DATA. YOU HEREBY INDEMNIFY AND AGREE TO HOLD HARMLESS THE SESAME PARTNERS FROM AND AGAINST CLAIMS, LOSSES, DAMAGES OR EXPENSES, BY WHOMEVER MADE, ARISING FROM YOUR POSSESSION OR USE OF THE SESAME TECHNOLOGY.

6. TERM.

The licence granted hereunder is effective until terminated. This licence shall automatically terminate without notice if you breach any of the provisions hereof. You may terminate it at any time by destroying the SESAME Technology copies in your possession and associated documentation.

7. GENERAL.

a. This Agreement shall be governed by the laws of France.

b. Address all correspondence regarding this licence to one of the SESAME partners :

Bull SA :
    Eric Baize
    Bull SA
    BP 68 - Rue Jean Jaures
    78340 Les Clayes sous Bois
    France
    Tel +33.1.30.80.77.78
    Fax +33.1.30.80.33.35
    Email : E.Baize@frcl.bull.fr

International Computers Ltd :
    Don Salmon
    ICL Enterprises
    Lovelace Road, Bracknell
    Berks, RG12 8SN
    United Kingdom
    Tel +44.1.344.473578
    Fax +44.1.344.473012
    Email : d.j.salmon@bra0108.wins.icl.co.uk

Software and Systems Engineering :
    Stephen Farrell
    Software and Systems Engineering Ltd
    Fitzwilliam Court
    Leeson Close
    Dublin, 2
    Ireland
    Tel +353.1.676.90.89
    Fax +353.1.676.79.84
    Email : Stephen.Farrell@sse.ie

References

[1] C. Adams. The Simple Public Key GSS-API Mechanism (SPKM), October 1996. RFC2025.

[2] C. Adams. The CAST-128 Encryption Algorithm, May 1997. RFC2144.

[3] C. Adams. Independent Data Unit Protection Generic Security Service Application Program Interface, May 1998. Internet Draft.

[4] K. Alagappan. Telnet Authentication : SPX, January 1993. RFC1412.

[5] Anonymous. Daemon9. *Phrack Magazine*, 9(49), 1997. Available at http://www.phrack.com/Archives/index.html.

[6] P. Ashley and B. Broom. Implementation of the SESAME Security Architecture for Linux. In *Proceedings of the AUUG Summer Technical Conference*, Brisbane, Qld., April 1997.

[7] P. Ashley, M. Vandenwauver, and B. Broom. A Uniform Approach To Securing Unix Applications Using SESAME. In C. Boyd and E. Dawson, editors, *Proceedings of the 3rd ACISP Conference - LNCS 1438*, pages 24–35. Springer-Verlag, 1998.

[8] P. Ashley, M. Vandenwauver, and J. Claessens. A Comparison of SESAME and SSL for Intranet and Internet Security. In *Proceedings of IFIP WG 11.2 Conference.*, Vienna, Austria, September 1998.

[9] P. Ashley, M. Vandenwauver, M. Rutherford, and S. Boving. Using SESAME's GSS-API to Add Security to Unix Applications. In *Proceedings of the Third International Workshop on Enterprise Security*, Stanford, CA., June 1998.

[10] R. Atkinson. IP Authentication Header, August 1995. RFC1826.

[11] R. Atkinson. IP Encapsulating Security Payload, August 1995. RFC1827.

[12] R. Atkinson. Security Architecture for the Internet Protocol, August 1995. RFC1825.

[13] E. Baize, S. Farrell, and T. Parker. The SESAME GSS-API Mechanism, November 1996. Internet Draft (expired).

[14] E. Baize and D. Pinkas. A Simple and Protected GSS-API Negotiation Mechanism, April 1998. Internet Draft.

[15] D. Balenson. Privacy Enhancement for Internet Electronic Mail: Part III – Algorithms, Modes, and Identifiers, February 1993. RFC1423.

[16] M. Bellare, R. Canetti, and H. Krawczyk. Keying Hash Functions for Message Authentication. In N. Koblitz, editor, *Advances in Cryptology, Proceedings of Crypto '96 - LNCS 1109*, pages 1–15. Springer-Verlag, 1996.

[17] M. Bellare and P. Rogaway. Entity Authentication and Key Distribution. In D. Stinson, editor, *Advances in Cryptology, Proceedings of Crypto '93 - LNCS 773*, pages 232–249. Springer-Verlag, 1993.

[18] S. Bellovin. Security Problems in the TCP/IP Protocol Suite. *Computer Communications Review*, 19(2):32–48, April 1989.

[19] S. Bellovin. There Be Dragons. In *Proceedings of the Third Usenix UNIX Security Symposium*, pages 1–16, 1992.

[20] S. Bellovin. Problem Areas for the IP Security Protocols. In *Proceedings of the Sixth Usenix Unix Security Symposium*, pages 1–16, 1996.

[21] S. Bellovin and M. Merritt. Limitations of the Kerberos Authentication System. In *Proceedings of the USENIX Winter '91 Conference*, pages 253–267, Dallas, Tx., 1991.

[22] S. Bellovin and M. Merritt. Encrypted Key Exchange: Password-Based Protocols Secure Against Dictionary Attacks. In *Proceedings of the IEEE Symposium on Security and Privacy*, pages 72–84, 1992.

[23] S. Bellovin and M. Merritt. Augmented Encrypted Key Exchange. In *Proceedings of the 1st ACM Conference on Communications and Computing Security*, pages 244–250, November 1993.

[24] E. Biham and A. Shamir. *Differential Cryptanalysis of the Data Encryption Standard*. Springer-Verlag, 1993.

[25] R. Bird, I. Gopal, A. Herzberg, P. Janson, S. Kutton, R. Molva, and M. Yung. Systematic Design of Two Party Authentication Protocols. In J. Feigenbaum, editor, *Advances in Cryptology, Proceedings of CRYPTO '91 - LNCS 576*, pages 44–61. Springer-Verlag, 1991.

[26] R. Bird, I. Gopal, A. Herzberg, P. Janson, S. Kutton, R. Molva, and M. Yung. Systematic Design of a Family of Attack-Resistant Authentication Protocols. *IEEE Journal on Selected Areas in Communications*, 11(5):679–693, June 1993.

[27] R. Bird, I. Gopal, A. Herzberg, P. Janson, S. Kutton, R. Molva, and M. Yung. The KryptoKnight Family of LightWeight Protocols For Authentication and Key Distribution. *IEEE/ACM Transactions on Networking*, 3(1):31–41, February 1995.

[28] A. Birrell, B. Lampson, R. Needham, and M. Schroeder. A Global Authentication Service Without Global Trust. In *IEEE Symposium on Security and Privacy*, pages 223–230, 1986.

[29] M. Blaze, W. Diffie, R. Rivest, B. Schneier, T. Shimomura, E. Thompson, and M. Wiener. Minimal Key Lengths for Symmetric Ciphers to Provide Adequate Commercial Security, January 1996. Available at ftp://ftp.research.att.com/dist/mab/keylength.ps.

[30] D. Borman. Telnet Linemode Option, October 1990. RFC1184.

[31] D. Borman. Telnet Data Encryption Option, 1992. Internet Draft (expired).

[32] D. Borman. Telnet Authentication and Encryption Option, 1993. Internet Draft (expired).

[33] D. Borman. Telnet Authentication Protocol, 1993. RFC1416.

[34] C. Boyd. Digital Multisignatures. In H.J. Beker and F.C. Piper, editors, *Cryptography and Coding*, pages 241–246. Clarendon Press, 1989.

[35] C. Boyd. Towards Extensional Goals in Authentication Protocols. In *DIMACS Workshop on Design and Formal Verification of Security Protocols*, 1997. Available at http://dimacs.rutgers.edu/Workshops/Security/program2/boyd/index.html.

[36] B. Broom and P. Ashley. A SESAME Environment. In *Australian Unix and Open Systems Group (AUUG) National Conference*, Sidney, Australia, September 1998.

[37] Open Group Technical Standard C707. Common Security: CDSA and CSSM, December 1997. Available at http://www.opengroup.org/publications/catalog/c707.htm.

[38] V. Cerf and R. Kahn. A Protocol for Packet Network Interconnection. *IEEE Transactions on Communications*, 22:637–648, May 1974.

[39] CERT. CERT Coordination Center, http://www.cert.org.

[40] CERT Coordination Center. CERT Advisory 88.01: ftpd Vulnerability, December 1988.

[41] CERT Coordination Center. CERT Advisory 90.11: Security Probes from Italy, December 1990.

[42] CERT Coordination Center. CERT Advisory 94.01: Ongoing Network Monitoring Attacks, February 1994.

[43] CERT Coordination Center. CERT Advisory 95.01: IP Spoofing Attacks and Hijacked Terminal Connections, January 1995.

[44] CERT Coordination Center. CERT Advisory 96.01: UDP Port Denial-of-Service Attack, February 1996.

[45] CERT Coordination Center. CERT Advisory 96.21: TCP SYN Flooding and IP Spoofing Attacks, September 1996.

[46] CERT Coordination Center. CERT Advisory 96.26: Denial of Service Attack via ping, December 1996.

[47] CERT Coordination Center. CERT Advisory 97.05: MIME Conversion Buffer Overflow in Sendmail Versions 8.8.3 and 8.8.4, January 1997.

[48] CERT Coordination Center. CERT Advisory 97.17: Vulnerability in suidperl, May 1997.

[49] CERT Coordination Center. CERT Advisory 97.18: Vulnerability in the at(1) Program, June 1997.

[50] CERT Coordination Center. CERT Advisory 97.23: Buffer Overflow Problem in rdist, September 1997.

[51] CERT Coordination Center. CERT Advisory 97.24: Buffer Overrun Vulnerability in Count.cgi cgi-bin Program, November 1997.

[52] CERT Coordination Center. CERT Advisory 97.25: Sanitizing User-Supplied Data in CGI scripts, November 1997.

[53] CERT Coordination Center. CERT Advisory 97.26: Buffer Overrun Vulnerability in statd Program, December 1997.

[54] CERT Coordination Center. CERT Advisory 97.27: FTP Bounce, December 1997.

[55] CERT Coordination Center. CERT Advisory 97.28: IP Denial-of-Service Attacks, December 1997.

[56] CERT Coordination Center. CERT Advisory 98.01: smurf IP Denial-of-Service Attacks, January 1998.

[57] CERT Coordination Center. CERT Advisory 98.03: Vulnerability in ssh-agent, January 1998.

[58] CERT Coordination Center. CERT Advisory 98.05: Multiple Vulnerabilities in BIND, April 1998.

[59] G. Champine, D. Geer, and W. Ruh. Project Athena as a Distributed Computer System. *IEEE Computer*, 23(9):40–51, September 1990.

[60] D. Chapman. Network (In)Security Through IP Packet Filtering. In *Proceedings of the Third Usenix Unix Security Symposium*, pages 63–76, September 1992.

[61] D. Chapman and E. Zwicky. *Building Internet Firwalls*. O'Reilly & Associates, Inc., 1995.

[62] L. Claesen, D. Beullens, R. Martens, R. Mertens, S. De Schrijver, and W. De Jong. SMARTpen: An application of integrated microsystem and embedded hardware/software codesign. In *Proceedings U.F., Electronic Design & Test Conference, ED&TC '96*, pages 201–205, March 1996.

[63] J. Claessens, M. Vandenwauver, B. Preneel, and J. Vandewalle. Setting up a Secure Server on an Intranet. In *Third International Workshop on Enterprise Security*, Stanford, CA., June 1998.

[64] D. Comer. *Internetworking with TCP/IP*, volume 1. Prentice Hall, Inc., 3rd edition, 1995.

[65] D. Crocker. Standard for the Format of ARPA Internet Text Messages, August 1982. RFC822.

[66] J. Daemen, L. Knudsen, and V. Rijmen. The Block Cipher Square. In E. Biham, editor, *Proceedings Fast Software Encryption '97 - LNCS 1267*, pages 149–165. Springer-Verlag, 1997.

[67] D. Davies and S. Murphy. Pairs and Triplets of DES S-Boxes. *Journal of Cryptology*, 8(1):1–25, 1995.

[68] DCE. Open Group's DCE Home Page, http://www.camb.opengroup. org/tech/dce.

[69] W.G. de Ru and J.P. Eloff. Enhanced Password Authentication through Fuzzy Logic. *IEEE Intelligent Systems & Their Applications*, 12(6):38–46, November/December 1997.

[70] S. Deering and R. Hinden. Internet Protocol, Version 6 (IPv6) Specification, December 1995. RFC1883.

[71] D. Denning. *Cryptography and Data Security*. Addison-Wesley Publishing Company, January 1983.

[72] D. Denning and G. Sacco. Timestamps in Key Distribution Protocols. *Communications of the ACM*, 24(8):533–536, August 1981.

[73] D.Icove, K.Seger, and W.VonStorch. *Computer Crime: A Crimefighter's Handbook.* O'Reilly & Associates, Inc., 1995.

[74] T. Dierks and C. Allen. The TLS Protocol Version 1.0, November 1997. Internet Draft (expired).

[75] W. Diffie and M. Hellman. New Directions in Cryptography. *IEEE Transactions on Information Theory*, 22(6):644–654, 1976.

[76] W. Diffie, P. van Oorschot, and M. Wiener. Authentication and Authenticated Key Exchanges. *Designs, Codes and Cryptography*, 2:107–125, 1992.

[77] H. Dobbertin. The Status of MD5 After a Recent Attack. *CryptoBytes*, 2(2):1–6, 1996.

[78] H. Dobbertin, A. Bosselaers, and B. Preneel. RIPEMD-160 : A strengthened Version of RIPEMD. In D. Gollmann, editor, *Proceedings Fast Software Encryption '96 - LNCS 1039*, pages 71–82. Springer-Verlag, 1996.

[79] S. Dussé, P. Hoffman, B. Ramsdell, L. Lundblade, and L. Repka. S/MIME Version 2 Message Specification, March 1998. RFC2311.

[80] ECMA 206. ECMA-206 Association Context Management Including Security Context Management, December 1993. European Computer Manufacturers Association.

[81] ECMA 219. ECMA-219 Security in Open Systems - Authentication and Privilege Attribute Security Application with Related Key Distribution Functionality, 2nd Edition, March 1996. European Computer Manufacturers Association.

[82] ECMA 235. ECMA-235 Security in Open Systems - The ECMA GSS-API Mechanism, March 1996. European Computer Manufacturers Association.

[83] EES. A proposed federal information processing standard for an escrowed encryption standard, July 30 1993. U. S. Federal Register.

[84] M. Eichlin and J. Rochlis. With Microscopes and Tweezers: An Analysis of the Internet Virus of November 1988. Technical report, MIT, February 1989.

[85] M. Eisler, A. Chiu, and L. Ling. RPCSEC-GSS Protocol Specification, September 1997. RFC2203.

[86] M. Eisler, R. Schemers, and R. Srinivasan. Security Mechanism Independence in ONC RPC. In *Proceedings of the 6th USENIX Security Symposium*, San Jose, CA., July 1996.

[87] M. Elkins. MIME Security with Pretty Good Privacy (PGP), October 1996. RFC2015.

[88] C. Ellison, B. Frantz, B. Lampson, R. Rivest, B. Thomas, and T. Ylonen. Simple Public Key Certificate, March 1998. Internet Draft.

[89] D. Farmer. Security Survey of Key Internet Hosts and Various Semi-Relevant Reflections, December 1996. Available at http://www.trouble.org/survey.

[90] D.F. Ferraiolo and R. Kuhn. Role-Based Access Control. In *Proceedings of the 15th NIST-NSA National Computer Security Conference*, Baltimore, MD., October 1992.

[91] A. Fiat and A. Shamir. How to Prove Yourself: Practical Solutions to Identification and Signature Problems. In A.M. Odlyzko, editor, *Advances in Cryptology, Proceedings Crypto '86 - LNCS 263*, pages 186–194. Springer-Verlag, 1987.

[92] FIPS 46. Data Encryption Standard. Federal Information Processing Standards Publication 46, U.S. Department of Commerce/National Bureau of Standards, National Technical Information Service, Springfield, Virginia, 1977 (revised as FIPS 46-1:1988;FIPS 46-2:1993).

[93] FIPS 81. DES Modes of Operation. Federal Information Processing Standards Publication 180-1, U.S. Department of Commerce/N.I.S.T., National Technical Information Service, Springfield, Virginia, April 17 1995.

[94] FIPS 180-1. Secure Hash Standard. Federal Information Processing Standards Publication 180-1, U.S. Department of Commerce/N.I.S.T., National Technical Information Service, Springfield, Virginia, April 17 1995.

[95] FIPS 181. Automated Password Generator. Federal Information Processing Standards Publication 181, U.S. Department of Commerce/National Bureau of Standards, National Technical Information Service, Springfield, Virginia, 1993.

[96] FIPS 186. Digital Signature Standard. Federal Information Processing Standards Publication 186, U.S. Department of Commerce/National Bureau of Standards, National Technical Information Service, Springfield, Virginia, 1994.

[97] W. Ford. *Computer Communications Security - Principles, Standard Protocols and Techniques*. Prentice-Hall, Inc., 1994.

[98] Electronic Frontier Foundation. *Cracking DES - Secrets of Encryption Research, Wiretap Politics & Chip Design.* O'Reilly & Associates, Inc., 1998.

[99] N. Freed and N. Borenstein. Multipurpose Internet Mail Extensions (MIME) Part One: Format of Internet Message Bodies, November 1996. RFC2045.

[100] A.O. Freier, P. Karlton, and P.C. Kocher. The SSL Protocol Version 3.0, March 1996. Internet Draft (expired).

[101] R. Ganesan. Bell Atlantic Yaksha Home Page, http://www.bell-atl.com/yaksha.

[102] R. Ganesan. Yaksha : Augmenting Kerberos With Public Key Cryptography. In *Proceedings of the Internet Society Symposium on Network and Distributed System Security*, pages 132–143, February 1995.

[103] R. Ganesan. The Yaksha Security System. *Communications of the ACM*, 39(3):55–60, March 1996.

[104] R. Ganesan and Y. Yacobi. A Secure Joint Signature and Key Exchange System. Technical report, Bellcore TM-24531, October 1994.

[105] S. Garfinkel and G. Spafford. *Practical Unix and Internet Security.* O'Reilly & Associates, Inc., 2nd edition, April 1996.

[106] M. Gasser, A. Goldstein, C. Kaufman, and B. Lampson. The Digital Distributed System Security Architecture. In *Proceedings of the 12th National Computer Security Conference*, pages 305–319, Baltimore, MD., October 1989.

[107] M. Gasser, C. Kaufman, J. Linn, Y. Le Roux, and J. Tardo. DASS - Distributed Authentication Security Service. In *Proceedings of the 1992 IFIP World Congress*, 1992.

[108] M. Gasser and E. McDermott. An Architecture for Practical Delegation in a Distributed System. In *Proceedings of the 1990 IEEE Symposium on Security and Privacy*, pages 20–30, Oakland, CA., May 1990.

[109] D. Gollman. What do we Mean by Entity Authentication. In *IEEE Symposium on Security and Privacy*, pages 46–54, 1996.

[110] L. Gong, T. Lomas, R. Needham, and J. Saltzer. Protecting Poorly Chosen Secrets from Guessing Attacks. *IEEE Journal on Selected Areas in Communications*, 11:648–656, June 1993.

[111] N. Haller. The S/KEY One-Time Password System, February 1995. RFC1760.

[112] B. Hancock. Windows-NT Network Attack Flavors of the Month. *Computers & Security*, 17(2):100–106, 1998.

[113] D. Harkins and D. Carrel. The Internet Key Exchange (IKE), June 1998. Internet Draft.

[114] D. Hartman. Unclogging Distributed Computing. *IEEE Spectrum*, 29(5):36–39, May 1992.

[115] R. Hauser, P. Janson, R. Molva, G. Tsudik, and E. Van Herreweghen. Robust and Secure Password/Key Exchange Method. In D. Gollmann, editor, *Proceedings of the Third European Symposium on Research in Computer Security (ESORICS) - LNCS 875*, pages 107–122. Springer-Verlag, November 1994.

[116] P. Hoffman. Enhanced Security Services for S/MIME, August 1998. Internet Draft.

[117] M. Horowitz. Kerberos Change Password Protocol, August 1998. Internet Draft.

[118] W. Hu. *DCE Security Programming.* O'Reilly & Associates, Inc., 1995.

[119] IBM. IBM Home Page, http://www.ibm.com.

[120] IBM. IBM SecureWay Key Recovery Technology. Available at http://www.ibm.com/security/html/wp_keyrec.html.

[121] IETF-CAT. IETF Common Authentication Technology (CAT) Working Group, http://www.ietf.org/html.charters/cat-charter.html.

[122] Intel. CDSA Home Page. http://www.intel.com/ial/security/index.htm.

[123] ISO 7498-1. Information processing – Open systems interconnection – Basic reference model – Part 1: The basic model. International Organization for Standardization, Geneva, Switzerland, 1994.

[124] ISO 7498-2. Information processing – Open systems interconnection – Basic reference model – Part 2: Security architecture. International Organization for Standardization, Geneva, Switzerland, 1989 (first edition).

[125] ISO 10181. Information technology – Open systems interconnection – Security Frameworks in Open Systems. International Organization for Standardization, Geneva, Switzerland, 1996.

[126] ISO/IEC 9594-8. Information Technology – Open systems interconnection – The directory: Overview of concepts, models, and services. International Organization for Standardization, Geneva, Switzerland, 1995.

[127] ISO/IEC 9796. Information technology – Security techniques – Digital signature schemes giving message recovery – Part 2: Mechanisms using a hash-function. Draft International Standard, December 1996.

[128] ISO/IEC 9798. Information technology – Security techniques – Entity authentication – Parts 1–5. International Organization for Standardization, Geneva, Switzerland, 1994 (first edition).

[129] ISO/IEC 10118-3. Information technology - Security techniques - Hash-functions - Part 3: Dedicated hash-functions. International Organization for Standardization, Geneva, Switzerland, 1997.

[130] ISO/IEC 11770. Information technology – Security techniques – Key management - Parts 1–3. International Organization for Standardization, Geneva, Switzerland, 1996.

[131] ITU. ITU-T Rec. X.509 (revised). The Directory - Authentication Framework, 1993. International Telecommunication Union, Geneva, Switzerland.

[132] P. Janson, G. Tsudik, and M. Yung. Scalability and Flexibility in Authentication Services: The Kryptoknight Approach. In *Proceedings of IEEE Infocom '97*, 1997.

[133] B. Jaspan. GSS-API Security For ONC RPC. In *Proceedings of the Symposium on Network and Distributed System Security*, pages 144–151, San Diego, CA., February 1995.

[134] L. Joncheray. A Simple Active Attack Against TCP. Technical report, Merit Network, Inc., April 1995.

[135] P. Kaijser. Secure Open Systems: Some Security Architectures. *Computer Fraud & Security Bulletin*, pages 12–18, November 1992.

[136] P. Kaijser. A review of the SESAME Development. In C. Boyd and E. Dawson, editors, *Proceedings of the 3rd ACISP Conference - LNCS 1438*, pages 1–8. Springer-Verlag, 1998.

[137] P. Kaijser, T. Parker, and D. Pinkas. SESAME: The Solution To Security for Open Distributed Systems. *Computer Communications*, 17(7):501–518, July 1994.

[138] B. Kaliski. Privacy Enhancement for Internet Electronic Mail: Part IV – Key Certification and Related Services, February 1993. RFC1424.

[139] B. Kaliski. PKCS #7: Cryptographic Message Syntax Version 1.5, March 1998. RFC2315.

[140] P. Karn and D. Feldmeirer. UNIX Password Security - Ten Years Later. In *Advances in Cryptology, Proceedings of Crypto ' 89 - LNCS 435*, pages 44–63. Springer-Verlag, 1990.

[141] P. Karn, P. Metzger, and W. Simpson. The ESP DES-CBC Transform, August 1995. RFC1829.

[142] P. Karn, P. Metzger, and W. Simpson. The ESP Triple DES Transform, September 1995. RFC1851.

[143] C. Kaufman. DASS Distributed Authentication Security Service, September 1993. RFC1507.

[144] C. Kaufman, R. Perlman, and M. Speciner. *Network Security: Private Communication in a Public World*. Prentice Hall, Inc., 1995. KryptoKnight Review, pages 438–431.

[145] C. Kaufman, R. Perlman, and M. Speciner. *Network Security: Private Communication in a Public World*. Prentice Hall, Inc., 1995. DCE Security Review, pages 455–459.

[146] S. Kent. Privacy Enhancement for Internet Electronic Mail: Part II – Certificate Based Key Management, February 1993. RFC1422.

[147] S. Kent and R. Atkinson. IP Authentication Header, July 1998. Internet Draft.

[148] S. Kent and R. Atkinson. IP Encapsulating Security Payload (ESP), July 1998. Internet Draft.

[149] S. Kent and R. Atkinson. Security Architecture for the Internet Protocol, July 1998. Internet Draft.

[150] Kerberos. MIT's Kerberos Home Page, http://web.mit.edu/kerberos/ www/index.html.

[151] D. Klein. Foiling the Cracker: A Survey of, and Improvements to, Password Security, 1992. Available at ftp://ftp.cert.org/pub/papers/ Dan_Klein_password.ps.

[152] L. Knudsen. Block Ciphers – Analysis, Design and Applications, 1994. PhD. Thesis, DAIMI PB 485, Aarhus University.

[153] L. Knudsen. Block Ciphers: A Survey. In B. Preneel, R. Govaerts, and J. Vandewalle, editors, *Proceedings Computer Security and Industrial Cryptography - State of the Art and Evolution - LNCS 1528*, pages 19–49. Springer-Verlag, 1998.

[154] J. Kohl. The Use of Encryption in Kerberos for Network Authentication. In G. Brassard, editor, *Advances in Cryptology - Crypto '89*, pages 35–43, 1989.

[155] J. Kohl. The Evolution of the Kerberos Authentication Service. In *Proceedings of the EurOpen Conference, Unix Distributed Open Systems in Perspective*, pages 295–313, Norway, May 1991.

[156] J. Kohl and C. Neuman. The Kerberos Network Authentication Service V5, September 1993. RFC1510.

[157] M. Krajewski. Concept For a Smart Card Kerberos. In *15th National Computer Security Conference*, pages 76–83, 1992.

[158] H. Krawczyk, M. Bellare, and R. Canetti. HMAC: Keyed-Hashing for Message Authentication, February 1997. RFC2104.

[159] KryptoKnight. IBM Zurich Research Laboratory KryptoKnight Home Page, http://www.zurich.ibm.com/~sti/g-kk/extern/kryptoknight.

[160] X. Lai, J. Massey, and S. Murphy. Markov Ciphers and Differential Cryptanalysis. In D. Davies, editor, *Advances in Cryptology, Proceedings of Eurocrypt '91 - LNCS 547*, pages 17–38. Springer-Verlag, 1991.

[161] L. Lamport. Password Authentication with Insecure Communication. *Communications of the ACM*, 24(11):770–772, November 1981.

[162] B. Lampson. Protection. *ACM Operating Systems Review*, 8(1):18–24, 1974.

[163] P. Leong and C. Tham. Unix Password Encryption Considered Insecure. In *Proceedings USENIX Winter Conference*, 1991.

[164] J. Linn. Practical Authentication for Distributed Computing. In *Proceedings of the 1990 IEEE Symposium on Security and Privacy*, pages 31–40, Oakland, CA., May 1990.

[165] J. Linn. Generic Security Services Application Program Interface, September 1993. RFC1508.

[166] J. Linn. Privacy Enhancement for Internet Electronic Mail: Part I – Message Encryption and Authentication Procedures, February 1993. RFC1421.

[167] J. Linn. Generic Interface to Security Services. *Computer Communications*, 17(7), July 1994.

[168] J. Linn. The Kerberos Version 5 GSS-API Mechanism, June 1996. RFC1964.

[169] J. Linn. Generic Security Service Application Program Interface Version 2, January 1997. RFC2078.

[170] T. Lomas, L. Gong, J. Saltzer, and R. Needham. Reducing Risks from Poorly Chosen Keys. *ACM Operating Systems Review*, 23:14–18, 1989.

[171] G. Lowe. Breaking and Fixing the Needham-Schroeder Public Key Protocol using FDR. In *Tools and Algorithms for the Construction and Analysis of Systems*, pages 147–166. Springer-Verlag, 1996.

[172] G. Lowe. Some New Attacks upon Security Protocols. In *9th IEEE Computer Security Foundations Workshop*, pages 162–169. IEEE Press, 1996.

[173] M. Matsui. Linear cryptanalysis method for DES cipher. In T. Helleseth, editor, *Advances in Cryptology, Proceedings Eurocrypt '93 - LNCS 765*, pages 386–397. Springer-Verlag, 1994.

[174] D. Maughan, M. Schertler, M. Schneider, and J. Turner. Internet Security Association and Key Management Protocol (ISAKMP), July 1998. Internet Draft.

[175] U. Maurer. New Approaches to the Design of Self-Synchronizing Stream Ciphers. In D. Davies, editor, *Advances in Cryptology, Proceedings Eurocrypt '91 - LNCS 547*, pages 458–471. Springer-Verlag, 1991.

[176] F. McKay. Fortify for Netscape. Available at http://www.fortify.net.

[177] P. McMahon. SESAME V2 Public Key and Authorisation Extensions To Kerberos. In *Proceedings of the Symposium on Network and Distributed System Security*, pages 114–131, February 1995.

[178] P. McMahon. GSS-API Authentication Method for SOCKS Version 5, June 1996. RFC1961.

[179] A. Medvinsky, J. Cargille, and M. Hur. Anonymous Credentials in Kerberos, September 1997. Internet Draft (expired).

[180] A.J. Menezes. *Elliptic Curve Public Key Cryptosystems*. Kluwer Academic Publishers, 1993.

[181] A.J. Menezes, P.C. van Oorschot, and S.A. Vanstone. *Handbook of Applied Cryptography*. CRC Press, 1997.

[182] P. Metzger and W. Simpson. IP Authentication using Keyed MD5, August 1995. RFC1828.

[183] C. Mitchell and L. Chen. Comments on the S/KEY User Authentication Scheme. *ACM Operating Systems Review*, 30(4):12–16, October 1996.

[184] R. Molva, G. Tsudik, E. Van Herreweghen, and S. Zatti. KryptoKnight Authentication and Key Distribution System. In *Proceedings of the European Symposium on Research in Computer Security (ESORICS)*, pages 155–174, Toulouse, France, 1992.

[185] R. Morris. A Weakness in the 4.2 BSD UNIX TCP/IP Software. Technical report, Computing Science TR-117, 1985.

[186] R. Morris and K. Thompson. Password security: A case history. *Communications of the ACM*, 22(11):594–597, November 1979.

[187] S. Muftic and M. Sloman. Security Architecture for Distributed Systems. *Computer Communications*, 17(7):492–500, July 1994.

[188] M. Nacht. The Spectrum of Modern Firewalls. *Computers and Security*, 17(1):54–56, 1997.

[189] R. Needham and M. Schroeder. Using Encryption for Authentication in Large Networks of Computers. *Communications of the ACM*, 21(12):993–999, December 1978.

[190] B. Neuman and S. Stubblebine. A Note on the Use of Timestamps and Nonces. *ACM Operating Systems Review*, 27:10–14, 1993.

[191] B. Neuman and T. Ts'o. Kerberos : An Authentication Service for Computer Networks. *IEEE Communication Magazine*, 32(9):33–38, September 1994.

[192] NIST.   SKIPJACK and KEA Algorithms Specifications, 1998. http://csrc.nist.gov/encryption/skipjack-1.pdf.

[193] A. M. Odlyzko. The Future of Integer Factorization. *CryptoBytes*, 1(2):5–12, 1995.

[194] OMG.   The   CORBA   Home   Page.   Available   at http://www.omg.org/corba.

[195] R. Oppliger. *Authentication Systems For Secure Networks*. Artech House, 1996.

[196] H. Orman. The OAKLEY Key Determination Protocol, 1998. Internet Draft.

[197] B. Page. A Report on the Internet Worm. Technical report, University of Lowell, Computer Science Department, November 1988.

[198] T. Parker and D. Pinkas. Extended Generic Security Services APIs: XGSS-APIs Access Control and Delegation Extensions, March 1997. Internet Draft (expired).

[199] T. Parker and C. Sundt. Role Based Access Control in Real Systems. In *Compsec '95*, October 1995.

[200] B. Preneel. Analysis and Design of Cryptographic Hash Functions, 1993. PhD Thesis, K.U.Leuven.

[201] B. Preneel, V. Rijmen, and A. Bosselaers. Recent Developments in the Design of Conventional Cryptographic Algorithms. In B. Preneel, R. Govaerts, and J. Vandewalle, editors, *Proceedings Computer Security and Industrial Cryptography - State of the Art and Evolution - LNCS 1528*, pages 106–131. Springer-Verlag, 1998.

[202] B. Preneel and P. van Oorschot. MDx-MAC and Building Fast MACs from Hash Functions. In D. Coppersmith, editor, *Advances in Cryptology, Proceedings of Crypto '95 - LNCS 963*, pages 1–14. Springer-Verlag, 1995.

[203] B. Preneel and P. van Oorschot. On the security of two MAC algorithms. In U. Maurer, editor, *Advances in Cryptology, Proceedings of Eurocrypt '96 - LNCS 1070*, pages 19–32. Springer-Verlag, 1996.

[204] B. Ramsdell. S/MIME Version 3 Message Specification, August 1998. Internet Draft.

[205] J. Reynolds. The Helminthiasis of the Internet, December 1989. RFC1135.

[206] V. Rijmen. Cryptanalysis and Design of Iterated Block Ciphers, 1997. PhD. Thesis, K.U.Leuven.

[207] R. Rivest. The MD5 Message-Digest Algorithm, April 1992. RFC1321.

[208] R. Rivest. The RC5 Encryption Algorithm. In B. Preneel, editor, *Proceedings Fast Software Encryption '94 - LNCS 1008*, pages 86–96. Springer-Verlag, 1995.

[209] R. Rivest. Description of the RC2(r) Encryption Algorithm, January 1998. RFC2268.

[210] R. Rivest and B. Lampson. SDSI - A Simple Distributed Security Infrastructure. Available at http://theory.lcs.mit.edu/~rivest/sdsi11.html.

[211] R. Rivest, A. Shamir, and L. Adleman. A Method for Obtaining Digital Signatures and Public Key Cryptosystems. *Communications of the ACM*, 21(2):158–164, February 1978.

[212] W. Rosenberry, D. Kenney, and G. Fisher. *Understanding DCE*. O'Reilly & Associates, Inc., 1992.

[213] R. Rueppel and P. van Oorschot. Modern Key Agreement Techniques. *Computer Communications*, 17:458–465, 1994.

[214] R. Sandhu, E.J. Coyne, H.L. Feinstein, and C.E. Youman. Role-Based Access Control Models. *IEEE Computer*, pages 38–47, February 1996.

[215] D. Seeley. A Tour of the Worm. In *Proceedings of 1989 Winter USENIX Conference*, February 1989.

[216] SESAME. The SESAME Home, https://www.cosic.esat.kuleuven.ac.be/sesame.

[217] E. Spafford. The Internet Worm Program: An Analysis. Technical report, Purdue CSD-TR-823, Department of Computer Sciences Purdue University, 1988.

[218] SPX. SPX Software Archive, ftp://ftp.funet.fi/pub/unix/security/login/SPX.

[219] SSH. IETF Secure Shell Working Group, http://www.ietf.org/html.charters/secsh-charter.html.

[220] J. Steiner, B. Neuman, and J. Schiller. Kerberos: An Authentication Service for Open Network Systems. In *Proceedings of the USENIX Winter Conference*, pages 191–202, Dallas, Tx., February 1988.

[221] M. Swift. Initial Authentication with Kerberos and the GSS-API, November 1997. Internet Draft (expired).

[222] M. Swift. User to User Kerberos Authentication using GSS-API, October 1997. Internet Draft (expired).

[223] M. Swift. Generating KDC Referrals, January 1998. Internet Draft (expired).

[224] A. Syukri, E. Okamoto, and M. Mambo. A User Identification System using Signature Written with Mouse. In C. Boyd and E. Dawson, editors, *Proceedings of the 3rd ACISP Conference - LNCS 1438*, pages 403–414. Springer-Verlag, 1998.

[225] J. Tardo and K. Alagappan. SPX: Global Authentication Using Public Key Certificates. In *Proceedings of the 1991 IEEE Symposium on Security and Privacy*, pages 232–244, May 1991.

[226] J. Trostle. Public Key Crytography for KDC Recovery in Kerberos V5, August 1998. Internet Draft.

[227] B. Tung, C. Neuman, J. Wray, A. Medvinsky, M. Hur, and J. Trostle. Public Key Cryptography for Initial Authentication in Kerberos, March 1998. Internet Draft.

[228] B. Tung, T. Ryutov, C. Neuman, G. Tsudik, B. Sommerfeld, A. Medvinsky, and M. Hur. Public Key Cryptography for Cross-Realm Authentication in Kerberos, March 1998. Internet Draft.

[229] P. van Oorschot and M. Wiener. On Diffie-Hellman Key Agreement with Short Exponents. In U. Maurer, editor, *Advances in Cryptology, Proceedings Eurocrypt '96 - LNCS 1070*, pages 332–343. Springer-Verlag, 1996.

[230] M. Vandenwauver, R. Govaerts, and J. Vandewalle. How Role Based Access Control is Implemented in SESAME. In *Proceedings of the 6-th Workshops on Enabling Technologies: Infrastructure for Collaborative Enterprises*, pages 293–298. IEEE Computer Society, 1997.

[231] M. Vandenwauver, R. Govaerts, and J. Vandewalle. Public Key Extensions used in SESAME V4, April 1997. Presented at Public Key Solutions 97. Available at http://www.esat.kuleuven.ac.be/~vdwauver/pks97/pks97.html.

[232] M. Vandenwauver, R. Govaerts, and J. Vandewalle. Role Based Access Control in Distributed Systems. In S. Katsikas, editor, *Communications and Multimedia Security*, volume 3, pages 169–177, 1997.

[233] M. Vandenwauver, R. Govaerts, and J. Vandewalle. Security of Client-Server Systems. In J. Eloff and R. von Solms, editors, *Information Security*, pages 39–54, 1997.

[234] G. Vernam. Cipher Printing Telegraph Systems for Secret Wire and Radio Telegraphic Communications. *Journal of the American Institute for Electrical Engineers*, 55:109–115, 1926.

[235] M. Warner, J. Trinkle, and G. Gaskell. Smart Card Integration with Kerberos. In *Proceedings of the 19th Australian Computer Science Conference (ACSC)*, 1996.

[236] M. Wiener. Performance Comparison of Public-Key Cryptosystems. *CryptoBytes*, 4(1):1–5, 1998.

[237] M.J. Wiener. Efficient DES Key Search. Presented at rump session of Crypto '93. Reprinted in W. Stallings, editor, *Practical Cryptography for Data Internetworks*, IEEE Computer Society Press, pp. 31–79, 1996. Currently available at ftp://ripem.msu.edu/pub/crypt/docs/des-key-search.ps.

[238] J. Wray. Generic Security Service API: C-Bindings, September 1993. RFC1509.

[239] Y. Xu and L. Harn. The Multi-Path Authentication of Kerberos (MPAKER), January 1998. Internet Draft (expired).

[240] T. Ylonen, T. Kivinen, M. Saarinen, T. Rinne, and S. Lehtinen. SSH Authentication Protocol, August 1998. Internet Draft.

[241] T. Ylonen, T. Kivinen, M. Saarinen, T. Rinne, and S. Lehtinen. SSH Connection Protocol, August 1998. Internet Draft.

[242] T. Ylonen, T. Kivinen, M. Saarinen, T. Rinne, and S. Lehtinen. SSH Protocol Architecture, August 1998. Internet Draft.

[243] T. Ylonen, T. Kivinen, M. Saarinen, T. Rinne, and S. Lehtinen. SSH Transport Layer Protocol, August 1998. Internet Draft.

Paul Ashley obtained BEng and BAppSc degrees in Electronic Engineering and Computer Science from the Queensland University of Technology (QUT) in 1990. From then to 1994 he was a software engineer at Honeywell Ltd.

From 1995 on he has been a member of the ISRC (Information Security Research Centre), part of the School of Data Communications, QUT. During this time he has worked as a lecturer and aims to complete his PhD titled "Smart Card Systems for Securely Managing Personal File Spaces" in 1999. He has also been involved in numerous consulting activities for the ISRC for industry and government, which has involved network security audits and design, firewall auditing, Smart Cards and physical security.

Mark Vandenwauver obtained BS and MS degrees in Electrical Engineering from the K.U.Leuven in 1990. Since then he has been a member of the COSIC (Computer Security and Industrial Cryptography) research group of the ESAT department. In 1998 he obtained a Ph.D. with his thesis entitled "Practical Network Security Aspects".

He has been involved as a consultant in evaluating cryptographic soft- and hardware for several companies including S.W.I.F.T., Banksys, Cetrel, Coopers & Lybrand and the Brussels Stock Exchange. He has also participated for 4 years in the EC-RACE project SESAME. He is a member of the Advisory Board of the Belgian "Kruispuntdatabank". He was also one of the co-founders of the Belinfosec group, a forum of experts in information security.

Index